Our Living History

EXPLORE AMERICA

Our Living History

Reader's
Digest

THE READER'S DIGEST ASSOCIATION, INC.
Pleasantville, New York / Montreal

OUR LIVING HISTORY was created and produced by ST. REMY MULTIMEDIA INC.

STAFF FOR OUR LIVING HISTORY
Series Editor: Elizabeth Cameron
Art Director: Solange Laberge
Editor: Elizabeth Warrington Lewis
Assistant Editor: Neale McDevitt
Photo Researcher: Geneviève Monette
Cartography: Hélène Dion, David Widgington
Designer: Anne-Marie Lemay
Research Editor: Robert B. Ronald
Contributing Researcher: Olga Dzatko
Researcher: Jennifer Meltzer
Copy Editor: Judy Yelon
Index: Christine Jacobs
System Coordinator: Éric Beaulieu
Technical Support: Mathieu Raymond-Beaubien, Jean Sirois
Scanner Operators: Martin Francoeur, Sara Grynspan

ST. REMY STAFF
PRESIDENT, CHIEF EXECUTIVE OFFICER: Fernand Lecoq
PRESIDENT, CHIEF OPERATING OFFICER: Pierre Léveillé
VICE PRESIDENT, FINANCE: Natalie Watanabe
MANAGING EDITOR: Carolyn Jackson
MANAGING ART DIRECTOR: Diane Denoncourt
PRODUCTION MANAGER: Michelle Turbide

Writers: Lori Erickson—Living History Farms
Rod Gragg—Battle at Gettysburg
Jim Henderson—King Ranch
Rose Houk—Taos
Steven Krolak—Columbia State Historic Park, Fort Clatsop
Neale McDevitt—Pennsylvania Dutch Country
Wendy Murphy—Historic Bath
James Wamsley—American Legacy, Savannah

Contributing Writers: Adriana Barton, Julie Crysler, Brian Polan

Address any comments about *Our Living History*
to U.S. Editor, General Books, c/o Customer Service,
Reader's Digest, Pleasantville, NY 10570

READER'S DIGEST STAFF
Editor: Kathryn Bonomi
Art Editor: Eleanor Kostyk
Assistant Production Supervisor: Mike Gallo
Editorial Assistant: Mary Jo McLean

READER'S DIGEST GENERAL BOOKS
Editor-in-Chief, Books and Home
Entertainment: Barbara J. Morgan
Editor, U.S. General Books: David Palmer
Executive Editor: Gayla Visalli
Art Director: Joel Musler

Opening photographs
Cover: Fort Union National Monument, New Mexico
Back Cover: Mission San Xavier del Bac, Arizona
Page 2: Old World Wisconsin, Wisconsin
Page 5: Gettysburg National Military Park, Pennsylvania

The credits and acknowledgments that appear on page 144
are hereby made a part of this copyright page.

Library of Congress Cataloging in Publication Data

Our living history.
      p.   cm.—(Explore America)
   Includes index.
   ISBN 0-89577-903-X
   1. United States—Description and travel. 2. United States—History,
Local   I. Reader's Digest Association. II. Series.
E169.04.094   1996
973—dc20   96-30610

CONTENTS

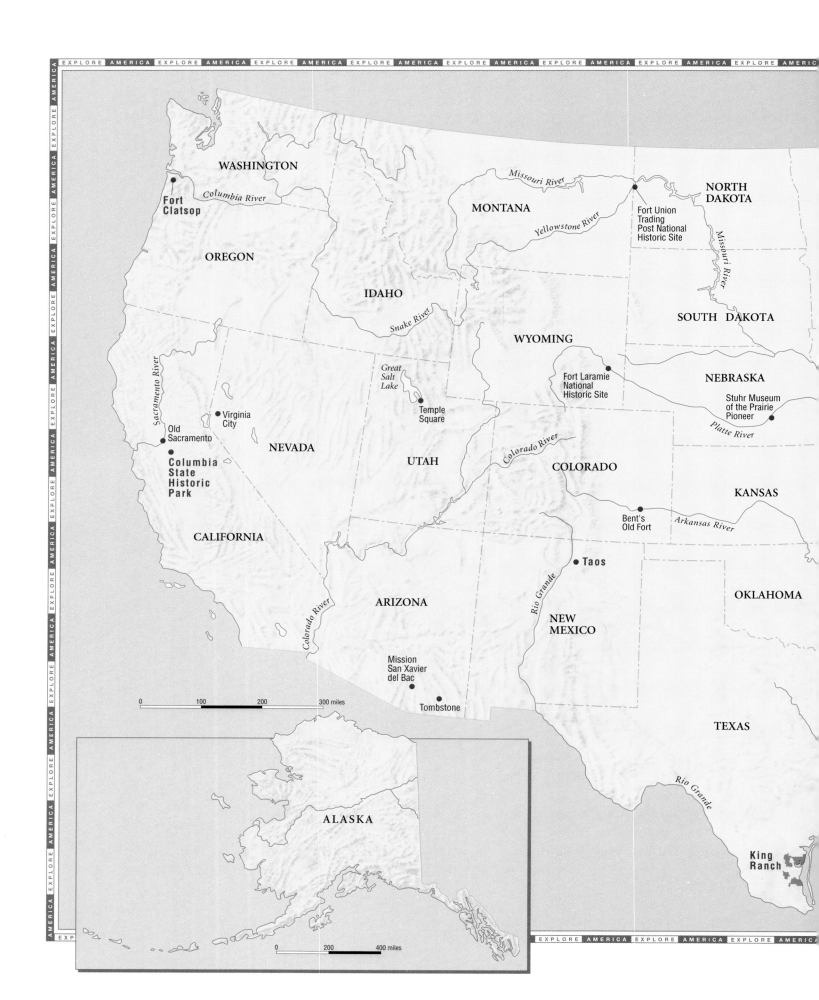

WASHINGTON

Fort
Clatsop

Columbia River

OREGON

Missouri River

MONTANA

Yellowstone River

Fort Union
Trading
Post National
Historic Site

NORTH
DAKOTA

Missouri River

IDAHO

Snake River

SOUTH DAKOTA

WYOMING

Sacramento River

Great
Salt
Lake

Temple
Square

Fort Laramie
National
Historic Site

NEBRASKA

Stuhr Museum
of the Prairie
Pioneer

Platte River

Virginia
City

Old
Sacramento

NEVADA

UTAH

Colorado River

COLORADO

Columbia
State
Historic
Park

KANSAS

Bent's
Old Fort

Arkansas River

CALIFORNIA

Taos

OKLAHOMA

Colorado River

ARIZONA

Rio Grande

NEW
MEXICO

Mission
San Xavier
del Bac

Tombstone

0   100   200   300 miles

TEXAS

ALASKA

Rio Grande

0   200   400 miles

King
Ranch

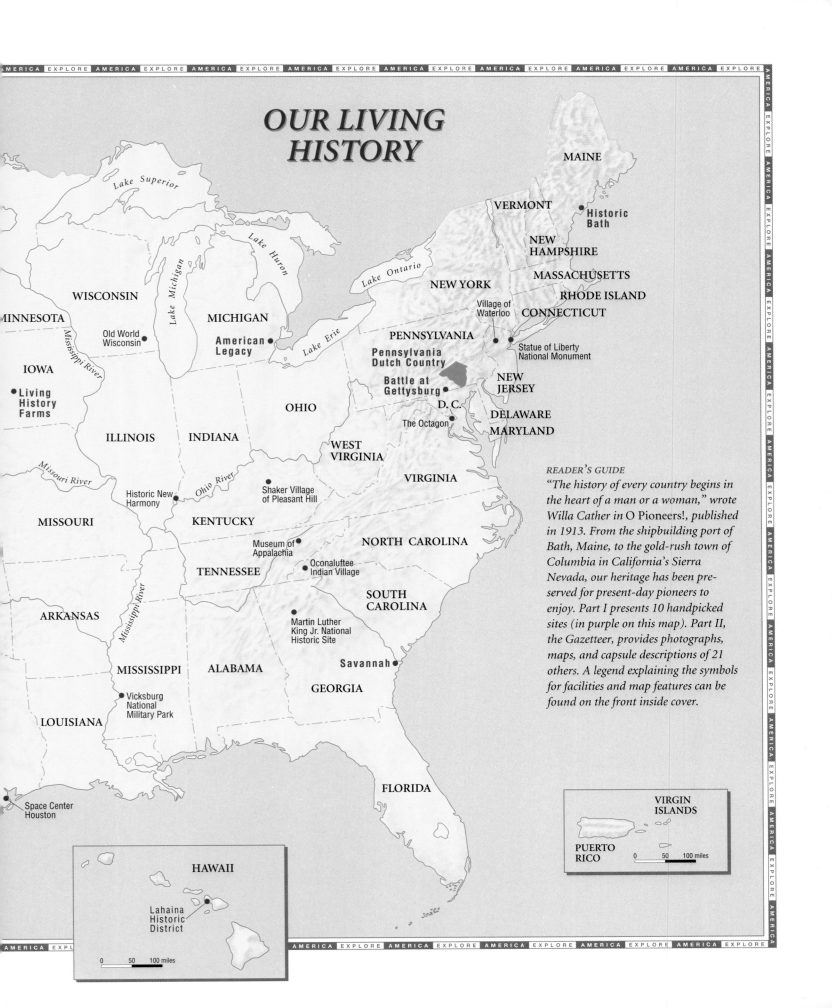

OUR LIVING HISTORY

Lake Superior

Lake Huron

Lake Michigan

Lake Ontario

Lake Erie

Mississippi River

Missouri River

Ohio River

Mississippi River

MAINE

VERMONT
• Historic Bath

NEW HAMPSHIRE

MASSACHUSETTS

RHODE ISLAND

CONNECTICUT

NEW YORK

Village of Waterloo

Statue of Liberty National Monument

NEW JERSEY

DELAWARE

MARYLAND

WISCONSIN

MINNESOTA

MICHIGAN

Old World Wisconsin •

American Legacy •

PENNSYLVANIA

Pennsylvania Dutch Country

Battle at Gettysburg

D. C.

The Octagon

IOWA

• Living History Farms

OHIO

INDIANA

ILLINOIS

WEST VIRGINIA

VIRGINIA

Historic New Harmony •

KENTUCKY

Shaker Village of Pleasant Hill •

MISSOURI

NORTH CAROLINA

Museum of Appalachia •

Oconaluftee Indian Village •

TENNESSEE

SOUTH CAROLINA

ARKANSAS

Martin Luther King Jr. National Historic Site •

MISSISSIPPI

ALABAMA

GEORGIA

Savannah •

LOUISIANA

• Vicksburg National Military Park

• Space Center Houston

FLORIDA

READER'S GUIDE

"The history of every country begins in the heart of a man or a woman," wrote *Willa Cather in O Pioneers!, published in 1913. From the shipbuilding port of Bath, Maine, to the gold-rush town of Columbia in California's Sierra Nevada, our heritage has been preserved for present-day pioneers to enjoy. Part I presents 10 handpicked sites (in purple on this map). Part II, the Gazetteer, provides photographs, maps, and capsule descriptions of 21 others. A legend explaining the symbols for facilities and map features can be found on the front inside cover.*

VIRGIN ISLANDS

PUERTO RICO

0   50   100 miles

HAWAII

Lahaina Historic District •

0   50   100 miles

HISTORIC BATH

*Nicknamed the City of Ships, this
quaint coastal town in Maine retains
the flavor of its salty past.*

Describing the port of Bath during the 19th century, writer Robert Tristram Coffin observed, "Bath was a city of sailors. Sailors with strange mustaches and sailors with rings in their ears. . . . The streets smelled of far countries. The shop windows were pages of a geography book. And all day long there was music through the air, the sound of a thousand wooden mallets driving home the treenails in the planking of a dozen hulls. . . . At the end of every street there were white sails, and ships were going by like high summer clouds."

Although Bath is no longer a port of call for vessels from around the world, it is still a place of unique charm. The oldest continuously active shipbuilding town in the United States, Bath also holds the coveted honor of making the list of the 100 Best Small Towns in America.

Bath's history and prosperity are due in large part to its location. It is surrounded on three sides by water: the mighty Kennebec River to the east, the confluence of four other rivers immediately to the north at Merrymeeting Bay, and the open seas of the Atlantic 12 miles to the south.

In its youth, Bath had ready access to the virgin timber of Maine's woods. The wood of the majestic ramrod-straight white pines was ideal for masts and spars, and oak made resilient and long-lived hulls. Growing in seemingly inexhaustible supply throughout the rivers' vast watershed, the trees provided tens of thousands of stout timbers for the shipbuilding enterprises that emerged as early as 1607.

Bath's gently sloping shoreline and the half-mile-wide river basin that forms its deep harbor created a near-perfect staging area for the building of oceangoing ships of almost any length and beam. Even Bath's distance from the open ocean worked in its favor, as its upriver location provided one of the most protected anchorages on the entire East Coast.

Hearing rumors of gold in the region, the British made their first formal attempt

BOUNTY FROM THE SEA
The Leon L. Bean Building at the Maine Maritime Museum, above, is devoted to the history of lobstering from Colonial times to the present. Six historical boats are on exhibit from oar- and sail-driven vessels to powerboats of the 1920's. Other displays show the evolution of lobster gear—from early hoop-net traps to modern wire-mesh ones.

WALKING TOUR
Overleaf: Front Street, located in Bath's main shopping district, is lined with 19th-century buildings. Brick sidewalks, front-lighted signs, and antique street lamps give visitors the impression that they have stepped back in time.

to settle the Kennebec region in 1607 when King James I gave an English investment group a charter to plant a colony. Sir George Popham, nephew of the lord chief justice of England, recruited 120 men and sailed for the Maine coast. They arrived in the balmy days of August 1607 at the mouth of the Kennebec, which had been explored two years earlier by Capt. George Waymouth. Finding timber and food sources plentiful, they constructed a small redoubt, complete with a storehouse, church, and a dozen or so shelters. But as cold weather set in, the men found themselves ill prepared and they began to succumb to despair, disease, and starvation. "Winter froze our hopes to death," wrote one survivor. When Sir George died, the remaining settlers decided to leave because the region was not rich in gold or silver. They mustered the strength to build a shallow-draft 30-ton pinnace, a vessel that holds the distinction of being the first English ship to be constructed in North America. Before the next summer was over, the boat, named *The Virginia of Sagadahoc*, had carried the men safely home to England.

LONG REACH HARBOR

Bath proper was first settled around 1660 when Britishers Christopher Lawson, Robert Gutch, and Alexander Thwaite bought titles to the land from the Abenaki Indians. Shortly afterward this area of Maine was annexed by the Massachusetts Bay Colony. The little hamlet—called Long Reach because of its spacious harbor and its location along a long and straight stretch of the Kennebec River—grew in spurts over the next hundred years, as settlers lived primarily on subsistence farming, fur trading, and lumbering. At the same

INFORMATION FOR VISITORS

To reach Bath from Portland, take I-95 north; from Augusta and Bangor, take I-95 south. At Brunswick, Hwy. 1 leads directly to Bath and also connects many of the small towns along the coast. The nearest airports are in Portland, Augusta, and Bangor. The Maine Maritime Museum and the Percy & Small Shipyard are open year-round except on Thanksgiving, Christmas, and New Year's Day. The Bath Iron Works is open to the public for launching and commissioning ceremonies. Sagadahoc Preservation, Inc., a nonprofit organization, offers walking tours through Bath's National Register Historic District. Heritage Days are celebrated in July.
For more information: Bath Area Chamber of Commerce, 45 Front St., Bath, ME 04530; 207-443-9751.

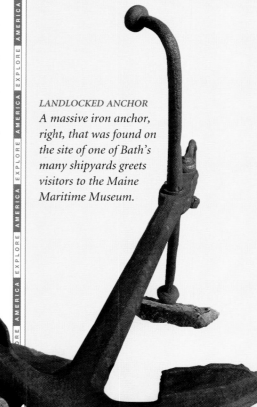

LANDLOCKED ANCHOR
A massive iron anchor, right, that was found on the site of one of Bath's many shipyards greets visitors to the Maine Maritime Museum.

10

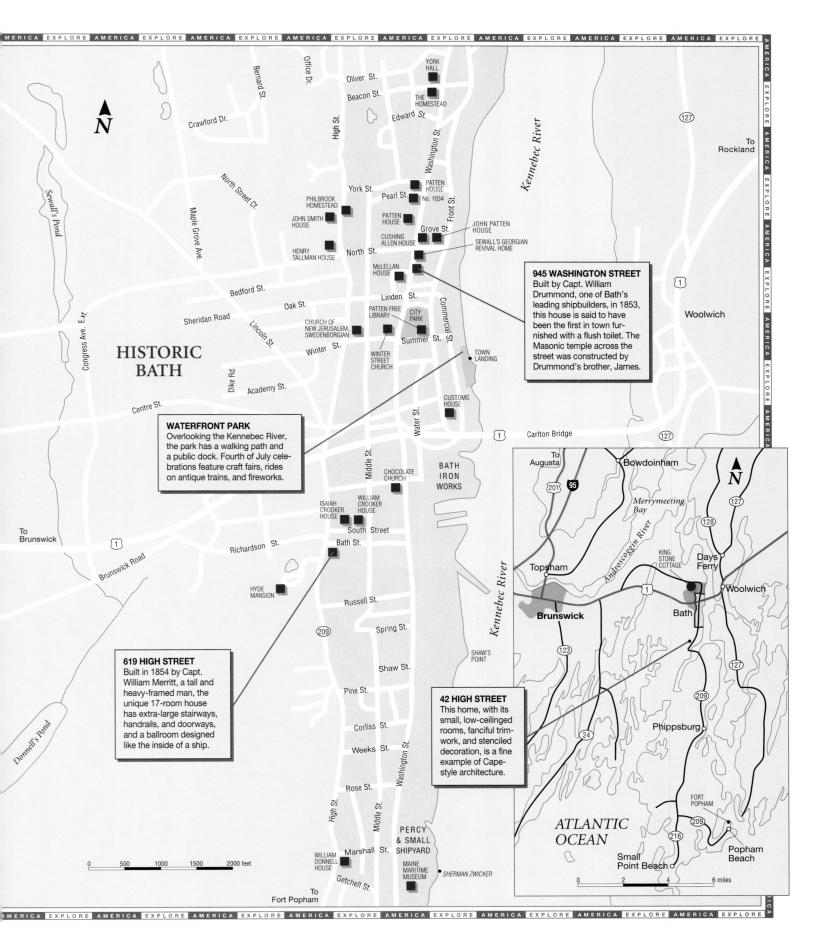

N

YORK HALL

THE HOMESTEAD

Oliver St.

Beacon St.

Edward St.

Bernard St.

Crawford Dr.

Office Dr.

High St.

Washington St.

Kennebec River

127

To Rockland

North Street Ct.

Maple Grove Ave.

York St.

PATTEN HOUSE No. 1034

Pearl St.

Front St.

PHILBROOK HOMESTEAD

JOHN SMITH HOUSE

PATTEN HOUSE

Grove St.

JOHN PATTEN HOUSE

CUSHING ALLEN HOUSE

SEWALL'S GEORGIAN REVIVAL HOME

1

Woolwich

HENRY TALLMAN HOUSE

North St.

McLELLAN HOUSE

Sewall's Pond

Congress Ave. Ext.

Bedford St.

Oak St.

Sheridan Road

Lincoln St.

Dike Rd.

Linden St.

945 WASHINGTON STREET
Built by Capt. William Drummond, one of Bath's leading shipbuilders, in 1853, this house is said to have been the first in town furnished with a flush toilet. The Masonic temple across the street was constructed by Drummond's brother, James.

PATTEN FREE LIBRARY

CITY PARK

Commercial St.

HISTORIC BATH

CHURCH OF NEW JERUSALEM, SWEDENBORGIAN

Summer St.

Winter St.

WINTER STREET CHURCH

Academy St.

Centre St.

TOWN LANDING

Water St.

CUSTOMS HOUSE

WATERFRONT PARK
Overlooking the Kennebec River, the park has a walking path and a public dock. Fourth of July celebrations feature craft fairs, rides on antique trains, and fireworks.

1

Carlton Bridge

127

To Brunswick

1

Brunswick Road

Richardson St.

Middle St.

CHOCOLATE CHURCH

BATH IRON WORKS

To Augusta

201

95

Bowdoinham

N

127

Merrymeeting Bay

128

ISAIAH CROOKER HOUSE

WILLIAM CROOKER HOUSE

South Street

Androscoggin River

KING STONE COTTAGE

Days Ferry

Bath St.

HYDE MANSION

Russell St.

Kennebec River

Topsham

1

Woolwich

Brunswick

Bath

209

Spring St.

SHAW'S POINT

123

619 HIGH STREET
Built in 1854 by Capt. William Merritt, a tall and heavy-framed man, the unique 17-room house has extra-large stairways, handrails, and doorways, and a ballroom designed like the inside of a ship.

Shaw St.

Pine St.

42 HIGH STREET
This home, with its small, low-ceilinged rooms, fanciful trimwork, and stenciled decoration, is a fine example of Cape-style architecture.

24

Phippsburg

Corliss St.

Weeks St.

Donnell's Pond

Rose St.

209

High St.

Middle St.

Washington St.

FORT POPHAM

209

0   500   1000   1500   2000 feet

ATLANTIC OCEAN

216

Marshall St.

WILLIAM DONNELL HOUSE

PERCY & SMALL SHIPYARD

Getchell St.

MAINE MARITIME MUSEUM

SHERMAN ZWICKER

Popham Beach

Small Point Beach

0   2   4   6 miles

To Fort Popham

AMERICA EXPLORE AMERICA EXPLORE AMERICA EXPLORE AMERICA EXPLORE AMERICA EXPLORE AMERICA EXPLORE AMERICA EXPLORE AMERICA EXPLORE AMERICA EXPLORE

HISTORIC BATH 11

KENNEBEC RIVER VIEW
The Kennebec River, opposite page, flows about 150 miles from Moosehead Lake—Maine's largest lake—to the sea.

LANDMARK CHURCH
The Chocolate Church, right, was named for its cocoa-colored exterior. Built in 1847 by the Congregationalists, the Gothic Revival structure now houses a center for the performing arts and an art gallery.

TOOLS OF THE TRADE
An exhibit room at the Maine Maritime Museum, below, displays tools used to repair steam engines, make iron and brass castings, and to build steel ships.

time, boatbuilding became an increasingly important industry for local craftsmen.

In 1781 Long Reach's several hundred inhabitants petitioned the newly formed Commonwealth of Massachusetts for incorporation as a town. Permission was granted, and shortly thereafter the town fathers decided to change its name to Bath, after the resort in England of the same name.

A TIME OF PROSPERITY

After America gained its independence from Britain in 1776, Bath enjoyed an era of genuine prosperity founded on the businesses of shipbuilding and mercantile shipping. Small schooners and brigantines built here plied the coastal water routes and short-haul routes to the West Indies. Before long Bath's merchants and shipbuilders set their sights on constructing deepwater merchant vessels. Except for the disruptions caused by the War of 1812, the port flourished, carrying lumber, cotton, and agricultural produce to the four corners of the globe. It was not uncommon for a shipowner to make his fortune within a very short time.

The population of the town soared, rising from 900 residents, according to the 1790 census, to some 11,000 people in 1850. Along the riverfront, warehouses, wharves, and sprawling shipyards vied for space. Sailors, harking from all over the world, walked the town's streets, lending it an exotic atmosphere. A short distance from the water's edge, various industries sprang up to serve the shipbuilding industry—sawmills, sail lofts, foundries, cordage

manufacturers, and ship chandlers, where ships could be outfitted with everything from canvas buckets and bronze quadrants to seagoing medicine chests, nautical charts, and crockery for the captain's table. In all but the coldest months of the year the sounds of broadaxes, caulking mallets, and a huffing steam engine resounded through the streets. More than 400 ships, brigs, schooners, and sloops were built between 1840 and 1850 alone.

KING OF BATH

Alongside the modest homes of earlier settlers rose residences in Georgian, Federal, Greek Revival, and Carpenter Gothic styles. One of the first Bath citizens to live on a grand scale was William King. He arrived from southern Maine in 1800 and got his start by opening a store. With the profits from that enterprise he invested first in warehouses, then in wharves and shipyards, and eventually he financed oceangoing vessels. One of King's ships, the *Reunion*, paid for itself three times over in as many voyages carrying cargo. Active in politics and a leader in the province's drive for independence from Massachusetts, King became Maine's first governor in 1820.

King was equally famous for his flamboyant lifestyle. In 1807, when the U.S. Congress passed the Embargo Act forbidding American vessels from sailing for foreign ports, King is reputed to have become a smuggler. King's Stone House, constructed in 1808, is one of the earliest Gothic Revival structures in America, and stands on Whiskeag Road, on the north side of the city. The two-and-a-half-story building has an exterior of carved granite. As his wealth grew, King built a more luxurious mansion on Front Street, which earned him the nickname, the King of Bath.

Bath's other famous shipbuilders included James McLellan, Levi Houghton, William Sewall, and the brothers Isaiah and William Crooker. McLellan's mansion, said at one time to have boasted five grand pianos, stands on Washington Street. George and John Patten also lived in high style. Captain John Patten's Federal-style house commands the foot of North Street, and two other Patten houses are located on Washington Street, along with William Sewall's elegant 28-room Homestead. Standing side by side on South Street are two Greek Revival houses that once belonged to the feuding Crooker brothers, Isaiah and William. William added a top story to his house to block Isaiah's view of the family shipyard. Some of these houses and their fine furnishings are largely intact and open to visitors and lodgers.

In 1850 Bath was poised to enter the most prosperous decade in its history, the heyday of the wooden ship. Some 20 shipyards employed more than 2,000 master craftsmen; another 1,000 men called themselves mariners; and nearly every other able-bodied man worked in some related trade. Based on the volume of wooden-hulled vessels produced at Bath, the city trailed only New York and Boston in tonnage.

| IRON SIDES | When the Civil War erupted, mercantile shipbuilding all but ceased and the town's main |

industry suffered a steady decline. In 1884, Bath's boatbuilding heritage was revived when young Thomas Hyde purchased the iron foundry on Water Street, leading the way for the ship industry's transition from wooden sailing ships to massive iron-and-steel vessels powered by steam.

Hyde had grown up in Bath and served as a brigadier general in the Union Army during the Civil War. He limited his business to the production of iron ship parts at first, and expanded the line by stages to include all manner of ship machinery. He also patented and manufactured his own

steam-driven deck capstans and windlasses. Plowing much of the profit back into the business, the General, as he came to be known among fellow citizens, bought up waterfront property in 1888 and renamed the business the Bath Iron Works. Two years later BIW went into full-scale operation when it got its first contract to build a vessel for the US Navy. Soon after, it became the state's leading employer and one of the primary commercial shipbuilders in the country.

WORKING HARBOR
The gigantic cranes of the Bath Iron Works, above, dominate the shipyards and give testimony to the community's ongoing maritime enterprises. BIW Corporation builds commercial vessels, as well as frigates and cruisers for the US Navy.

BIW arranged lucrative contracts with the navy early on, starting with the gunboats *Machias* and *Castine*—the first steel ships built in Maine. Thirty more commissions for both naval ships and commercial vessels followed.

MARITIME PRINCE

Meanwhile, though the wooden sailing ships of old were on their way out, Bath's other shipbuilding efforts enjoyed a brief economic boom. In order to protect American trading routes from overseas competition, a law had been passed in 1817 stipulating that only vessels built in the United States were entitled to carry goods between U.S. ports. As California and other Western states entered the Union in the mid-1800's, Bath's shipyards were kept busy constructing vessels that transported sugar, coal, and lumber from ports on the East Coast and returned with grain from West Coast ports.

In this era, shipowner Arthur Sewall operated the largest fleet of vessels under the American flag from his Bath headquarters, earning him the nickname America's Maritime Prince. Several sizable square-riggers were built at Sewall's yards along the Kennebec, including, in 1894, the first steel sailing ship built in America, the 310-foot *Dirigo*. At Nathaniel Palmer's yards, work crews completed a five-master in 1898, and two years later the newly formed Percy & Small Shipyard, run by Capt. Samuel R. Percy and Frank Small, produced their first six-masted schooner.

During the 20th century Bath's fortunes have waxed and waned with the nation's economy, military commitments, and maritime interests. Today BIW continues to build sophisticated naval vessels, and Bath takes great pride in the shipyard's well-deserved fame. The town is also supportive of the unique resource of its historic city and port, and has done a notable job of reviving and maintaining it. From its humble beginnings in 1962 the Maine Maritime Museum has grown to become one of the country's leading institutions for preserving maritime history.

Located on the 10-acre site of the venerable Percy & Small Shipyard, the museum displays thousands of artifacts attesting to the high degree of skill, artistry, and inventiveness that are a part of the

New England maritime legacy—everything from captains' portraits and ship models to fancifully carved figureheads, craftsmen's tools, and navigational equipment. A half-dozen shops nearly a century old—including a mill and joiner shop, a caulker's shed, a paint and treenail shop, and a molding loft—illustrate many of the shipbuilding trades. Berthed on the waterfront and open for inspection during the summer is a 142-foot fishing schooner, the *Sherman Zwicker*. Visitors who wish to try out their sea legs can enjoy a 30-minute cruise along the Kennebec aboard the museum's tour boat. The narrated tour features excellent views of the sprawling Bath Iron Works, whose 400-foot-tall red-and-white-striped crane can be seen some 30 miles away.

The Sagadahoc Preservation has led the fight to restore the city's historic houses and buildings and its waterfront. The preservation's effort would have pleased the famed novelist Harriet Beecher Stowe, who lived in nearby Brunswick. "A shipbuilding, ship-sailing community," Stowe said, "has an unconscious poetry underlying its existence." That poetry still works its magic in Bath.

MARITIME PRINCE'S CASTLE
Erected around 1840 by Capt. Asa Palmer, this stately house, above, passed through several owners before being bought by the prominent Sewall shipping family in 1894. The house was acquired by the Maine Maritime Museum and now serves as a function hall.

VILLAGE GREEN
The Winter Street Church, with its splendid steeple, looks over City Park, left. The church, built in 1843, combines elements of Greek and Gothic Revival architecture.

NEARBY SITES & ATTRACTIONS

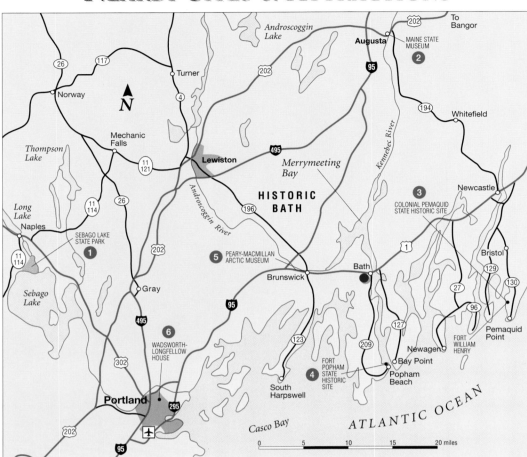

The Wadsworth-Longfellow House in Portland, above, was donated to the Maine Historical Society in 1901 by the poet's sister, Anne Longfellow Pierce.

An 1827 lighthouse peers over a rocky bluff at Pemaquid Point, right. The lighthouse keeper's home now displays a collection of old charts, photographs, and fishing equipment that represent Maine's 400-year fishing history.

① SEBAGO LAKE STATE PARK

Fine sandy beaches rim the northern shore of Sebago Lake where this 1,295-acre state park is located. There are more than 250 campsites scattered throughout the park, most of them situated along the shoreline of Maine's second-largest lake. Many fishing boats troll the lake, which is stocked annually with salmon and brook trout, and provides an ample spawning habitat for lake trout, smallmouth bass, largemouth bass, cusk, lake whitefish, and rainbow smelt. Nature trails wind through the wooded hills, and rangers are on hand to answer questions about the park's wildlife and terrain. Located 5 miles south of Naples off Hwy. 114.

② MAINE STATE MUSEUM

Maine's natural environment, prehistory, social history, and manufacturing heritage are celebrated in the programs and tours offered by this museum. The state's numerous wildlife habitats are portrayed in five natural history dioramas, which depict plants and animals that thrive in its woodlands, mountains, inland waters, marshlands, and coastal areas. Archeological artifacts, dating from the end of the last ice age to the 19th century, represent 12,000 years of human habitation in the region. They include reproductions of pictographs, authentic arrowheads,

ancient tools, and baskets and basketmaking materials. A permanent exhibit entitled "Made in Maine" is dedicated to the industries that dominate the state's economic history. On view are a water-powered woodworking mill, a two-story textile factory, and a 40-foot interior section of a square-rigged Downeaster called *The St. Mary*. Representing the agricultural industry are plows, harrows, and a Fordson tractor, as well as harvesting and processing equipment. Visitors can view The Lion—a steam locomotive built for the Whitneyville and Machiasport Railroad—and investigate a Lombard log hauler and an up-and-down sawmill. Artifacts retrieved from the sunken Revolutionary War ship *Defence* are also on display. Located at 162 State St. in Augusta.

3 COLONIAL PEMAQUID STATE HISTORIC SITE

In the mid-1620's English settlers established one of northern New England's earliest Colonial communities in the sheltered harbor where the state historic site is located. The settlers farmed the land, fished, and traded with the Abenaki and Micmac Indians. In 1677 the community was caught in a tug-of-war between the English to the south and the French to the north. Fort Charles, the first of three forts to be erected here, was constructed to protect the settlement against attack. It was razed 12 years later by the Abenakis. In 1692 the Massachusetts Bay Colony erected a second fort, Fort William Henry, to protect the settlers against further attacks; but four years later that fort was leveled by the French and Abenakis. For the next 30 years the site was left abandoned. In the 1720's an English colonel, David Dunbar, built Fort Frederick on the foundations of Fort William Henry. This fort survived until 1776 when the citizens of Bristol tore it down to prevent the British from occupying it. A modern replica of Fort William Henry stands on the site, and a museum displays some of the 75,000 artifacts that have been unearthed here. Located north of Pemaquid Point off Hwy. 130.

4 FORT POPHAM STATE HISTORIC SITE

Named in honor of George Popham, who founded the nearby settlement of Bath in 1607, Fort Popham occupied a strategic position at the mouth of the Kennebec River. The fort was erected in 1861 to protect the fledgling town against invasion by Confederate troops and their European allies at the beginning of the Civil War. The crescent-shaped fort's 30-foot-high granite walls are pierced by two stories of vaulted openings for cannons. The interior of the fort had two barrack blocks, subterranean cisterns that supplied the fort with its water, and four magazines to store gunpowder. Although the interior of the fort is closed off, visitors can tour the parade ground of the massive redoubt. Located just off Hwy. 209 at Popham Beach.

5 PEARY-MACMILLAN ARCTIC MUSEUM

Exhibitions and displays of polar artifacts, equipment, and journals commemorate the Arctic explorations of two Bowdoin College alumni: Adm. Robert Edwin

Peary (class of 1877) and Adm. Donald Baxter Macmillan (class of 1898). Peary is credited with being one of the first men (along with his assistant Matthew Henson and the Polar Eskimos Ootaq, Ooqueah, Segloo, and Egingwah) to reach the North Pole. Macmillan accompanied Peary on his 1908–09 North Pole expedition and made 26 trips of his own to the far north. Much of the memorabilia on display was donated to the college by the Peary and Macmillan families. One of the exhibits highlights Peary's trip to the North Pole with displays of his equipment, private journals and log books, maps, navigational instruments, and one of the five sledges the explorer took to the pole. An exhibit that focuses on Macmillan's expeditions contains snow goggles, soapstone pots and lamps, ivory and soapstone carvings, bone and antler tools, hunting weapons, and a full-size skin kayak given to Macmillan by the Inuit peoples of the Arctic. Located in Hubbard Hall at Bowdoin College in Brunswick.

6 WADSWORTH-LONGFELLOW HOUSE

The boyhood home of poet Henry Wadsworth Longfellow was built in 1785 by his grandfather, Gen. Peleg Wadsworth, a Revolutionary War hero. Longfellow lived in the house until 1821 when he left to study at nearby Bowdoin College. His first published poem, titled "The Battle of Lovell's Pond," was printed in the *Portland Gazette* when he was just 13 years old. Two of Longfellow's best-loved works are *Evangeline* and *The Song of Hiawatha*. On display are his desk, family mementoes, and portraits. Located at 487 Congress St. in Portland.

In the rugged upland region off the northwestern shore of Sebago Lake, above, the elevation rises from 1,000 feet near the shoreline to 4,000 feet in the White Mountains, 40 miles to the northwest. The pristine waters of the lake supply Greater Portland with its water.

PENNSYLVANIA DUTCH COUNTRY

Rural Lancaster County is home to people whose lives illuminate simple truths in traditional ways.

The rhythmic clip-clop of horse hooves echoes across a glen in rural Pennsylvania as a chestnut mare pulling a closed gray carriage dips over the crest of a hill. Gently rolling expanses of wheat that shimmered green in summer winds now blaze gold beneath a fading autumn sun. Fields of lustrous green alfalfa alternate with the ripened wheat, giving the valley the look of a patchwork quilt. The carriage is driven by a bearded man, dressed in a solid blue shirt, black straight-cut coat, and suspenders, a broad-brimmed black hat on his head. His daughter leans against him, gazing at distant trees painted yellow and rust. Her modest green dress is partially hidden by a black cloak and her hair is worn in a bun and covered by a *Kapp*, or prayer covering. In the back, two boys, looking like smaller replicas of their father, poke playfully at each other.

The scene seems to come straight out of the 18th century, but it takes place in modern-day

Overleaf: Willow trees thrive near an old stone mill in Lancaster County. The Amish still use such mills to grind wheat into flour. Although sometimes sold commercially, the flour is more often kept for the community's use.

SOLITARY PLAY

Too young to attend school, an Amish girl, wearing a white prayer covering, plays alone on her family's farm, right. At the age of six, she will go to one of the one-room Amish schoolhouses. Her formal schooling will end at the eighth grade, when she will turn her attention to farming and homemaking skills. Young Amish women wear black prayer coverings after their baptism, which takes place between the ages of 16 and 21, and before their marriage.

COMPANY FOR BREAKFAST

A pair of Amish dolls joins some visitors at the breakfast table, far right, at historic Smithton Inn, located next to the Ephrata Cloister.

Lancaster County, where many of the farm families are Old Order Amish—people taught by tradition and religion to remain aloof from the concerns and practices of the 20th century. Living apart from, yet in harmony with, their non-Amish neighbors, they farm the fertile valleys that crease the region and hold on to their old ways of life.

The Amish, along with several other German-speaking religious groups such as the Mennonites, are known as the Pennsylvania Dutch—a misnomer based on a misspelling of *Deutsch*, the German word for their language. Their ancestors came to William Penn's colony—the area now known as Lancaster County—in the early 1700's, drawn by the promise of religious tolerance, something they did not experience in their homeland. The Amish trace their roots to the Anabaptists, or rebaptizers (as the Swiss Mennonites were called), who had suffered persecution for their convictions, including the belief that only willing adults should

be baptized. The Amish who stayed in Europe were either killed or absorbed by other sects.

Penn, who was a Quaker, had welcomed other persecuted groups, including the Swiss Mennonites, Scottish Presbyterians, French Huguenots, and English Quakers to the haven provided by his colony. The Amish settled here in the hope of carving out new lives for themselves in peace. They live today in a handful of communities in the United States, Canada, and Central and South America. While some have adopted modern conveniences, such as cars and electricity, the Old Order Amish cling to traditional ways.

PLAIN PEOPLE

Visitors to Lancaster County will come to appreciate the modest dignity of Old Order Amish people, whose lives are governed by their religious convictions. Easily identified by their humble attire, the Amish reject the trappings of modernity to better devote themselves to the word of God. Visitors will notice that married Amish women always wear white prayer coverings on their heads and never don jewelry. Also, the jackets worn by the men are fastened with hooks and eyes, perhaps because buttons have been historically associated with the military and nobility or because buttons are equated with finery.

While Old Order Amish are an independent and reserved people, they are no longer as shut off from the outside world as they used to be. Some have gone so far as to build telephone booths on their property, tiny outbuildings that can be spotted here and there in the fields near farmhouses.

Yet for the most part, Old Order Amish continue to model their lives on a literal interpretation of the Bible and follow an unwritten set of rules called the *Ordnung*, which prescribes behavior, appearance, and other aspects of Amish life. They are reluctant to use devices, such as television and tractors, for fear that technology might tempt them to leave their close-knit community. Cars are shunned because the ability to travel long distances is believed to weaken ties. The taking of photographic portraits is prohibited as a violation of the biblical Second Commandment —"Thou shalt not make to thyself a graven image." Ironically, this

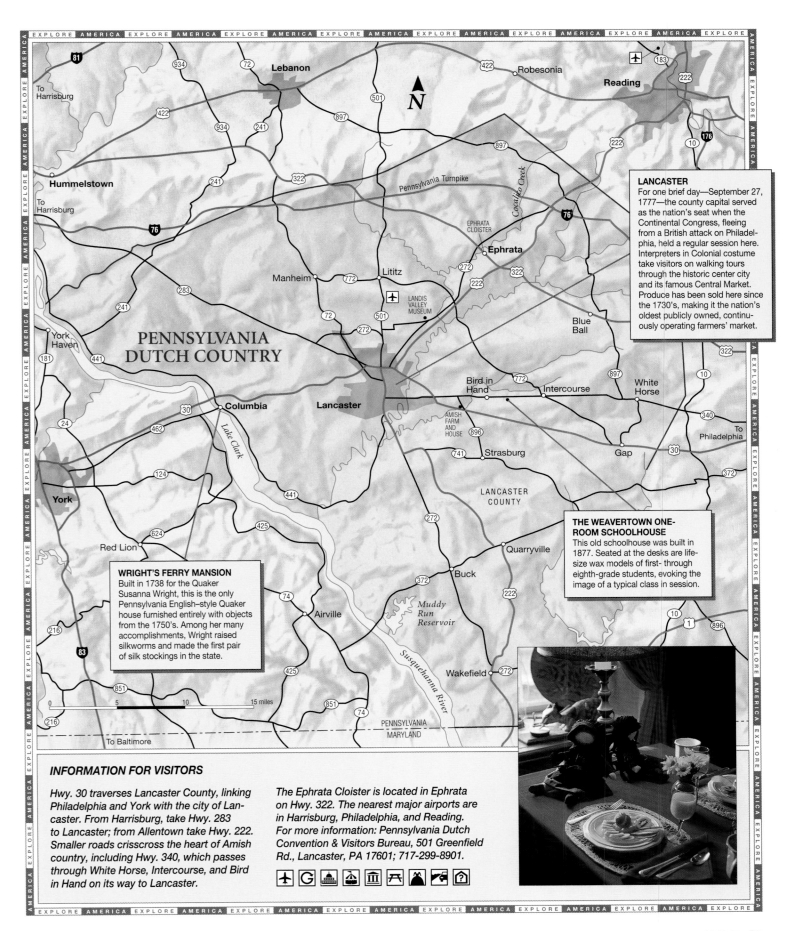

To Harrisburg

81

934

72

Lebanon

422

Robesonia

183

Reading

222

422

241

934

241

501

897

N

897

222

176

10

322

Pennsylvania Turnpike

76

76

To Harrisburg

EPHRATA
CLOISTER

LANCASTER
For one brief day—September 27, 1777—the county capital served as the nation's seat when the Continental Congress, fleeing from a British attack on Philadelphia, held a regular session here. Interpreters in Colonial costume take visitors on walking tours through the historic center city and its famous Central Market. Produce has been sold here since the 1730's, making it the nation's oldest publicly owned, continuously operating farmers' market.

Hummelstown

Ephrata

Manheim

772

Lititz

272

322

222

LANDIS
VALLEY
MUSEUM

Blue
Ball

**PENNSYLVANIA
DUTCH COUNTRY**

283

72

501

241

272

322

York
Haven

181

441

Bird in
Hand

772

Intercourse

897

White
Horse

10

Columbia

30

Lancaster

340

To
Philadelphia

24

462

AMISH
FARM
AND
HOUSE

896

Gap

30

372

Lake Clark

741

Strasburg

York

124

LANCASTER
COUNTY

441

THE WEAVERTOWN ONE-ROOM SCHOOLHOUSE
This old schoolhouse was built in 1877. Seated at the desks are life-size wax models of first- through eighth-grade students, evoking the image of a typical class in session.

425

272

Quarryville

222

Red Lion

624

WRIGHT'S FERRY MANSION
Built in 1738 for the Quaker Susanna Wright, this is the only Pennsylvania English–style Quaker house furnished entirely with objects from the 1750's. Among her many accomplishments, Wright raised silkworms and made the first pair of silk stockings in the state.

74

Airville

372

Buck

Muddy
Run
Reservoir

10

1

896

216

425

83

Wakefield

272

Susquehanna River

0   5   10   15 miles

851

851

74

216

PENNSYLVANIA
MARYLAND

To Baltimore

INFORMATION FOR VISITORS

Hwy. 30 traverses Lancaster County, linking Philadelphia and York with the city of Lancaster. From Harrisburg, take Hwy. 283 to Lancaster; from Allentown take Hwy. 222. Smaller roads crisscross the heart of Amish country, including Hwy. 340, which passes through White Horse, Intercourse, and Bird in Hand on its way to Lancaster.

The Ephrata Cloister is located in Ephrata on Hwy. 322. The nearest major airports are in Harrisburg, Philadelphia, and Reading. For more information: Pennsylvania Dutch Convention & Visitors Bureau, 501 Greenfield Rd., Lancaster, PA 17601; 717-299-8901.

rejection of the modern world is one reason some 5 million tourists make a pilgrimage to Lancaster County every year.

Although the Amish willingly pay taxes, they do not believe in insurance or government aid. Instead, they rely on one another in a crisis. When a fellow farmer, including a non-Amish one, is too sick to work his fields, his neighbors pitch in by plowing, planting, and harvesting for him. When a barn is destroyed by fire, the community gathers to build a new one. The air resounds with the methodic beat of hammers and the rasp of handsaws, and before long, bearded carpenters have raised the skeleton of a new barn where only grass stood hours before. In the kitchen of the white clapboard farmhouse nearby, a group of Amish women and girls

CLOSE FAMILIES
A high-stepping chestnut mare pulls an open buggy bearing an Amish mother and daughter along a road outside Bird in Hand, above. Older family members are cared for by their children, and grandparents are often provided with a separate dwelling on the family farm known as the Grossdawdy.

cooks food for the workers on a stove fueled with wood. They prepare sausage and apple casserole, smoked ham, pepper cabbage, and sweet shoofly pie— traditional Pennsylvania Dutch specialties.

Museums across the county provide travelers with a deeper understanding of the Pennsylvania Dutch. Tours of the Amish Farm and House, located about three miles east of Lancaster, offer a look at an 1805 stone house that is decorated and furnished in the style of the Old Order Amish people. The house was originally built by a Quaker family. It was bought by Mennonites and then by an Amish family, who lived here until 1955. A long wooden table inside the kitchen is set for dinner after a hard day's work in the fields. Outside, visitors learn how farmers managed to get by without the modern amenities: a waterwheel down by a creek and a windmill set near the house pump

water for the kitchen and barn; a kiln produces lime for the fields; and an operational blacksmith shop hammers out horseshoes and other ironworks. In the nearby fields, tobacco, alfalfa, and corn are cultivated. The farm contains the usual roster of livestock, with the addition of peacocks, which the Amish and other local farmers employ as guard animals.

Exhibits at the Landis Valley Museum near Lancaster describe Pennsylvania's German rural heritage using restored and re-created period settings such as a 1760 log farmstead, an 1800's hotel, and an 1890 schoolhouse. Agricultural equipment and vehicles, from hay wagons to sleighs, are also on display, as are several Conestoga wagons. These wagons were the tractor-trailers of the 18th to mid-19th centuries, carrying such items as grain, tobacco, and whiskey. They lumbered along the first long-distance hard-surfaced road in the country—the Philadelphia-to-Lancaster Turnpike. Special horses, bred for strength and durability, drew the wagons, whose hard-living drivers often smoked long, thin cigars called stogies, a derivation of the word Conestoga.

The museum hosts several kinds of craft demonstrations, including traditional spinning, weaving, and quilt-making, for which Pennsylvania Dutch women are renowned. Amish and Mennonite women still gather in sewing circles to fashion these practical and delightful works of art. An expression of frugality and self-sufficiency, quilting offers the women a chance to socialize with their neighbors as they skillfully stitch the pieces together.

SPIRITUAL NEIGHBORS
Mennonite and Amish farmers were just two of several German-speaking groups to find in Lancaster County a refuge for practicing their beliefs. Not long after these groups settled here, a German monastic community began to take root on the banks of Cocalico Creek, situated about 11 miles northeast of Lancaster. The medieval-style buildings of Ephrata Cloister, the home of this unique communal society, have been meticulously preserved and are open to the public.

Once 300-strong, the Ephrata Cloister followed the teachings of Georg Conrad Beissel from Eberbach, Germany, the former leader of a sect of German Baptists known as Dunkers because they believed in baptism by total immersion. After seven years, Beissel broke away so that he could adhere to his own ideas of observing the Sabbath on Saturday and practicing celibacy. In 1732 he and his followers founded Ephrata. The community survived for 200 years, first as a primarily celibate order and gradually as one that included many married members. They became known as Seventh-Day German Baptists. Self-purification and rigorous self-discipline guided the members in all aspects of their daily lives.

AUSTERE LIFESTYLE

During Beissel's lifetime, the society constructed a settlement of log, stone, and half-timbered buildings that echoed the architecture of their German homeland. Ten buildings remain, their simple and austere design reflecting the group's commitment to humility and self-discipline. The cloister corridors are narrow and straight, reminders to follow the straight path. The doorways are low so that members had to bend to pass through them, reinforcing their humility. Modern-day visitors—generally taller than their 18th-century predecessors—often need to stoop to enter these rooms.

The community consisted of three orders: a celibate brotherhood, a celibate sisterhood, and a married order of householders. In the beginning the celibates lived on the cloister property and were engaged in fruit growing, carpentry, papermaking, bookmaking, and other activities, while the householders were farmers or craftsmen who lived nearby, worshiped at the cloister and supported the community's economy. Visitors who tour Ephrata

HEADING HOME
Driving a wagon laden with corn stalks, an Amish farmer heads back to his farm, left. Once there, he will chop up the stalks and store them in his silo.

PLAIN KITCHEN
Each of the three floors in the Saron, where the celibate sisters of the Ephrata Cloister lived, has a kitchen, left. The sisters prepared one meal a day using vegetables harvested from their garden. The order's brothers and sisters rarely ate meat and dined separately unless called together by their pastor for a communal meal, which was called a love feast.

23

GROCERY SHOPPING
Two Amish women load their groceries into the back of a horse-drawn carriage in Bird in Hand, right. Amish women spend much of their time caring for their families—which tend to be large—and rarely work outside the home.

Cloister can see the *Saron*, or Sister House, which is still intact with its workrooms, kitchens, sleeping cells, and the adjoining *Saal*, a meetinghouse for worship. Each cell is furnished with a simple bare bench for a bed and a hard wooden block pillow. Another building, probably used at one time as a dormitory for celibate brothers, has been furnished as it would have been for a householder, once householders began to live in Ephrata Cloister. The furnishings are in a style similar to that of a Pennsylvania-German interior of the early 19th century. Visitors will take note that married members were allowed a great deal more comfort than were celibate members.

The orders were renowned for their calligraphy, printing, and bookmaking, as well as their choral music and composition. In 1748 they produced the 1,200-page *Martyrs Mirror*, the story of Mennonite persecution in Europe and the longest book printed in Colonial America up to then.

In the Beissel House where the society's charismatic leader lived until his death in 1768, there are regularly scheduled demonstrations of the art of calligraphy. *Frakturschriften*, or broken script, as the form of calligraphy practiced by the sisters was called, got its name from the multiple strokes of the pen used to write each letter. The sisters developed their skills by rendering music for the choir. Calligraphy was encouraged as a sacred exercise.

Beissel composed hymns for the members of the cloister that exalted the spiritual life. The a cappella chorus followed strict diets, designed for each voice by Beissel. They sang in falsetto through slightly parted lips. Visitors who attend the concerts held on special occasions in the *Saal* have a chance to hear the eerie effect of this unusual music.

In Pennsylvania Dutch country the past merges with the present in telling vignettes and fleeting impressions: a lone farmer perched on the back of a plow leads his team of mules as they churn through soil tinged red by the sunrise; a young girl beguiles motorists with her shy wave from the back window of a closed family carriage; a woman, her face obscured by a white cowl, bends over a manuscript, silently crafting a beautiful script. Visitors to Lancaster County come to understand the attraction of an old-world existence and the simple truths such a life reveals.

NEARBY SITES & ATTRACTIONS

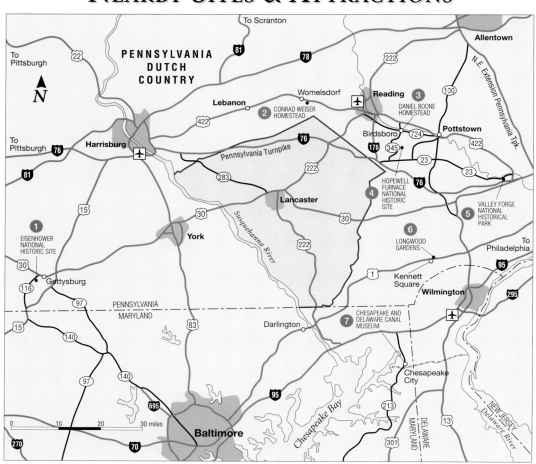

During the Revolutionary War colonists produced arms for the Casting House, below, now part of Hopewell Furnace National Historic Site.

1 EISENHOWER NATIONAL HISTORIC SITE, PENNSYLVANIA

Although in his lifetime he occupied more than 35 residences, including the White House for eight years, Dwight D. Eisenhower owned only one home—built on this 690-acre site. The two-story Georgian-style house was constructed in 1955 according to the specifications of Eisenhower's wife, Mamie. Within these walls, the 34th president of the United States hosted Charles de Gaulle, Winston Churchill, and Nikita Khrushchev. A landscape painting left unfinished by Eisenhower, as well as the putting green and sand trap behind the house, gives visitors a hint of the private man. Located on Taneytown Rd. in Gettysburg.

2 CONRAD WEISER HOMESTEAD PENNSYLVANIA

German-born Conrad Weiser was a friend of the Iroquois chief, Shikellamy, and became an important force in the mid-1700's during negotiations to maintain peace on the frontier. His house, built about 1729, is furnished with period pieces. The Weiser family burial plot is situated on a nearby hill. Located 1 mile east of Womelsdorf on Hwy. 422.

3 DANIEL BOONE HOMESTEAD, PENNSYLVANIA

Daniel Boone, America's most famous frontiersman, was born here in 1734. The restored Boone House and six other 18th-century buildings reveal what life was like for the early settlers. As visitors stroll the 579-acre grounds, they may spot woodchuck dens, painted turtles in the lake, and various songbirds. Located at 400 Daniel Boone Rd. in Birdsboro.

4 HOPEWELL FURNACE NATIONAL HISTORIC SITE, PENNSYLVANIA

More than a dozen restored and reconstructed buildings, including a casthouse and blast furnace, an ironmaster's house, and a company store, help bring this 18th- and 19th-century iron-making village back to life. During the summer, costumed interpreters re-enact the activities that made the company town run. Located south of Birdsboro on Hwy. 345.

5 VALLEY FORGE NATIONAL HISTORICAL PARK, PENNSYLVANIA

Although no battle was fought here, Valley Forge is one of the most important sites of the Revolutionary War. On December 19, 1777, George Washington led 12,000 exhausted troops to the site and set up camp until spring. The men were so undernourished and poorly clothed that more than 2,000 of them died. The military training and reorganization conducted at Valley Forge that winter enabled the army to succeed in America's war for independence.

The stately Isaac Potts House, in the Valley Forge National Historical Park, above, served as George Washington's headquarters from December 1777 to June 1778.

Washington's headquarters and a visitor center are open to the public. Located 18 miles northwest of Philadelphia on Hwy. 23.

6 LONGWOOD GARDENS, PENNSYLVANIA

Longwood Gardens is one of the world's premier horticultural displays, reminiscent of the great pleasure gardens of Europe. Some 11,000 species of plants flourish throughout 1,050 acres of formal gardens, meadows, and woodlands. About four acres are enclosed within the Conservatory. The Topiary section displays shrubs clipped in elegant geometric shapes. Other areas of interest include the Wisteria Garden, Peony Garden, Hillside Garden and the Rose Arbor. Roses and orchids bloom year-round within the Conservatory. Located near the town of Kennett Square.

7 CHESAPEAKE AND DELAWARE CANAL MUSEUM, DELAWARE

The canal connecting Chesapeake Bay and the Delaware River was opened in 1829 and has become one of the busiest canals in the world. The museum celebrates the waterway's rich history. There are models of a canal barge and a pipeline dredge, and a working model shows how the canal's lift lock is operated. On view in the Old Lock Pump House are steam-driven pumping engines and an antique cypress-wood waterwheel. Located off the Canal Bridge in Chesapeake City.

Pierre du Pont, the creator of Longwood Gardens, left, was inspired by his European travels. He kept his childhood promise that if he ever built a greenhouse it would be open to the public.

BATTLE AT GETTYSBURG

The pivotal battle of the Civil War was fought near this small Pennsylvania town.

Across the pastoral fields and burly ridges that surround the small town of Gettysburg, amid its wooded hills and peach orchards, lingers the memory of a terrible three-day battle fought here in the summer of 1863. An enduring shadow of warriors in blue and gray still hovers in this place, luring modern pilgrims to walk the ground hallowed by the monumental events of that July long ago. The town was a rural backwater before the bloody clash of arms that saw some 51,000 American soldiers killed, wounded, or captured. Today it draws 1.7 million people annually. They come to awaken their imaginations to the fighting that raged on here in what proved to be the turning point of the Civil War. It involved more than 163,000 troops and was the largest battle ever fought on American soil.

Gettysburg was a likely place for the Union and Confederate armies to meet: all roads in the region converged here. Today the town square remains a busy crossroads, lined by historic buildings, souvenir shops, and sites such as the Lincoln

HIGH GROUND
The statue of Brig. Gen. G. K.
Warren, above, overlooks the
battlefield from Little Round Top.
Warren wisely placed artillery
on the summit, allowing Federal
troops to defend the strategic hill.

SILENT WEAPONS OF WAR
Overleaf: Once fire-breathing
messengers of death, the cannons
positioned along the fenceline on
Seminary Ridge now stand as silent
reminders to the horrors of war.

Room Museum. The battlefield, by contrast, is striking in its understatement. The sheer size of the park comes as a surprise to many. Gettysburg National Military Park, which almost completely surrounds the town, is a sprawling 5,733 acres. The overall terrain has changed little since the summer of 1863, when Gen. Robert E. Lee's Army of Northern Virginia marched into the region.

The Confederate soldiers tramped along the dusty roads of Pennsylvania in three long, ragged columns—70,000 strong wearing gray and butternut uniforms—followed by artillery caissons and supply wagons. Although the invading army was orderly, it was disheveled in appearance: "Most of the men were exceedingly dirty, some ragged, some without shoes," noted an eyewitness, "[but they were] well armed and under perfect discipline. They seemed to move like one vast machine."

Fresh from a major victory at the Battle of Chancellorsville, Virginia, Lee's army was at the peak of its strength and confidence. The general hoped a successful invasion in the very heart of Union territory would force the North to make peace, or else spur France and England to recognize the Confederacy officially. But most important, it would produce a decisive victory that would end the war and result in Southern nationhood.

On June 30, 1863, Lee was unsure as to the exact whereabouts of the Northern army. Gen. J. E. B. Stuart, whom Lee called his eyes and ears, had taken his cavalry on a raid to Hanover, 12 miles east of Gettysburg, and was unable to report on the Federal position. Lee dispersed his army across south-central Pennsylvania: one corps was stationed near Chambersburg, a second north of Gettysburg, and a third at Cashtown, between Chambersburg and Gettysburg. In the meantime, President Lincoln's Army of the Potomac under Gen. George G. Meade was making its way into Pennsylvania to intercept the Confederate invaders.

INFORMATION FOR VISITORS

To reach Gettysburg from Philadelphia take the Pennsylvania Turnpike to Harrisburg. From Harrisburg, take Hwy. 15 south. The park includes 35 miles of roads and 17 miles of hiking and horse-back trails. It is dotted with 1,340 battle-related monuments, memorials, and markers, a visitor center and museum, a battlefield cyclorama, and three park service observation towers. Maps and directions can be obtained at the visitor center, which also provides licensed guides and rents audiotapes for self-guided tours. Commercial bus tours are available from town. For more information: Superintendent, Gettysburg National Military Park, Gettysburg, PA 17325; 717-334-1124.

FOR VALOR
The 42nd New York Infantry—called the Tammany Regiment after the Delaware Indian chief—was honored for its part in Pickett's Charge with a memorial, above, erected near the High Water Mark.

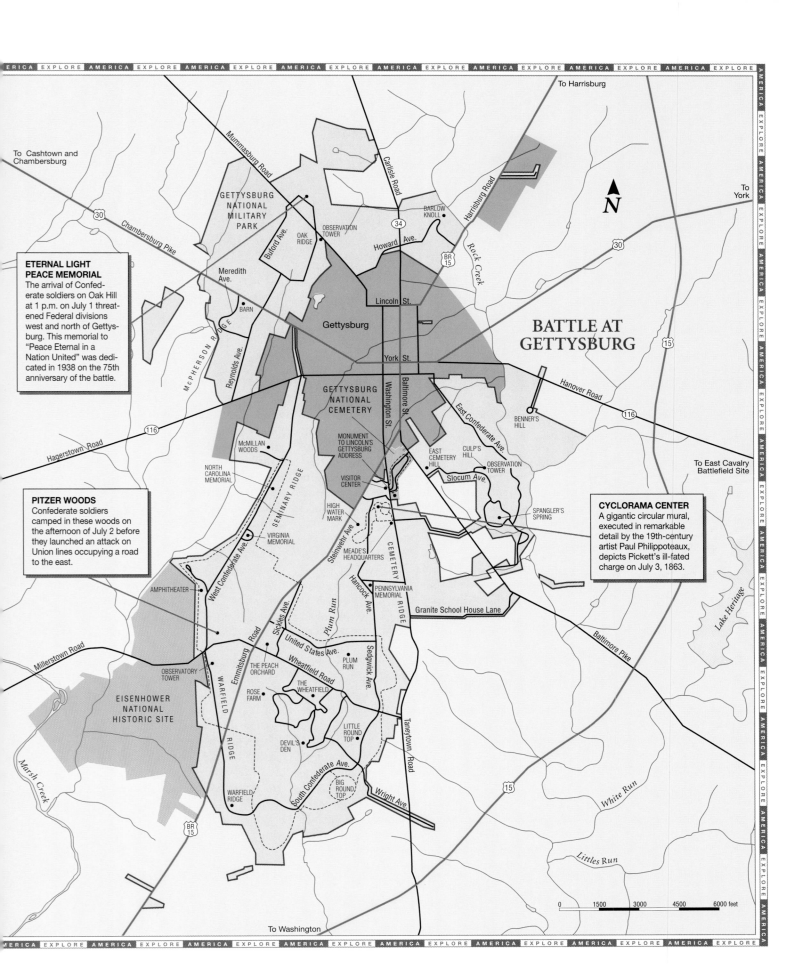

To Harrisburg

To Cashtown and
Chambersburg

To York

30

Chambersburg Pike

Mummasburg Road

Carlisle Road

Harrisburg Road

34

BARLOW KNOLL

OBSERVATION TOWER

Rock Creek

GETTYSBURG NATIONAL MILITARY PARK

Buford Ave.

OAK RIDGE

Howard Ave.

BR 15

30

15

ETERNAL LIGHT PEACE MEMORIAL
The arrival of Confederate soldiers on Oak Hill at 1 p.m. on July 1 threatened Federal divisions west and north of Gettysburg. This memorial to "Peace Eternal in a Nation United" was dedicated in 1938 on the 75th anniversary of the battle.

Meredith Ave.

BARN

McPHERSON RIDGE

Reynolds Ave.

Lincoln St.

Gettysburg

BATTLE AT GETTYSBURG

York St.

Washington St.

Baltimore St.

Hanover Road

East Confederate Ave.

BENNER'S HILL

116

116

Hagerstown Road

GETTYSBURG NATIONAL CEMETERY

McMILLAN WOODS

SEMINARY RIDGE

NORTH CAROLINA MEMORIAL

MONUMENT TO LINCOLN'S GETTYSBURG ADDRESS

VISITOR CENTER

EAST CEMETERY HILL

CULP'S HILL

OBSERVATION TOWER

Slocum Ave.

To East Cavalry Battlefield Site

PITZER WOODS
Confederate soldiers camped in these woods on the afternoon of July 2 before they launched an attack on Union lines occupying a road to the east.

VIRGINIA MEMORIAL

HIGH WATER MARK

Steinwehr Ave.

MEADE'S HEADQUARTERS

CEMETERY RIDGE

SPANGLER'S SPRING

CYCLORAMA CENTER
A gigantic circular mural, executed in remarkable detail by the 19th-century artist Paul Philippoteaux, depicts Pickett's ill-fated charge on July 3, 1863.

AMPHITHEATER

West Confederate Ave.

Hancock Ave.

PENNSYLVANIA MEMORIAL

Granite School House Lane

Baltimore Pike

Lake Heritage

Emmitsburg Road

Sickles Ave.

Plum Run

United States Ave.

THE PEACH ORCHARD

Wheatfield Road

PLUM RUN

Sedgwick Ave.

Millerstown Road

Observatory TOWER

EISENHOWER NATIONAL HISTORIC SITE

WARFIELD RIDGE

ROSE FARM

THE WHEATFIELD

DEVIL'S DEN

LITTLE ROUND TOP

Taneytown Road

Marsh Creek

WARFIELD RIDGE

South Confederate Ave.

BIG ROUND TOP

Wright Ave.

15

White Run

BR 15

Littles Run

To Washington

0   1500   3000   4500   6000 feet

The Virginia Memorial, right, stands on Seminary Ridge near where Gen. Robert E. Lee surveyed Pickett's Charge on the afternoon of July 3, 1863. The figures of a youth, farmer, businessman, and plantation owner on horseback represent the people from different walks of life who fought in the battle.

DEVIL'S DEN
From their shelter inside Devil's Den, comprised of a group of house-sized granite boulders positioned here by glaciers, above, Confederate sharpshooters picked off Federals stationed 500 yards away on the slope of Little Round Top.

A good place to hold a battlefield reconnaissance today is at the park's visitor center, where Gettysburg's famous electric map helps orient visitors with colored lights that illustrate troop movement during the battle.

OPENING BATTLE The fighting started on the northwestern side of town, just after daybreak on July 1. Two divisions of Confederate troops marched down the road from Cashtown and attacked the Union cavalry under the command of Gen. John Buford just beyond McPherson's barn on the ridge by that name. Although outnumbered, Buford's cavalry was able to stall the Confederate advance until reinforcements arrived. Today the equestrian statue of Gen. John F. Reynolds, commander of the reinforcements, stands watch over the Chambersburg Pike (U.S. 30 West) near the intersection of Reynolds Avenue, facing toward the advancing Confederates. Nearby is a statue of Buford, who survived the carnage of Gettysburg only to die six months later of an illness he contracted in the field. The Southern troops were repulsed and many were captured before the tide shifted in their favor. During the valiant Union stand, Reynolds was shot from the saddle and killed at a point south of where his statue now stands.

Some of the fiercest fighting of the day took place on what is now Meredith Avenue, which runs to McPherson Ridge. On one side of the avenue stands a monument to the Iron Brigade, a unit of Midwesterners known for their courageous fighting, and on the other side is a memorial to the 26th North Carolina. Led by 26-year-old Col. Henry Burgwyn, the North Carolina troops fought their way up the wooded ridge. They suffered horrible casualties—Colonel Burgwyn himself was mortally wounded—but they finally defeated the much heralded Iron Brigade.

The drive north on Reynolds Avenue crosses the Chambersburg Pike, traverses the railroad, and heads in the direction of the Eternal Light Peace Memorial. Barlow Knoll is located north of the town of Gettysburg, and is the site where a bold afternoon assault by Confederate troops breached the Federal line, causing it to collapse all the way along McPherson Ridge. The badly outnumbered Northern forces made a hasty retreat. However, about a half mile south of town on East Cemetery Hill, they rallied and organized a strong defensive position along Cemetery Ridge.

From the observation tower atop Culp's Hill—a rocky, wooded peak situated on the eastern edge of town—visitors can reexamine the overall strategy and tactics employed by both sides during the battle. When the second day's fighting began, the Federal defensive line formed a fishhook shape, with the hook bending west from Culp's Hill to Cemetery Ridge and the shank stretching south along Cemetery Ridge to the base of Little Round Top. Lee's army had established its position along a parallel course that stretched along Emmitsburg Road and Seminary Ridge and curled at the southern edge of Gettysburg; they were ready to face the enemy, now dug in on Culp's Hill.

Lee was advised that the Federal positions on Culp's Hill and East Cemetery Hill were too strong to assault so he ordered an attack on the Federal left. The time-consuming deployment of troops delayed the attack until almost four o'clock. By then the Union forces had strengthened their line along Cemetery Ridge and on a rise known as the Peach Orchard, quite close to the intersection of Emmitsburg Road and Wheatfield Road.

Today a road takes drivers past the Peach Orchard, where peach trees still grow, and the Wheatfield, then on to Devil's Den. Ferocious fighting continued to rage here throughout the afternoon and spread to Little Round Top. At the peak of the battle, Confederate forces appeared on the verge of breaking through the Federal line north of Little Round Top, but a courageous stand by 262 troops of the 1st Minnesota preserved the line, at the heavy toll of 215 dead and wounded.

On the southern slope of Little Round Top is a ridge marked by a stone wall and a modest monument. It was here that the decisive moments of the battle unfolded.

BAYONET CHARGE

This was the site of a last stand similar to that taken by the 1st Minnesota—and perhaps an even closer call for the Union forces. On July 2 this position represented the extreme left flank of the Federal line, and was defended by the 20th Maine Infantry commanded by a former college professor, Col. Joshua Lawrence Chamberlain. Ordered by Chamberlain to hold its position "at all hazards," the regiment repelled Confederate attacks repeatedly. They were almost out of ammunition and on the verge of being overrun, when Chamberlain ordered his troops to prepare for a surprise bayonet charge. The soldiers

CEMETERY HILL
The area known as Cemetery Hill, below, was the site of several skirmishes. On July 1 Union soldiers rallied here after their retreat from the northern end of town. The hill was occupied by the Federal line for the next two days, and on July 3, the artillery forces helped repulse Pickett's Charge.

During the summer months volunteers reenact the battle in Gettysburg National Military Park using period firearms and swords such as the ones pictured, right. The Lincoln Address Memorial, below, is one of Gettysburg's most poignant sites. The memorial commemorates the eloquent words spoken by President Lincoln at the dedication of the Gettysburg National Cemetery on November 19, 1863.

from Maine affixed bayonets on their guns and met the next Southern assault with a counterattack, pushing back the exhausted Confederates.

Near dark, the Confederates attempted a long-delayed assault on the Federal right flank. They scrambled up Culp's Hill, but failed to capture either that hill or nearby Cemetery Hill. The Southerners tried a second time before dawn, but their valiant assault did little but slash the trees and end with scores of dead Southerners.

On July 2 Stuart and his cavalry returned from their raid. Lee ordered him to send in his 6,500-man cavalry to attack the Federal position from the rear. Stuart's assault was blocked by a fierce counterattack of 4,500 Union cavalrymen. The battle was waged three miles east of Gettysburg at what is now called the East Cavalry Battlefield Site. Having failed either to break the Union flanks or to attack them from the rear, Lee decided to strike at the center of the enemy line.

DAY OF RECKONING

Hoping to shatter the Federal center, Lee ordered a massive infantry assault, organized by Gen. James Longstreet and directed by Gen. George E. Pickett, whose division of Virginians had just arrived. "The enemy is there," Pickett said, pointing to Cemetery Ridge, "and I am going to strike him." At one o'clock on July 3, as many as 170 Confederate artillery pieces opened fire, pounding at the very heart of the Federal line. The Northern artillery returned fire, and soon the battleground was enveloped in smoke and dust. Along West Confederate Avenue, which follows the western rim of the military park, 400 field pieces remain at the approximate site of the Confederate artillery position that day. The present-day visitor to the North Carolina Memorial can cast his or her gaze across the wide-open fields toward Cemetery Ridge and try to visualize the chaos and carnage that once permeated this tranquil pastoral scene with the blood of both sides.

At one point the Federal artillery fire slackened, raising Confederate hopes that their relentless bombardment had overwhelmed the Northerners. Longstreet signaled General Pickett, who rallied his men with the words "Up men, and to your posts! Don't forget today that you are from old Virginia!" At about three o'clock in the afternoon, some 13,000 veteran Confederate troops emerged from the woods on Seminary Ridge, reached today by West Confederate Avenue. The ill-fated Pickett's Charge had begun.

Advancing across the rolling Pennsylvania countryside holding aloft battle flags as if on parade, the mile-long line of infantrymen moved resolutely toward the now famous clump of trees at the center of the Federal line on Cemetery Ridge. It was a magnificent spectacle—"fearfully irresistible" according to one Union observer. But the mood of triumph would be short-lived.

RETRACING BRAVE STEPS

The Union artillery opened fire on the Southern ranks. Still the Confederate soldiers advanced. They clambered over rail fences, crossed Emmitsburg Road, and charged up the smoke-filled field toward the stone fence atop Cemetery Ridge. Visitors today can walk the route of Pickett's Charge. They leave Seminary Ridge between the North Carolina and Virginia memorials, and head across the field, climb or pass through the reconstructed post-and-rail fence, carefully cross Emmitsburg Road, and make the final hike toward the distant clump of trees and the stone wall atop Cemetery Ridge. Solemnly and thoughtfully, today's marchers—like the Southern troops on that fiery day—follow the route, trying to imagine the thoughts that raced through the minds of the brave Confederate soldiers as artillery shells exploded all around them and their comrades fell to the deadly rake of rifle fire.

Few Southerners made it to the ridge. The storm of Northern fire devastated their ranks, leaving great gaps in the line and piles of bodies strewn on the ground. The troops of the 26th North Carolina —the battered survivors of McPherson Ridge— had joined the charge and advanced the farthest. They reached the stone wall on Cemetery Ridge, near a place indicated today by a modest stone marker. There the stouthearted North Carolinians withered before a double blast of canister from the 1st Rhode Island Light Artillery.

At Cemetery Ridge, some 200 Virginians, led by Gen. Lewis A. Armistead, scaled the stone wall and pierced the Union line. For an instant, Pickett's Charge appeared close to succeeding. Then a surge of Northern troops drove the Southerners back, mortally wounding General Armistead. It was the high-water mark of the Confederacy. Never again would the Confederate goal of independence seem within reach. Amid wild cheers by the victorious Northern troops, the Confederate survivors of Pickett's Charge streamed back across the corpse-littered field in defeat. At the present-day site of the Virginia Memorial they were met by Lee. "It's all my fault," the general told them.

Pickett's Charge ended the battle of Gettysburg. An estimated 28,000 Confederate and 23,000 Union troops lost their lives in this battle. Although the bloody war would wage for almost two more years, the victory at Gettysburg preserved the Union for the North and doomed the Confederate quest for nationhood. Across Taneytown Road from the visitor center lies the Gettysburg National Cemetery. It was here on November 19, 1863, that Pres. Abraham Lincoln delivered his famous Gettysburg Address. Lincoln's words that day befit all who fought and died at Gettysburg: "We cannot dedicate, we cannot consecrate, we can not hallow this ground. The brave men living and dead who struggled here have consecrated it far above our poor power to add or detract."

SIMPLE LODGING
Union General Meade set up his headquarters in the farmhouse of the widow Lydia Leister, below. It was here, on the night of July 2, 1863, that he and his top officers decided to stand and fight.

NEARBY SITES & ATTRACTIONS

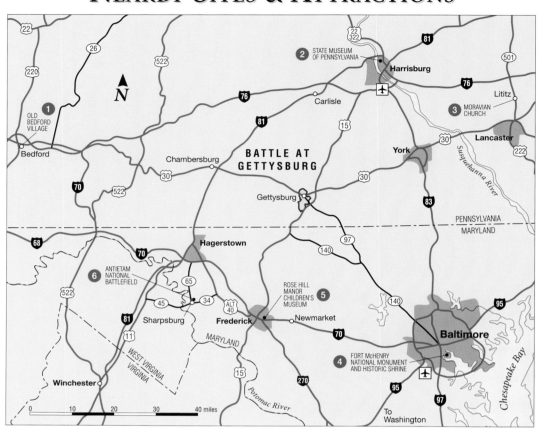

Among the weaponry on display at Fort McHenry is the Rodman gun, below, which was designed specifically to penetrate ironclad vessels.

1 OLD BEDFORD VILLAGE, PENNSYLVANIA

With numerous restored and reconstructed buildings, this living history museum captures the spirit of Pennsylvania frontier life. The re-created Colonial settlement extends over 72 acres and includes 40 log cabin homes, workshops, barns, and several one-room schoolhouses. Original buildings date between 1750 and 1850. Costumed interpreters reenact Colonial rural activities such as tinsmithing, basket weaving, potting, gun making, tanning, broom making, and cooking over an open hearth. Theater performances and special events take place from May to December. Located in Bedford off Hwy. 220.

2 STATE MUSEUM OF PENNSYLVANIA, PENNSYLVANIA

Established in 1905, this museum traces the colorful history of the Keystone State from prehistoric times to the present. Displays range from natural science and the military to fine arts and industry; there is something of interest for everyone. Visitors can peruse exhibits of pewter, furniture, and ironwork, and examine Peter F. Rothermel's *Battle of Gettysburg*, one of the largest frame paintings in the world, or the original Pennsylvania charter issued to William Penn by King Charles II. The museum also contains a full-scale re-created Pennsylvania town with cobblestone streets lined with small shops and homes, and a Native American village. Other popular exhibits

include the Planetarium, the Hall of Mammals, and the Carboniferous Forest. Located at the junction of Third and North streets in Harrisburg.

❸ MORAVIAN CHURCH, PENNSYLVANIA

Founded 60 years before the Reformation in 1457, the Moravian Church claims to be the oldest organized Protestant religious group. The first Moravian church in the United States was erected in Lititz in 1749, and a village soon grew up around it. The community was named after the castle in Lititz, Bohemia, where the first Moravians made their headquarters under their leader John Hus. The present church was built in 1787 and is the fifth church to be built here. The belfry of the church soars above the town. The bell is rung at 11:30 a.m. Monday through Friday, a custom that began in 1787 to notify farmers that noontime was at hand. The adjacent Moravian Home, erected in 1908, houses the church's archives. It also serves as a small museum for the display of a collection of artifacts, manuscripts on the history of the church, and musical instruments going back to the early days of the community. Located at 8 Church Sq. in Lititz.

❹ FORT McHENRY NATIONAL MONUMENT AND HISTORIC SHRINE, MARYLAND

Built in the late 18th century and designed to protect the city of Baltimore from a naval attack, this fort is best known as the inspiration for Francis Scott Key's "Star-Spangled Banner," written during the War of 1812. After British forces attacked and burned Washington, D.C., they sailed on to Baltimore and on September 13 and 14, 1814, bombarded the fort. Francis Scott Key—a Baltimore lawyer—witnessed the attack from a ship in the harbor. When, after 25 hours, the smoke from more than 1,800 British bombs had cleared, Key was astounded to see that the American flag still flew. Today visitors can view a replica of the 30-by-42-foot flag, with its 15 stars. The fort has been restored to its mid-19th-century appearance and displays artifacts from the War of 1812, the Civil War, and World War I. British bombs

and rockets are on exhibit in the museum. During the summer interpreters dressed in American military uniforms perform drills and flag-raising ceremonies. Located on East Ford Ave. in Baltimore.

❺ ROSE HILL MANOR CHILDREN'S MUSEUM, MARYLAND

Housed in a Georgian manor, this museum permits visitors to handle originals and reproductions of 18th-century tools, toys, clothing, and other artifacts. The kitchen alone contains 300 artifacts. With the assistance of costumed interpreters, visitors young and old can operate a butter churn and roll dough for biscuits. In the textile room, guides help visitors card wool and teach them how to sew quilts. A collection of 18th-century toys is popular with young visitors. Several second-floor rooms contain the possessions of Thomas Johnson, the first elected governor of Maryland. Located in Frederick.

❻ ANTIETAM NATIONAL BATTLEFIELD, MARYLAND

This is the site of one of the bloodiest single days of the Civil War, whose outcome profoundly influenced international politics and the duration of the war. At the end of the day on September 17, 1862, more than 23,000 Confederate and Union soldiers lay dead or wounded. The battle marked the first attempt by Confederate general Robert E. Lee to cross into Union territory. Unable to break through the Union forces led by Gen. George B. McClellan, Lee failed to gain a foothold in the North, effectively dashing Confederate hopes of being aided by the British. An eight-and-a-half-mile automobile tour winds past small exhibits in the battle area. The visitor center displays battlefield artifacts, including medical equipment, uniforms, and swords, as well as paintings of the battle; a film depicting the battle is also presented. During the summer visitors can watch costumed interpreters perform firing drills using authentic reproductions of Civil War equipment. The visitor center is located 1 mile north of Sharpsburg off Hwy. 65.

Burnside Bridge, above, was the scene of a heroic Confederate stand during the Battle of Antietam, in which some 400 Georgian riflemen held off the superior Union forces for four hours.

The dignified Moravian Church building in Lititz, left, is surmounted by a belfry, which was designed by David Tanneberger, a noted Colonial organ builder.

SAVANNAH

*Squares, parks, and architectural
treasures retain the graciousness
of the past in this seaport city.*

Sunrise in Savannah is a magical time. Golden shafts of light slice through moss-draped branches of ancient oaks and illuminate the cobblestone streets. As the sun climbs higher, the intricate detail of the sweeping staircases and cast-iron work that embellish the historic downtown's 18th- and 19th-century buildings is brought to the fore. Grecian fountains gleam in the orderly squares, and the air is perfumed by the sweet scent of magnolia. In the distance the muffled sounds of a horse-drawn carriage rattling through the streets can be heard, heightening the impression that Savannah is a city frozen in time.

Yet Savannah is no museum village, no quaint Olde Towne contrived for tourists. Just under the beguiling surface, hard and often tragic contours trace the old port city's journey through time. Here is a town founded on lofty ideals that was the setting for one of the Revolutionary War's most bloody battles. It surrendered bitterly to Union forces during the Civil War, suffered hideous epidemics and destructive fires, and watched its commercial life flourish and decline as the price of cotton rose and fell precipitously.

OLD-WORLD CHARM
Overleaf: Restored 19th-century row houses on West Charlton Street display Savannah's elegant architecture. The stately buildings encircle Madison Square, named for Pres. James Madison.

NEW LIFE ON THE RIVER
Many of the buildings along the Rousakis Riverfront Plaza, right, began as cotton warehouses. Today they house boutiques, artists' studios, restaurants, and pubs.

KING COTTON
Savannah became a prosperous link in the cotton trade in the 19th century. The money made in cotton, opposite page, fueled the building boom that transformed the city from a modest town to a grand Southern metropolis.

Today in Chippewa Square the bronze statue of Gen. James Oglethorpe gazes out upon the city he founded in 1733. A high-minded English army officer and member of Parliament, Oglethorpe was moved by the plight of England's debtors, dissenters, and working poor. His plan was to give these social outcasts a fresh start harvesting silks, wines, and spices for Britain in a new colony called Georgia. Oglethorpe's vision included banning rum, slavery, and the selling of large land tracts to speculators. The British government supported the idea of a colony as a buffer zone between Spanish Florida and the English Carolinas, and gave Oglethorpe its financial backing.

In 1733 Oglethorpe sailed up the Savannah River in search of a site for his settlement. He chose a spot about 15 miles from the ocean: a valuable chunk of high ground on the riverbank surrounded by fertile marshland that was easy to defend and which became known as Yamacraw Bluff. One of the first planned cities in America, Savannah's original layout was based on a series of wards, or neighborhoods, each of which was centered on a public square. Happily, 21 of the original 24 squares remain today.

Despite his lofty intentions, Oglethorpe could not meet all his goals. Efforts to establish wine and silk industries failed, and in order to compete with other slave-holding states, the settlement's trustees began allowing slave labor by the 1740's.

Nevertheless, the colony flourished in the mid-1700's, thanks to healthy profits from the rice and tobacco crops and its prosperous seaport. Savannah's reputation for tolerance of cultural and religious differences attracted people of many different ethnic backgrounds including Scots, Moravians, Sephardic Jews, and French Huguenots. One immigrant was John Wesley, who served as Oglethorpe's Anglican chaplain before he returned to England and became the founder of Methodism. By the start of the Revolutionary War in 1776, the city's population had swelled to over 2,000 people.

Captured by the British in 1778, Savannah was attacked by the Continental forces the following year. During the bloody Battle of Savannah, Casimir Pulaski, the Polish-born hero of the American Revolution and the father of the American calvary was fatally wounded when he led a charge into the teeth of the English defense. Repulsing the attack, the British held Savannah until July 1782.

RISING FROM THE ASHES

Disaster struck again in 1796, when two-thirds of the city was destroyed in a huge fire. Displaying characteristic pluck, Savannah's residents rebuilt their city on top of the ashes. One of the improvements made during the reconstruction was the planting of pride-of-China trees throughout Savannah to beautify the city and provide much-needed shade.

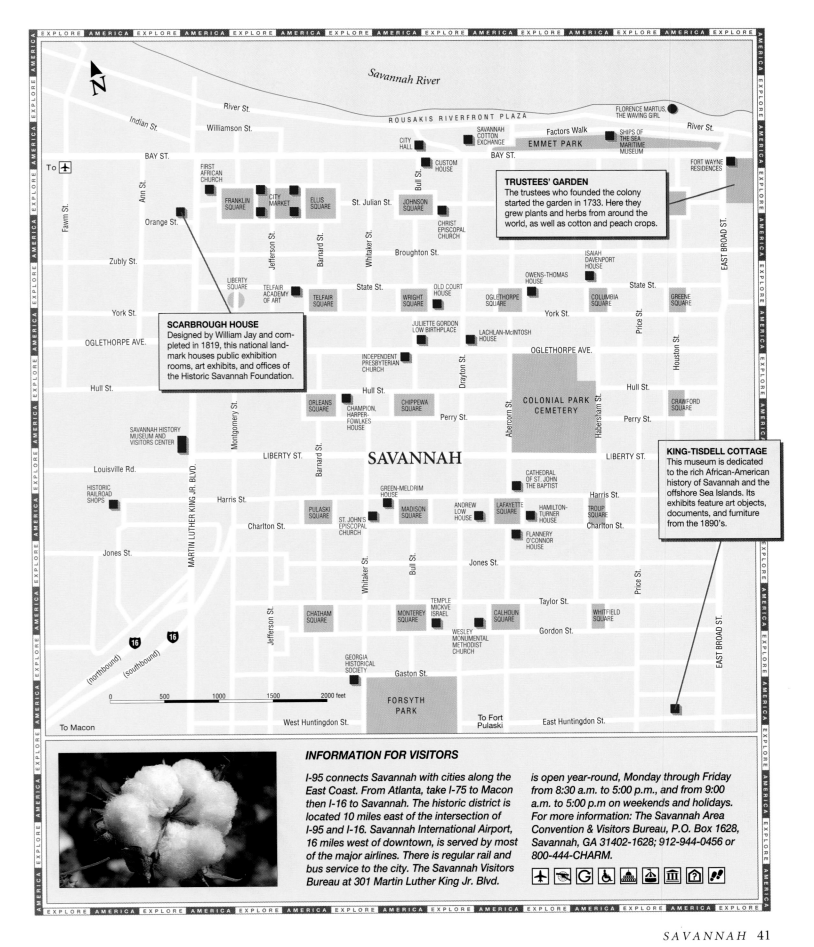

N

Savannah River

River St.

Indian St.

Williamson St.

ROUSAKIS RIVERFRONT PLAZA

FLORENCE MARTUS, THE WAVING GIRL

River St.

BAY ST.

To ✈

SAVANNAH COTTON EXCHANGE

Factors Walk

EMMET PARK

SHIPS OF THE SEA MARITIME MUSEUM

CITY HALL

BAY ST.

FIRST AFRICAN CHURCH

CUSTOM HOUSE

FORT WAYNE RESIDENCES

Ann St.

Fawm St.

FRANKLIN SQUARE

CITY MARKET

ELLIS SQUARE

St. Julian St.

Bull St.

JOHNSON SQUARE

TRUSTEES' GARDEN
The trustees who founded the colony started the garden in 1733. Here they grew plants and herbs from around the world, as well as cotton and peach crops.

Orange St.

CHRIST EPISCOPAL CHURCH

EAST BROAD ST.

Zubly St.

Jefferson St.

Barnard St.

Whitaker St.

Broughton St.

ISAIAH DAVENPORT HOUSE

York St.

LIBERTY SQUARE

TELFAIR ACADEMY OF ART

TELFAIR SQUARE

State St.

WRIGHT SQUARE

OLD COURT HOUSE

OGLETHORPE SQUARE

OWENS-THOMAS HOUSE

State St.

COLUMBIA SQUARE

Price St.

GREENE SQUARE

York St.

SCARBROUGH HOUSE
Designed by William Jay and completed in 1819, this national landmark houses public exhibition rooms, art exhibits, and offices of the Historic Savannah Foundation.

OGLETHORPE AVE.

JULIETTE GORDON LOW BIRTHPLACE

LACHLAN-McINTOSH HOUSE

Houston St.

Hull St.

INDEPENDENT PRESBYTERIAN CHURCH

Drayton St.

OGLETHORPE AVE.

Hull St.

CRAWFORD SQUARE

Hull St.

ORLEANS SQUARE

CHAMPION, HARPER-FOWLKES HOUSE

CHIPPEWA SQUARE

Perry St.

Abercorn St.

COLONIAL PARK CEMETERY

Habersham St.

Perry St.

SAVANNAH HISTORY MUSEUM AND VISITORS CENTER

Montgomery St.

Barnard St.

LIBERTY ST.

SAVANNAH

LIBERTY ST.

KING-TISDELL COTTAGE
This museum is dedicated to the rich African-American history of Savannah and the offshore Sea Islands. Its exhibits feature art objects, documents, and furniture from the 1890's.

Louisville Rd.

MARTIN LUTHER KING JR. BLVD.

Harris St.

CATHEDRAL OF ST. JOHN THE BAPTIST

Harris St.

HISTORIC RAILROAD SHOPS

GREEN-MELDRIM HOUSE

PULASKI SQUARE

MADISON SQUARE

ANDREW LOW HOUSE

LAFAYETTE SQUARE

HAMILTON-TURNER HOUSE

TROUP SQUARE

Charlton St.

Charlton St.

ST. JOHN'S EPISCOPAL CHURCH

FLANNERY O'CONNOR HOUSE

Jones St.

Jones St.

Whitaker St.

Bull St.

Price St.

Taylor St.

16 (northbound) 16 (southbound)

Jefferson St.

CHATHAM SQUARE

MONTEREY SQUARE

TEMPLE MICKVE ISRAEL

CALHOUN SQUARE

WHITFIELD SQUARE

Gordon St.

WESLEY MONUMENTAL METHODIST CHURCH

EAST BROAD ST.

0 500 1000 1500 2000 feet

GEORGIA HISTORICAL SOCIETY

Gaston St.

FORSYTH PARK

To Macon

West Huntingdon St.

To Fort Pulaski

East Huntingdon St.

INFORMATION FOR VISITORS

I-95 connects Savannah with cities along the East Coast. From Atlanta, take I-75 to Macon then I-16 to Savannah. The historic district is located 10 miles east of the intersection of I-95 and I-16. Savannah International Airport, 16 miles west of downtown, is served by most of the major airlines. There is regular rail and bus service to the city. The Savannah Visitors Bureau at 301 Martin Luther King Jr. Blvd.

is open year-round, Monday through Friday from 8:30 a.m. to 5:00 p.m., and from 9:00 a.m. to 5:00 p.m on weekends and holidays. For more information: The Savannah Area Convention & Visitors Bureau, P.O. Box 1628, Savannah, GA 31402-1628; 912-944-0456 or 800-444-CHARM.

STATELY MANSION
The Owens-Thomas House, above, stretches the length of a city block. Two wrought-iron stair rails lead to a porticoed entrance supported by columns. The house overlooks Oglethorpe Square, which was laid out in 1742 in honor of the founder of Savannah, Gen. James Edward Oglethorpe.

HISTORIC PARK
Forsyth Park is dominated by an ornate fountain erected in 1858, right. A monument dedicated to the Confederate soldiers who lost their lives in the Civil War was set up in the park by the United Daughters of the Confederacy.

Along with the physical resurrection of the city came a period of economic boom. Eli Whitney had invented the cotton gin in 1793, on a plantation outside of town, making it possible to process huge quantities of cotton in little time. Cotton quickly replaced tobacco as the dominant cash crop in the South. And if King Cotton, as it was called, had a throne, it was Savannah's waterfront, where, by the early 19th century, cotton brokers had developed a major commercial hub. A row of connected buildings along the riverbank grew and expanded, from River Street at the bottom of the 40-foot-high bluff to Bay Street on the town's upper level. Cotton and naval stores were located in river-level buildings, and the cotton factors, or brokers, occupied offices in the upper levels, which afforded them views of the town and harbor.

Riding the crest of this wave of prosperity, Savannah city planners and private citizens took pride in developing their city. Improvements to the waterfront included the installation of multilevel walkways and circular stone stairways, giving the area a vaguely medieval look. A lane called Factors Walk, where busy cotton brokers plied their trade, became the heart of the cotton enterprise.

GRACIOUS BUILDINGS

Residents and visitors, instead of the high-hatted merchants, now walk Savannah's maze of ramps and cobblestoned alleys, and the area's historic buildings have been converted to homes and businesses. On the eastern edge of the waterfront the Ships of the Sea Museum offers visitors the opportunity to explore its extensive collection of ship models, artifacts, and other maritime objects. The waterfront is also enhanced by the Rousakis Riverfront Plaza, a nine-block brick concourse perfect for strolling and observing the harbor activity. At the top of the bluff and across Bay Street lies more of the two-and-a-half-square-mile historic district.

In 1816 a home began to rise on Oglethorpe Square that was unlike anything that preceded it. Commissioned by the wealthy cotton merchant Richard Richardson, the house had been designed a year earlier by a young British architect named

William Jay. The talented 24-year-old, attracted to Savannah by commissions from cotton brokers, incorporated into his design many of the great neoclassical and Regency architectural elements popular in his hometown of Bath.

It took Jay three years to complete his masterpiece. He adopted the region's building materials, and used tabby—a Southern low-country concrete made of oyster shells, lime, sand, and water—for the structure. But Jay's design was unmistakably English. A winding double stairway leads to the columned entrance portico, and the front door opens on a classical foyer adorned with busts of Lord Byron and Sir Walter Scott. Above the interior stairs soars an arched bridge that connects the front of the second floor to the rear. Other touches include a trompe l'oeil ceiling that gives the illusion that the square room is round. Magnificent furnishings express the period's romantic classicism—with an English slant. Often described as the finest Regency house in America, this building, now known as the Owens-Thomas House, was

PLACES OF BUSINESS
The Savannah Cotton Exchange, above, was erected in 1886 by William G. Preston. The facade of this outstanding example of romantic revival architecture is made of red brick and terra-cotta, with iron window lintels and copper finials. Entrepreneurs such as the flower vendor, left, enliven the street life of Savannah today.

A statue of Florence Martus, known as The Waving Girl, *right, stands on the site where she hailed returning ships as they passed the lighthouse on Cockspur Island. Legend says that Florence's lover left for sea in 1887 and, between then and 1931, she waved a white cloth by day and lit a lantern by night, so she would be the first person to welcome him home to Savannah. He never did return.*

the setting for a speech the Marquis de Lafayette delivered to Savannahians during his famous 1825 American tour.

Among the other masterpieces erected by William Jay during his four-year sojourn in Savannah was an 1819 Regency mansion for Alexander Telfair, which stayed in the family for 50 years before it was turned into a museum. It is said to be the oldest public art museum in the South and boasts an impressive collection of American, French, and German Impressionist paintings. The magnificent rooms of the house appear as Jay designed them, including the octagonal library/receiving room and the dining room, complete with its original furniture.

Another mansion attributed to William Jay is the birthplace of Juliette Gordon Low, founder of the Girl Scouts of America. Today the regal building serves a dual function as a memorial to Mrs. Low and a program center for the Scouts. Named Savannah's first National Historic Landmark in 1965, the Low House's graceful architecture and original furnishings make it one of the major historic sites in Savannah.

The Girl Scouts organization itself was set up in a downtown mansion, known as the Andrew Low House, after Mrs. Low's father-in-law, which was

HISTORIC SAVANNAH
With the Savannah River in the background, some of Savannah's many church spires soar above the historic district, right.

designed by New York architect John Norris. Built in 1849, this Greek Revival house represents an era of renewed affluence after the city had recovered from the triple ravages of economic depression, a second devastating fire, and a yellow fever epidemic. A new generation of cotton kings, which included Andrew Low, soon rose to power. Robert E. Lee and William Makepeace Thackeray were among the many distinguished guests Low entertained in his home. Today the elegantly furnished house is owned by the Georgia chapter of the National Society of the Colonial Dames of America.

SHERMAN'S MARCH At the height of Savannah's antebellum prosperity, the architect who designed the Andrew Low House created one of the most refined Gothic Revival mansions in the city. The elegant 1853 home of wealthy cotton merchant Charles Green now serves as the parish house for St. John's Episcopal Church. The house was equipped with black walnut woodwork and silver-plated hardware, a huge round skylight ringed with gas jets, and intricate ironwork. Gen. William T. Sherman used the house as his headquarters at the end of his infamous march to the sea during the Civil War. It was in the Green-Meldrim

House that the respected military man composed his famous telegram on December 22, 1864, offering Pres. Abraham Lincoln the city of Savannah as a Christmas present. Unlike Atlanta, which was burned to the ground by Sherman's forces one month earlier, Savannah was not destroyed. Experts are at odds as to why the city was spared. Some say that the port was of strategic value to the Union, while others believe that it was because Savannah's leaders capitulated without a fight.

In fact, the only real Civil War battle in the area took place two years earlier at Fort Pulaski. Built

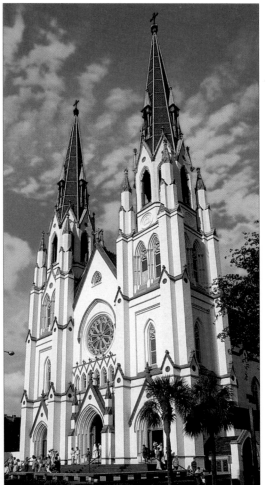

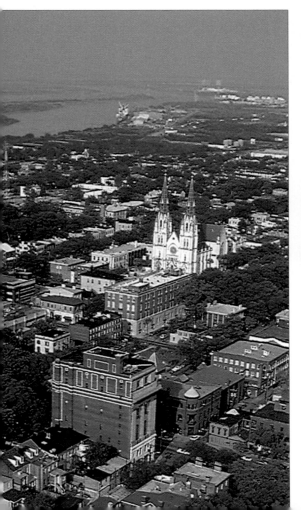

CHURCH HISTORY
The congregation of St. John the Baptist, the oldest Roman Catholic parish in Georgia, sponsored the building of its first church in 1799 on Liberty Square; in the 1830's the original church was demolished and the imposing Cathedral of St. John the Baptist, left, rose on the site. It was dedicated in 1876. The cathedral's twin spires are typical of French Gothic architecture. The church is renowned for its stained-glass windows, detailed murals, and Oriental rugs.

on Cockspur Island to guard the sea approaches to the city, the mammoth structure was equipped with towering walls and a wide moat. Once thought impregnable, the fort crumbled under 30 hours of relentless Union bombardment. Although they are more than 130 years old, the scars left by Yankee artillery on Fort Pulaski's massive brick walls seem curiously fresh, and speak of the horrors of war. Today the fort, on the road to Tybee Island, Savannah's beachfront, is a national monument administered by the National Park Service.

DOWNTOWN REVIVAL

A look in any direction reveals an extraordinary architectural panorama. Greek, Federal, and Renaissance building styles grace Savannah's historic district, with more congruency than one might expect: dignified Colonial buildings stand beside their ornate Victorian counterparts. But saving the edifices was a close call. With cotton crops suffering under the onslaught of the boll weevil in 1914, the city's economy faltered. This situation, along with the development of property on the outskirts of town, led to the deterioration of the city core. Wrecking crews salvaged valuable old brick and fixtures, and tore down the rest. The doorway of the Gibbons House now serves as the entrance to the Early American Wing of the Metropolitan Museum of Art in New York.

Preservationists came to the rescue in 1954 after a 19th-century shopping district known as the City Market was flattened to make way for a parking lot. Years later, four blocks along West St. Julian

preservation of Savannah's architectural legacy. The foundation bought imperiled buildings and resold them to people interested in restoring them. As the preservation movement grew, the Historic Savannah Foundation became increasingly successful, and it now claims to have saved more than 1,700 architecturally significant buildings. Some of them, including the Davenport House, are open for public inspection.

Today it seems almost unimaginable that the Davenport House came so close to extinction. This noble example of late-Federal architecture was created by master builder Isaiah Davenport, a transplanted resident of Rhode Island. A successful tradesman and the son of a shipbuilder, Davenport could afford the best, and the interior of his house displays examples of his lavish but refined taste: handsome original woodwork and ornamental plaster, Chippendale, Hepplewhite, and Sheraton furniture, and a first-class collection of china.

The loving restoration of Savannah has breathed new life into old buildings. A perfect example of this splendid rebirth is the Savannah Visitors Center, located in the antebellum station of the Central of Georgia Railroad. When completed in 1860, it was acclaimed as the nation's finest station. Today this national historic landmark does double duty as the the Savannah History Museum. Its collection includes an antique cotton gin, a

HISTORIC GRAVEYARD
Colonial Park Cemetery, above, dates to 1753 and is the burial place of Button Gwinnet, a signer of the Declaration of Independence, Hugh McCall, Georgia's first historian, and Edward Green Malbone, a renowned painter of miniatures.

Street were renovated and turned into a lively row of restaurants, taverns, and art galleries.

The Isaiah Davenport House, a mansion erected on Columbia Square between 1815 and 1820, was also slated to become a parking lot in the 1950's. A group of seven outraged citizens, all women, formed the Historic Savannah Foundation and raised $22,500 to buy the house—less than 24 hours before the wrecking crew arrived. The foundation established a revolving fund earmarked for the steam locomotive, relics from various wars, and a diorama showing the British victory during the Revolution. A film outlines the history of the city's founding. Adjacent to the station, railroad buffs can explore Savannah's historic railroad shops, built in 1855, and said to be the country's oldest and most complete locomotive repair complex.

TOURING
THE SQUARES

Although visitors can tour Savannah by car, bus, or horse-drawn carriage, they will find that the city was designed to be seen on foot. Savannah's famous wards were built so that public buildings and churches occupied the east and west sides of the squares, and lots on the north and south sides were sold for private homes. Today these havens are shaded by live oaks and magnolia trees and flame-blossomed shrubs. Most of the squares are associated with an interesting story. Johnson Square, laid out in 1733 in honor of Gov. Robert Johnson of South Carolina, is the oldest in Savannah. In past centuries many of the city's significant public events occurred here, such as the 1860 unveiling of the Secession flag. The picturesque square was the meeting place for early colonists, who would come here to find out the time of day on the square's sundial. The original sundial was replaced with a replica in 1933 by the Society of Colonial Wars in Georgia. In Chippewa Square, situated near the middle of the landmark district, Tom Hanks, as the movie character Forrest Gump, sat under moss-bearded oaks with his box of chocolates and philosophized about life. (The Gump bench is now on display at the Savannah History Museum.)

Because each square has its own unique quality, travelers often find that a particular one strikes a chord with them. Whether standing in the shadow of the obelisk dedicated to Revolutionary general Nathanael Greene in Johnson Square, or marveling at the cast iron–festooned mansions that line Monterey Square, visitors feel vitally connected to the city of yesteryear. In contemporary Savannah, history is not relegated to the dusty past, it plays an important role in the present and the future. In a world where old things are often forgotten, the historic center continues to thrive. It is a testament to the man whose brilliant vision created Savannah —and to those who continue to work to preserve the city's rich heritage.

CITY OF GARDENS
Walls enclose a private garden, below, with beautifully manicured hedges. Savannah offers an annual garden and home tour beginning in early spring, when the public is invited to enjoy the beauty of these urban oases.

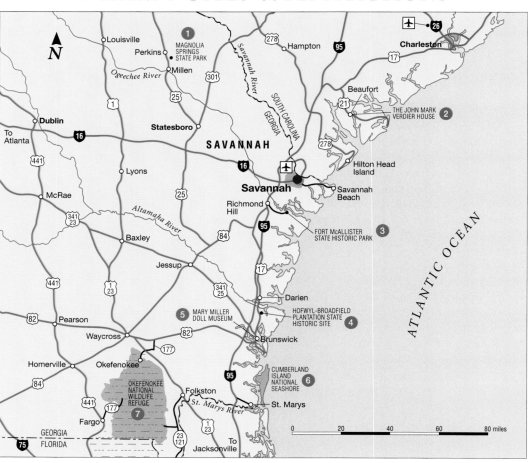

The Southern leopard frog, above, lives in the swamps of the Okefenokee National Wildlife Refuge, where its distinctive snoring call can often be heard.

① MAGNOLIA SPRINGS STATE PARK, GEORGIA

The ruins of a Confederate prisoner-of-war camp where 10,000 Union soldiers were incarcerated are located at the main entrance to this 948-acre park. The freshwater springs that supplied the camp during the war continue to flow at the rate of 9 million gallons per day and feed a 15-foot-deep pool that draws ducks, herons, egrets, deer, and alligators. Extensive stands of dogwood, magnolia, live oak, and pine along the Woodpecker Woods Nature Trail are astir with the activity of seven species of resident woodpeckers. Upper Lake, one of two lakes in the park, has a launch ramp and a boat dock, and water-skiing is permitted there. The park offers cottages, boats, and canoes for rent and there is a campground and a picnic area. Located 5 miles north of Millen on Hwy. 25.

② THE JOHN MARK VERDIER HOUSE, SOUTH CAROLINA

John Mark Verdier, one of Beaufort's leading merchants and planters, built this graceful Federal-style home in the 1790's. Its architectural features include a symmetrical facade, a double portico, and a hipped roof. The aging Marquis de Lafayette, hero of both the American and the French revolutions, was entertained here in 1825. A tour of the interior includes the paneled reception parlor and the drawing room. During the Civil War, Union forces used the house as their headquarters. It fell into disrepair during the Great Depression and was condemned in 1942. Public-minded citizens had the building faithfully restored to its original design in 1975. Period furnishings are on display throughout the mansion. Located at 801 Bay St. in Beaufort.

③ FORT McALLISTER STATE HISTORIC PARK, GEORGIA

Reconstructed Fort McAllister is the highlight of this 1,700-acre park on the Ogeechee River. The original earthen fortification was built in 1861–62 to guard one of the approaches to Savannah. A year later the fort repulsed seven attacks by armored Union vessels, demonstrating that earthen fortifications were capable of withstanding the heaviest naval ordnance of the time. It did not survive the onslaught of Union Forces, however, who captured it in 1864 during the final days of Maj. Gen. William Tecumseh Sherman's march to the sea. Guides in Civil War uniforms interpret the history of the fort. Fishing, crabbing, and shrimping are permitted year-round, and a campground is located in a stand of hardwood on Red Bird Creek. Located 10 miles east of Richmond Hill.

4 HOFWYL-BROADFIELD PLANTATION STATE HISTORIC SITE, GEORGIA

In the early 19th century, rice was cultivated in the freshwater marshland along the coast of Georgia, giving rise to properties such as the Hofwyl-Broadfield Plantation, which harvested rice crops from 1806 to 1915. The family fled during the Civil War and returned to find the fields in ruins. The operation was restored, but by the turn of the century Georgia's rice industry was in decline, and eventually the plantation was transformed into a dairy farm. Museum displays and a video presentation recall the history of the plantation era. Visitors can tour the plantation house, which contains all of its original furnishings. Outbuildings open to the public include the dairy barn, bottling house, and commissary, which displays farm implements. The surrounding 1,268-acre preserve encompasses wetlands that attract native and migratory birds. Visitors can follow a half-mile trail through a coastal forest of live oak and pine. Located 5 miles south of Darien on Hwy. 17.

5 MARY MILLER DOLL MUSEUM, GEORGIA

Some 3,000 dolls, dating from the mid-1860's to the present, from more than 90 countries are on display here. The antique dolls are made of porcelain, corn cobs, wood, and papier-mâché, and sport authentic clothing, hair styles, and accessories. The collection also includes doll clothing, dollhouses, and furniture. Located at 1523 Glynn Ave. in Brunswick.

The modest house at the Hofwyl-Broadfield Plantation, above, was built for the Dent family in the 1850's, on a piece of land called Broadfield. When George Dent became master of the plantation, he added Hofwyl to the name, after the prestigious agricultural academy he attended in Switzerland. Five generations of the Dent family lived here up until the house was opened to the public in the 1970's.

6 CUMBERLAND ISLAND NATIONAL SEASHORE, GEORGIA

A forest of live oak, magnolia, palmetto, devilwood, and pine trees covers much of this 16-mile-long island and serves as a nesting ground for many of the 300 species of birds native to the island. Sand dunes on the eastern side of the island shelter breeding loggerhead turtles. There are several man-made constructions of interest as well, including the burial site of Henry Lee, Robert E. Lee's father, and the remains of a mansion built by Thomas Carnegie, brother of Andrew, the financier. A maximum of 300 visitors are permitted on the island in a single day, and permits must be obtained for overnight camping. The only access to this fragile marine wilderness is via ferry from St. Marys on the mainland.

7 OKEFENOKEE NATIONAL WILDLIFE REFUGE, GEORGIA

About 11,000 alligators lurk in the cypress swamps of this 396,000-acre refuge, and countless herons and egrets nest and roost along its shores. Boardwalks cross the prairies, from which visitors can watch sandhill cranes court their mates. Several trails lead into the woodlands, whose silence is often broken by the hammering of flame-crested pileated woodpeckers and the endangered red-cockaded woodpecker. Strategically placed observation towers offer visitors the opportunity to see the refuge's 250 to 300 resident black bears. The park is accessible at three points: Okefenokee Swamp Park (13 miles south of Waycross via Hwys. 1/23 and 177), which also presents films and exhibits on the wildlife and vegetation; Suwannee Canal Recreation Area (11 miles southwest of Folkston off Hwy. 23/121), where visitors can rent boats or enjoy a nine-mile scenic drive; and Stephen C. Foster State Park (17 miles northeast of Fargo on Hwy. 177), which offers overnight lodging.

Yucca plants, left, take root in the white sands of Cumberland Island. Where the shore turns into sand dunes at Sea Camp Beach, a boardwalk has been constructed to allow visitors to cross the dunes without damaging the fragile sea oats that stabilize them.

AMERICAN LEGACY

Henry Ford had the vision to re-create the story of America's development on a grand scale.

Contrary to popular myth, Henry Ford was not dismissing history altogether when he uttered the memorable words, "History is more or less bunk." He was talking about textbook accounts, which he felt focused on "guns and speeches" at the expense of the everyday concerns of ordinary people. What Ford believed in—and what the Henry Ford Museum & Greenfield Village celebrates—is Americans' daily lives. For Ford that meant paying tribute to the spirit of ingenuity and innovation that is an important part of the American heritage.

At Henry Ford Museum & Greenfield Village in Dearborn, Michigan, visitors learn how their forefathers lived and worked. Although most indoor/outdoor museums concentrate on a particular time and place, the buildings and objects on display here span the period from Colonial times to the present and are drawn from sites across the continent. The result is an eclectic mix of artifacts and historical themes, which give the museum and village a distinctly personal flavor.

THE WRIGHT STUFF
Orville and Wilbur Wright were living in Dayton, Ohio, in the Wright family home, above, when they built Flyer I *in 1903. The house, which was constructed in 1870, was moved to Greenfield Village in 1938.*

GREENFIELD VILLAGE
Overleaf: Greenfield Village, established in 1929, was the first reconstructed village of its kind in the nation. Between 1933 and 1947, scarcely a year passed without several new buildings being added to the site.

FORD'S DREAM

It is not clear when the concept of a museum and historic village began to take root in Henry Ford's mind. However, as far back as 1919 Ford had said, "I'm going to start up a museum and give people a true picture of the development of this country." Already his Model T had revolutionized the automotive industry doing the lion's share of putting America on motorized wheels: the Ford Motor Company's moving assembly line had reduced the time it took to produce a car from 12-and-a-half hours to 90 minutes, bringing the cost of a car within reach of ordinary families. The American way of life was changing rapidly and much of the past was disappearing. Ever the innovator and by then a major collector of Americana, Ford wanted to capture some of that history—and, as he told his secretary, Ernest G. Liebold, "It won't be bunk!"

Ford caught the collecting bug early on. His first acquisition, made in 1904, was ironically his own prototype for the automobile, the 1896 single-cylinder Quadricycle, which he repurchased for $65. Soon thereafter, he turned his sights on the early phonographs of his lifelong hero, Thomas Edison; in 1914 Ford bought McGuffey's *Eclectic Readers*, the textbooks used in many of the one-room school-houses across America; in 1919

To
Detroit

(westbound) 12

(eastbound) 12

River Rouge

N

A TASTE OF HISTORY
A Taste of History Restaurant serves dishes culled from the recipes of famous Americans, including those of Henry Ford, made from soybeans, and George Washington Carver's peanut recipes.

VILLAGE GREEN
During the summer, the Village Green offers visitors a place to relax and play some of the games that were popular in the 19th century.

SMITH'S CREEK DEPOT

EAGLE TAVERN

MARTHA-MARY CHAPEL

EDISON ILLUMINATING COMPANY

PHOENIXVILLE POST OFFICE

J. R. JONES GENERAL STORE

RAILROAD TURNTABLE

DR. HOWARD'S OFFICE

SCOTCH SETTLEMENT SCHOOL

TRAIN STOP

TRIPP UP & DOWN SAWMILL

PRINTING SHOP

RICHART CARRIAGE SHOP

TINSMITH SHOP

GLASS SHOP

THE WORKSHOP

HANK'S SILK MILL

PLYMOUTH CARDING MILL

SIR JOHN BENNETT JEWELRY STORE

TOWN HALL

LOGAN COUNTY COURTHOUSE

CHAPMAN HOUSE

Suwanee Lagoon

POTTERY SHOP

TEXTILES SHOP

GRIMM JEWELRY STORE

HEINZ HOUSE

GEORGE WASHINGTON CARVER MEMORIAL

ADAMS HOUSE

STEINMETZ CABIN

GROUP EDUCATION CENTER

MARTINSVILLE CIDER MILL

ARMINGTON & SIMS MACHINE SHOP

COHEN MILLINERY

VILLAGE BANDSTAND

McGUFFEY SCHOOL

SUWANEE PARK

CAROUSEL

PETER'S FIELDS

58 BAGLEY AVENUE SHOP

WRIGHT HOME

MATTOX HOUSE

HERMITAGE SLAVE HOUSES

GREENFIELD VILLAGE

MACK AVENUE

WRIGHT CYCLE SHOP

STEPHEN FOSTER MEMORIAL

LORANGER GRISTMILL

MILLER SCHOOL

EDISON'S MENLO PARK LABORATORY

SARAH JORDAN BOARDING HOUSE

BURBANK BIRTHPLACE

ANN ARBOR HOUSE

HENRY FORD BIRTHPLACE

BURBANK GARDEN OFFICE

EDISON HOMESTEAD

NOAH WEBSTER HOUSE

ACKLEY COVERED BRIDGE

SECRETARY PEARSON HOUSE

COTSWOLD COTTAGE

VILLAGE ENTRANCE BUILDING

SUSQUEHANNA PLANTATION

PLYMPTON HOUSE

COTSWOLD FORGE

AMERICAN LEGACY

CAPE COD WINDMILL

DAGGETT FARMHOUSE

VILLAGE ROAD

TRAIN TOUR
The oldest steam locomotive operating on a daily basis in the United States offers tours of the village from mid-April through mid-October.

PROVING GROUND

0   200   400   600   800 feet

WORK OF ART
A beautifully carved horse, left, takes a turn around the carousel that was constructed by the Herschell-Spillman Company in 1913 and restored for Suwanee Park. The horse, a frog, sea dragon, and giraffe are just a few of the carousel's colorful animals.

INFORMATION FOR VISITORS

Henry Ford Museum & Greenfield Village is located in the Detroit suburb of Dearborn, Michigan, near I-94. From Detroit, take Michigan Ave. to the site of the museum and village. From Kalamazoo, Battle Creek, Jackson, and Ann Arbor, take I-94 east; from Grand Rapids and Lansing, take I-96 east; from Toledo, take I-75 north. The nearest airports are the Detroit Metro Airport and Detroit City Airport. The Dearborn Amtrak Station is located two miles away. The museum and village are open daily year-round from 9:00 a.m. to 5:00 p.m. except Thanksgiving and Christmas.

Some transportation services, such as horse-drawn carriage rides and the Suwanee riverboat tour, operate on a seasonal basis. Although admission to the Henry Ford Museum & Greenfield Village can be paid for separately, the best value is a combination ticket that allows entrance to both facilities.
For more information: Henry Ford Museum & Greenfield Village, 20900 Oakwood Blvd., P.O. Box 1970, Dearborn, MI 48121-1970; 313-271-1620.

AMERICA EXPLORE AMERICA EXPLORE AMERICA EXPLORE AMERICA EXPLORE AMERICA EXPLORE AMERICA EXPLORE AMERICA EXPLORE AMERICA EXPLORE AMERICA EXPLORE AMERICA EXPLORE

AMERICAN LEGACY 53

he began to track down furnishings to complete the restoration of his birthplace at Dearborn. His agents scoured the countryside for artifacts and acquired enough to fill several buildings. By 1922 Ford's tractor plant office overflowed with an incredible array of household objects.

It was just a matter of time before Ford's reach was extended from plows and player pianos to buildings. He bought the 1686 Wayside Inn in 1924. The dilapidated old building in South Sudbury, Massachusetts, had held a privileged place in the American imagination ever since Henry Wadsworth Longfellow immortalized it in his 1863 collection of poems, *Tales of a Wayside Inn*. Ford restored the inn and began acquiring other nearby buildings to preserve its setting.

Sometime in the mid-1920's Ford started to envision a way to combine his immense Americana collection with his belief in learning by doing. What better way for people to understand the past than to tangibly re-create it? The notion of a combined museum and learning center began to take shape:

GOG AND MAGOG
When Ford, an avid watch and clock collector, heard that the Sir John Bennett Jewelry Store of London, England, was for sale, he had the facade and clockworks, right, transported to Dearborn. The original five-story building was scaled down to fit in its new setting, but the figures of the mythical British giants, Gog and Magog, still strike the quarter-hour.

that machines needed only to be studied closely to be understood. Most people, however, require some assistance to figure out how machines work and to imagine how they once fit into their historical context. Following a total redesign in the late 1970's, the museum reopened in 1979, complete with a 30,000-square-foot Interpretive Center geared toward unlocking the mysteries of machines. Today, hands-on computer stations allow children and adults to tinker with cutting edge technology.

TOURING THE MUSEUM

"Made in America," one of the museum's permanent exhibits, tells the story of the country's manufacturing history through the use of hands-on activities, films, and videos. A core display of more than 1,500 artifacts plays a supporting role to the stars of this exhibit— machines that had a powerful impact on American production. There's a mammoth generator from Thomas Edison's first New York power plant; an assembly-line painting robot; a 1910 windmill; and an automated assembly system that demonstrates how 1,500 electric automobile components can be assembled within an hour. Some of the machines are beautiful in their own right, for instance, the gleaming white 19th-century steam engine with its Gothic-style pointed arches.

a huge indoor space in which his artifacts would be arranged to tell the story of man's technological and cultural progress, and a village that would show how Americans lived and worked at various times in the past. In 1927 the first village buildings arrived in Dearborn. Two years later ground was broken for the museum building, a one-story structure modeled on an assembly-line factory and fronted by a monumental facade based on Independence Hall in Philadelphia. Thomas Edison dedicated the enterprise in October 1929—the 50th anniversary of the incandescent light.

The display areas within the 12-acre museum contain artifacts that touch on nearly all facets of daily life. Ford had tried, as he put it, "to assemble a complete series of every article used or made in America from the days of the first settlers down to the present time." One area is devoted to land and air transportation and includes horse-drawn vehicles, bicycles, locomotives, automobiles, and streetcars. Another area, which focuses on the development of agriculture, displays everything from 18th-century hand tools and horse-drawn equipment to modern tractor-powered machinery. In a third area, the history of the household arts in America is portrayed. One exhibit here shows a 1930's kitchen replete with a green porcelain kitchen table, white kitchen cabinet, long-legged gas range, and coil-topped refrigerator. The scene takes older visitors back to their childhoods and gives younger ones a vivid sense of American domestic life in that decade.

Most of the buildings and collections that exist today were acquired by Henry Ford before his death in 1947. Ford was a mechanical genius who felt

CLASSIC STATION WAGON
A 1931 Model A "woody," below, is one of several vintage cars driven around Greenfield Village. Vehicles such as this were used as shuttle buses to transport people from railway station to residence during the 1930's.

MICHIGAN COTSWOLD
In 1930 Ford had a 17th-century limestone cottage and barn from Chedworth, Gloucestershire, right, dismantled and transported to Greenfield Village, Michigan. To enhance the farmstead's authenticity, Ford even bought Cotswold sheep and a sheepdog named Rover.

TRAGIC RIDE
The black limousine, above, was an open car when President John F. Kennedy rode in it through the streets of Dallas on November 22, 1963. After JFK's assassination, the car was extensively rebuilt, and it continued to be used by American presidents until 1977.

The "Made in America" exhibit is designed to appeal to visitors of all ages. Cartoons explain industrial processes such as light bulb manufacturing and how a plastic injection molding machine works. Hands-on activities allow visitors young and old to operate a robot, examine microchips through a microscope, and don the protective clothing worn by the workers who handle hazardous material. Special films and videos go behind the scenes to give a picture of factory life from 1880 to the present. Rare film footage reveals how Ford's moving assembly line made possible the mass production of automobiles in the 20th century. And a collection of vintage commercials shows how companies used television to sell their products.

While "Made in America" explains the nuts and bolts of technological progress in a clear and interesting way, it also examines the broader ethical issues raised by industrialization. Materialism, pollution, and recycling are treated as by-products of mass production and mass consumption. Visitors can flip through the pages of a collection of quotations criticizing 19th-century materialism, or watch a film that examines the long-range costs of traditional energy sources, such as coal, and newer technologies like nuclear power.

It should come as no surprise that the automobile collection at Henry Ford's museum is one of its major attractions. Where else could a car buff find the only surviving 1896 Duryea from America's first automotive production run of 13? Or a 1931 Bugatti Royale Type 41 Cabriolet, one of only six built. Included in the extensive roster of cars on exhibit are Pierce Arrows, Packards, and Peerlesses, the White House limousines of several presidents, including Franklin D. Roosevelt and Dwight D. Eisenhower, and cars owned by Henry Ford, Thomas Edison, and Walter P. Chrysler.

CARS, CARS, CARS

For many years, the museum's car collection was lined up in glittering phalanxes, accompanied only by labels. Today the 60,000-square-foot display, called "100 Years of the Automobile in American Life," outlines the century-long journey through automotive history. More than 100 cars and thousands of artifacts, supported by video and audio presentations, are

This car-lover's paradise is also prized by railroad buffs. The locomotive collection includes turn-of-the-century high-wheeled passenger locomotives as sleek as mechanical thoroughbreds, and Big Al, a 1941 C&O Allegheny class coal burner whose mighty boiler generated 8,000 horsepower, a record for steam locomotives. The museum's woodburners go back to before the Civil War.

Ford also amassed a sizable collection of furniture by the country's finest craftsmen, ranging from Puritan to Victorian pieces, with emphasis on the late 18th and early 19th centuries. Along with the furniture are glassware, ceramics, lighting fixtures, musical instruments, guns, and toys that accurately reflect the distinct tastes of each period. The fine arts and natural history are not well represented here as Ford showed little interest in these areas.

THE VILLAGE THAT NEVER WAS

Greenfield Village is located a short walk from the museum. At the village more than 100 historic buildings on 81 developed acres provide a panorama of American life. The structures were all taken apart before being transported to Dearborn and reassembled there. Each offers a different view of American life, and together, like pieces of a puzzle, they create a vivid portrait of the nation's history. Modern preservation purists balk at the idea of moving historic buildings out of their original settings. But Ford would no doubt have scorned such orthodoxy and pointed out that many

SUMMER BOAT RIDE
The Suwanee, *below, is a reconstruction of the sternwheel paddle steamer used by Edison during his winters in Florida. After the boat sank, Ford hired its one-time captain, Conrad Menge, to build a replica of it in Dearborn between 1929 and 1930.*

arranged to present a clear chain of events—in reverse order. The trip begins in the near future as visitors are introduced to the Ghia Via, a prototype sports car for the year 2000. The lineup of cars stretches backward in time along a raised, curved highway. Multimedia exhibits take visitors back to the early days of the 20th century, when road conditions were treacherous and black Model T's rolled off the assembly line.

Several of the roadside exhibits steal the show. On display is a World War II–era Texaco gasoline station with its distinctive white exterior and red gas pumps, and Lamy's Diner, a classic chrome-sided diner that opened in Worcester, Massachusetts, in 1946. An early Holiday Inn bedroom, a 1950's McDonald's neon sign, and vintage camping vehicles, including a 1959 Volkswagen camper and a 1949 Airstream trailer are also featured. Smaller items vie for the visitor's attention, such as a letter sent to Henry Ford by Clyde Barrow: "While I still have got breath in my lungs, I will tell you what a dandy car you make." A month and a half later Clyde and his partner, Bonnie Parker, were shot at the wheel of a Ford V8.

MARTHA-MARY CHAPEL
A Universalist church in Bradford, Massachusetts, was the inspiration for the Martha-Mary Chapel, above, completed in 1929. The Martha-Mary was one of six non-denominational chapels Ford built around the country in honor of his mother, Mary Litogot Ford, and his mother-in-law, Martha Bryant.

was within these walls that Edison enjoyed his most creative years, devising the first practical electric lighting system and the tinfoil phonograph, and making significant improvements to the telephone and telegraph. In his lifetime, Edison developed 1,093 patents, 420 of them at Menlo Park. When, in 1929, Edison saw the reincarnation of his lab at Greenfield Village he pronounced it "accurate . . . except for the fact that it was too tidy."

The two-story clapboard building containing the fully equipped laboratory dominates a cluster of reconstructed buildings that includes the Sarah Jordan Boarding House, a frame structure that accommodated Edison's unmarried employees and was run by the widow Sarah Jordan, her daughter Ida, and a domestic servant, Kate Williams. In 1879 it became one of the world's first buildings to be illuminated by the inventor's incandescent lights. A sense of the real lives of the workers has been re-created at the boardinghouse by a marvelous attention to detail—even the beds are rumpled as one might expect from men who kept long erratic hours. A sitting room, complete with a chess game in progress and a dining room table set for a swarm of hungry boarders, helps round out the picture of the daily lives of Edison's workers.

FLYING BROTHERS

The Wright brothers' buildings in Greenfield Village were moved from Dayton, Ohio, under the direction of Orville Wright himself. The white clapboard Victorian-style home even retains the Wrights' window curtains. The brothers modernized the 1870 house around the turn of the century, adding gas lighting, heat, and a kitchen pump, but they abstained from wiring it for electricity. The Wrights upgraded the house when they were conducting their historic experiments in early flight, and it retains the very essence of that time.

Next door to the Wright house stands the brick Wright Cycle Company Shop. Orville and Wilbur built, sold, and repaired bicycles in the front of the store while they conducted their experiments in aviation out back. Around 1900 the brothers began constructing the gliders that would eventually carry a man aloft. In 1903 they built the spindly gasoline-powered airplane, *Flyer I*, that was to become the first manned, powered, heavier-than-air craft to achieve sustained flight.

One of the more recent additions to Greenfield Village also bears a legendary name: Firestone. A brick farmhouse, transplanted from eastern Ohio, was the childhood home of the industrialist Harvey Firestone, founder of the Firestone Tire and Rubber Company and a friend of Henry Ford's. Surrounded by seven acres, the original Firestone house and

of the structures would have been demolished had he not had the foresight to move them to Greenfield Village. The historic community includes homes, farms, schools, a chapel, workshops, and stores from different periods.

Among the first projects Ford completed was a reconstruction of Thomas Edison's 1870's "invention factory," in Menlo Park, New Jersey, a world-famous research and development complex. The inventor's presence is almost palpable here, for it

barn have been set up as they were in the 1880's. Costumed interpreters plant and plow the fields with horses, tend livestock, and do various domestic chores such as boiling laundry, cooking, and canning vegetables. The interior of the house is a case study in the tastes and wherewithal of a late-19th-century American farmer. Factory-made furniture and mass-produced fabrics and wallpaper in floral, paisley, and striped patterns express the exuberance of the period.

ORDINARY PEOPLE   Ever mindful of the role ordinary Americans played in the building of their nation, Ford found a place in Greenfield Village for their homes and workplaces. The era of the Colonial settlers is represented by the Plympton House of Massachusetts and the Daggett House of Connecticut. Relocated from Georgia, a pair of slave cabins and the Mattox House, the modest rural home of three generations of a black American family, provide a poignant glimpse into the lives of African-Americans. The Susquehanna House from Maryland offers a view of plantation life in the mid-1800's; its original owners, the Carroll family, grew tobacco and corn on 700 acres of land worked by 64 slaves. As early-20th-century machinery hums away at the Armington & Sims Machine Shop, visitors learn how the workers at this small business built the high-speed engines that powered Edison's early electrical plants.

Oddly, Henry Ford's own childhood home was the last building he moved to the village, although it had been restored in 1919 and was only a few miles away. The house was sliced in two and hauled there by truck in 1944. In 1995 the building caught fire, but a fast response saved it and most of its contents. Ford Museum & Greenfield Village had, once again, foiled both time and the elements.

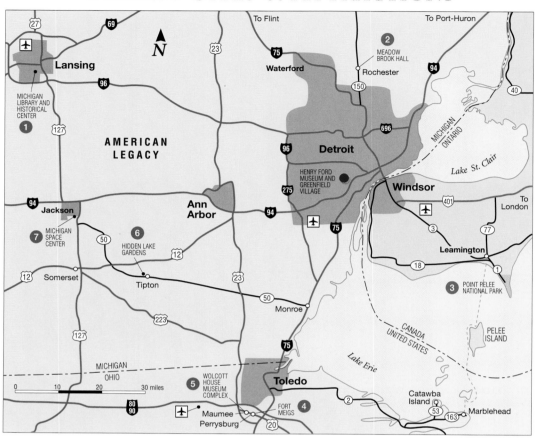

The Library of Michigan, above, is a repository for more than 5 million books and documents stored on some 27 miles of shelving. The library has an extensive collection of genealogical information.

① MICHIGAN LIBRARY AND HISTORICAL CENTER, MICHIGAN

This center includes the Michigan Historical Museum, the Library of Michigan, and the State Archives. Artifacts, dioramas, and walk-through sets bring 10,000 years of Michigan history to life. The exhibits range from a diorama on the Paleo-Indians, Michigan's earliest known inhabitants, to displays on the state's contribution to modern manufacturing and technology. Local mining history is re-created in an Upper Peninsula copper mine, and a film on the lumber trade illustrates that industry's importance to the state. The nose of the *Liberator*, a B-24 bomber built in Michigan during World War II, is the centerpiece of an exhibit on the state's contribution to the war effort. A 1957 Detroit Auto Show displays vintage cars, such as a '57 red Corvette and a Plymouth Fury. The library, which offers public tours, is the second-largest state library building in the nation, and the state archives contain about 80 million documents, 330,000 photographs, and 500,000 maps. Located at 717 West Allegan St. in Lansing.

② MEADOW BROOK HALL, MICHIGAN

Alfred Wilson and his wife, Matilda Dodge Wilson, the widow of auto magnate John Dodge, built this 100-room mansion in the 1920's at a cost of $4 million. It was inspired by Elizabethan and Tudor period architecture. Crystal chandeliers, Oriental carpets, stained-glass windows, gold bathroom fixtures, and Tiffany glass adorn rooms with elaborately carved paneling, gargoyles, and corbels. The 1,400-acre estate has beautifully manicured lawns and lovely gardens. The entire Meadow Brook Hall estate was donated by the Wilson family in 1957 to establish Oakland University. Since that time seminars, meetings, and educational and cultural events have been held here. Located on the Oakland University campus in Rochester.

③ POINT PELEE NATIONAL PARK, ONTARIO

Measuring a mere six square miles and located at the southernmost point of the Canadian mainland, Point Pelee is a bird-watcher's paradise. The tapered sandpit is renowned as a stopover for large numbers of birds during their spring and fall migrations. Point Pelee offers the birds their last chance to rest and feed before crossing Lake Erie to fly south in the autumn. It is also the first stretch of land they encounter on their flight north during the spring. Some 357 species have been spotted in the wetland park since it was established in 1918, including rusty blackbirds, long-billed dowitchers, dark-eyed juncos, and ruby-crowned kinglets. As many as 124,000 common terns, 30,000 blue jays, and 7,000 purple martins have been counted in the park on a single day. In autumn the colorful display of birds is complemented by the sight of roosting monarch butterflies. It is easy to spot birds from numerous walking

Greek Revival home; a saltbox farmhouse from the same period; and the Monclova Country Church. Located at 1031 River Rd. in Maumee.

6 HIDDEN LAKE GARDENS, MICHIGAN

When Harry Fee bought this property tucked away in the scenic Irish Hills of southwestern Michigan 1926, he envisioned a beautiful garden for it. The garden has since grown to 755 acres and contains more than 2,500 species of trees, flowers, and shrubs. Greenhouses, measuring more than 8,000 square feet, shelter bonsai, banana, tapioca, camphor, palm, and vanilla plants. Magnolias, azaleas, rhododendrons, conifers, ashes, and pines grow in abundance outdoors. Knolls, valleys, and funnel-like depressions distinguish the landscape, which is also remarkable for the many rounded boulders that were transported here from north of Georgian Bay, Canada, by advancing glaciers. A six-mile loop takes drivers through the gardens, and visitors can walk along five miles of nature trails. Located 2 miles west of Tipton off Hwy. 50.

7 MICHIGAN SPACE CENTER, MICHIGAN

Devoted to the NASA Space Program, this museum includes hands-on exhibits. The 83-foot-tall Mercury Redstone rocket is on display outside the center. Exhibits inside trace the history of space flight from its beginnings to the present era of the space shuttle. Items on display include a lunar rover, the Mercury and Gemini command modules, space food, and astronauts' space suits. Visitors can view a moon rock through a microscope, put on a space helmet, and climb aboard the Apollo 9 capsule. They can also step on a scale to see what they would weigh on Venus or Mars. An exhibit on the space shuttle Challenger includes a tribute to the crew that perished in the 1986 explosion and a 14-foot model of a shuttle. Located at 2111 Emmons Rd. in Jackson.

An elegant fountain graces the eastern side of Meadow Brook Hall, left. The house is built in the style of an English country home.

and biking trails and from a boardwalk that extends to the tip of the park. Visitors are welcome to canoe, fish, and picnic in the park. Located 5 miles south of Leamington on Hwy. 1.

4 FORT MEIGS, OHIO

In the initial stages of the War of 1812 British forces held the Great Lakes region. Determined to swing the momentum to the U.S. side, Gen. William Henry Harrison ordered his troops to construct a stockade fort on the banks of the Maumee River in February 1813. In a matter of weeks the soldiers erected a fort that enclosed 10 acres and included blockhouses with two-foot-thick walls. The fort was completed in May 1813, just in time to withstand a week-long siege by the united forces of British, Canadian, and Native American troops. This authentic reconstruction of the fort includes cannon batteries, earthen traverses, and seven blockhouses. Exhibits on the War of 1812 and the fort's construction are on display in some of the blockhouses. Costumed interpreters re-enact the defense of the fort on weekends during the summer. Located at 29100 West River Rd. (Hwy. 65) in Perrysburg.

5 WOLCOTT HOUSE MUSEUM COMPLEX, OHIO

Several 19th-century architectural styles are on display at this complex in the Maumee Valley. Six buildings with period furnishings and household objects evoke local life in the 1800's. Wolcott House is a Federal-style structure built between 1827 and 1836. Other buildings include a fully furnished log cabin that once sat on the banks of the Miami and Erie Canal; the Clover Leaf Railroad Depot, built during the early 1800's, plus a boxcar and a caboose; an 1840

Stately landscaping with trees, shrubs, and flowers gives shape and color to the glacier-carved terrain of Hidden Lake Gardens, below.

LIVING HISTORY FARMS

An open-air museum tells the story of how Iowans transformed prairie into productive farmland.

It's laundry day in a small log cabin on the Iowa prairie and a farm wife in a worn cotton dress bustles about making sure she has everything she needs. She checks the temperature of a pot of water that hangs on a rack over the fire, then returns to the table where two tubs, a washboard, and a bowl of lye soap await. "I need another bucket of cold water," she tells a young man. "Could you go out to the well and draw me one?"

A while later the young man staggers back into the cabin. "That's heavy!" he exclaims, as he puts the bucket down. "Think of that next time you put a load of clothes in a washing machine," says the farm wife, smiling as she hefts the pail easily up to the table.

At Living History Farms in the Des Moines suburb of Urbandale, such anachronisms crop up all the time—contrasts between the frontier era and the present, and also among each of the five periods of American agricultural history that

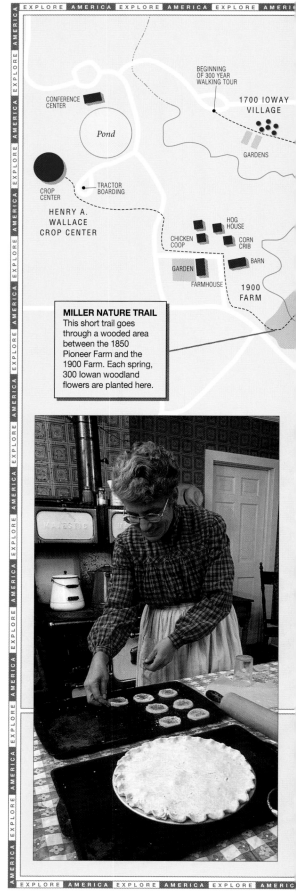

MILLER NATURE TRAIL
This short trail goes through a wooded area between the 1850 Pioneer Farm and the 1900 Farm. Each spring, 300 Iowan woodland flowers are planted here.

ONE-STOP SHOPPING
The Greteman General Store, above, is typical of many stores of the era. Built in 1887 by the Greteman brothers in the town of Willey, Iowa, it was dismantled and rebuilt at the 1875 Walnut Hill frontier town.

PIONEER HOMESTEAD
Overleaf: The rustic interior of a log dwelling at the 1850 Pioneer Farm displays many of the household items typically used by the region's settlers. Food was cooked in cast-iron pots over an open hearth. A handmade broom, lye candles, and dyed yarn hang from the wall.

are brought to life here. Living History Farms tells the story of the changes that have occurred in Midwestern agriculture through actual working farms, which showcase the animals, crops, and the different farming techniques used by the people who have made their living off the land.

FARMING MUSEUM

The directors of Living History Farms ensure the authenticity of the sites through the use of original sources such as diaries and letters. The gardens are planted with heirloom varieties, and breeds of livestock similar to those of the era are raised on each farm. Cultivation and building methods also fit each period.

Three decades after its founding in 1967 this living museum encompasses 600 acres of farmland and sites that link the years 1700, 1850, 1875, and 1900 to the present. Although the crops, livestock, living quarters, outbuildings, and daily routines of the people who lived in these eras vary dramatically, they are united by the land—the Iowa soil—among the world's most fertile. In 1850 about 90 percent of Iowa was covered with prairie, and wild grasses such as the big bluestem reportedly reached heights of 12 feet. When the grasses died, their deep root system created Iowa's rich topsoil. During

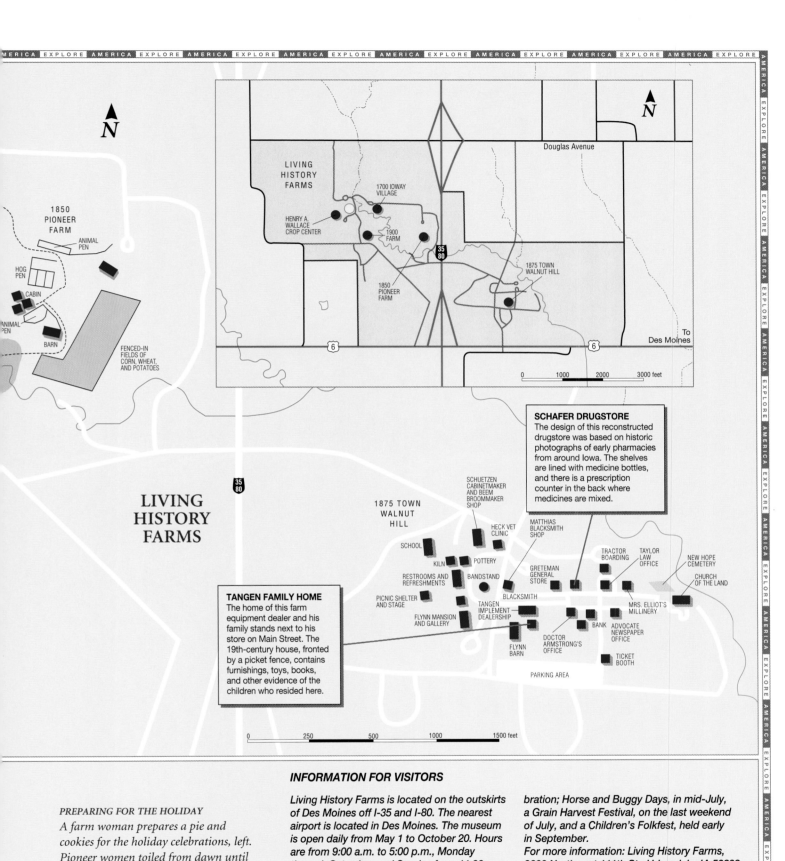

N

1850 PIONEER FARM

ANIMAL PEN

HOG PEN

CABIN

ANIMAL PEN

BARN

FENCED-IN FIELDS OF CORN, WHEAT, AND POTATOES

N

LIVING HISTORY FARMS

Douglas Avenue

1700 IOWAY VILLAGE

HENRY A. WALLACE CROP CENTER

1900 FARM

35 80

1875 TOWN WALNUT HILL

1850 PIONEER FARM

To Des Moines

6

6

0   1000   2000   3000 feet

SCHAFER DRUGSTORE

The design of this reconstructed drugstore was based on historic photographs of early pharmacies from around Iowa. The shelves are lined with medicine bottles, and there is a prescription counter in the back where medicines are mixed.

35 80

LIVING HISTORY FARMS

1875 TOWN WALNUT HILL

SCHUETZEN CABINETMAKER AND BEEM BROOMMAKER SHOP

HECK VET CLINIC

MATTHIAS BLACKSMITH SHOP

SCHOOL

KILN

POTTERY

RESTROOMS AND REFRESHMENTS

BANDSTAND

GRETEMAN GENERAL STORE

BLACKSMITH

TRACTOR BOARDING

TAYLOR LAW OFFICE

NEW HOPE CEMETERY

CHURCH OF THE LAND

PICNIC SHELTER AND STAGE

TANGEN FAMILY HOME

The home of this farm equipment dealer and his family stands next to his store on Main Street. The 19th-century house, fronted by a picket fence, contains furnishings, toys, books, and other evidence of the children who resided here.

FLYNN MANSION AND GALLERY

TANGEN IMPLEMENT DEALERSHIP

MRS. ELLIOT'S MILLINERY

BANK

ADVOCATE NEWSPAPER OFFICE

FLYNN BARN

DOCTOR ARMSTRONG'S OFFICE

TICKET BOOTH

PARKING AREA

0   250   500   1000   1500 feet

PREPARING FOR THE HOLIDAY
A farm woman prepares a pie and cookies for the holiday celebrations, left. Pioneer women toiled from dawn until dusk, doing household chores, looking after the children, and helping out in the fields during harvesttime.

INFORMATION FOR VISITORS

Living History Farms is located on the outskirts of Des Moines off I-35 and I-80. The nearest airport is located in Des Moines. The museum is open daily from May 1 to October 20. Hours are from 9:00 a.m. to 5:00 p.m., Monday through Saturday, and Sunday from 11:00 a.m. to 6:00 p.m. The farms hold several special events throughout the season, including an extravagant old-fashioned Fourth of July cele-

bration; Horse and Buggy Days, in mid-July, a Grain Harvest Festival, on the last weekend of July, and a Children's Folkfest, held early in September.
For more information: Living History Farms, 2600 Northwest 111th St., Urbandale, IA 50322; 515-278-5286.

MERICA EXPLORE AMERICA EXPLORE AMERICA EXPLORE AMERICA EXPLORE AMERICA EXPLORE AMERICA EXPLORE AMERICA EXPLORE AMERICA EXPLORE AMERICA EXPLORE

LIVING HISTORY FARMS 65

PECKING ORDER
At the 1850 farm, a costumed guide feeds the hungry chickens that scurry around her long skirt, right. Along with chickens, the pioneers' livestock included hogs, milk cows, and sheep.

IOWAY VILLAGE
A typical Ioway bark lodge, below, stands in a clearing in the middle of the woods. Cooking pots were suspended above wood-burning fires on tripods such as the one shown in the foreground.

the spring and fall, fires regenerated the plants for yet another growing season.

The trip back in time begins with a ride in a cart drawn by a tractor down a winding gravel road. The tractor pulls to a halt at the entrance to a path that leads into a heavily shaded wood under a high canopy of tall bur oak trees. A few yards into the forest, visitors arrive at a clearing, the first stop along the agricultural timeline: It is a village of Ioway Indians from the year 1700. A half-dozen bark lodges called *na-ha-ches* (Ioway for "tree skin houses") lie in a cluster next to a small stream, a luxuriant garden plot, racks of drying corn, and tanned animal skins.

An interpreter in modern dress emerges from one of the lodges; because of cultural sensitivity issues, staff members do not assume the roles of the Native Americans who would once have lived in such a village. "We don't know exactly how these people lived," the interpreter explains. "In 1700 the Ioway were just beginning to have some contact with the French, but their culture was largely untouched by European influences."

The interpreter describes the Ioway villages, how they planted their vegetable gardens in the river

valleys and in wooded areas on the bluffs and high lands. In the garden next to a stream, an interpreter explains the methods used by the Ioways to grow the vegetables they called the Three Sisters of Life. Red bean runners grow in profusion on tripods made of branches alongside stalks of blue corn and yellow squash vines.

As the group of visitors steps inside one of the lodges, the interpreter points out wooden beds attached like shelves to the walls of the lodge. Visitors can see examples of Ioway pottery used to store seeds, prepare food, and cook in. Some of the ceramic vessels are decorated with designs that were incised or stamped into the clay surface before the pots were fired slowly at low temperatures in open fires in pits. Also on exhibit are projectile points, fishhooks, and agricultural tools such as hoes and rakes made of deer and elk antlers and animal bones. Outside again, visitors can try their hands at tanning deerhide with a bone scraper or grinding corn into a thickener for the vegetable stew simmering above the fire.

This is a peaceful place, shaded from the hot sun by towering oaks and filled with the gentle sound of singing birds and the murmur of the stream. It is a way of life that existed for many generations before Europeans came to the New World.

TIME TRAVELING	The next stop on the timeline is 1850, 150 years after the first but only a few minutes' walk along a woodland path. The

site, a typical Iowa farm a few years after the state was opened to American settlement, is on the crest of a windswept hill. The center of the homestead is a simple one-room cabin and small barn made of rough-hewn logs. Split-rail fences separate animal pasture from the fields of corn, wheat, and potatoes.

A farmer wearing simply tailored breeches, vest, and shirt calls a hearty greeting. "Welcome to the year 1850!" he says, laying down the tool he's been using to repair a wagon wheel. Although the scene may seem far removed from the modern era, it is in many respects more distant from the Ioway settlement just up the path. Unlike the Ioway, who hunted and cultivated garden crops, the frontier farmers bought large tracts of open land that had access to water and timber supplies. A typical pioneer farm consisted of 40 acres. Farmers also benefited from advances in technology. They plowed their vast properties using steel plows pulled by oxen. Instead of hunting for game, the farmers of the 1850's raised their own livestock, including milk cows, sheep, and pigs.

During a tour of the pastures and fields, a farmer tells how oxen do most of the heavy work, their slow pace offset by their stamina and the fact that

they need only the nutrition the pasture provides. The farm's hogs are a surprise to anyone familiar with the lean pigs raised on modern farms: these are porkers indeed, with long snouts and spindly legs. "In 1850 the more lard a hog had, the better," explains the farmer. The hogs fattened rapidly and were the main source of lard for the farmers.

Inside the log cabin, the farmer's wife is busy doing her weekly washing with lye soap made from a mixture of hog lard and wood ash. The one-room cabin contains the basic necessities, which were hauled overland from the East—cooking utensils, dishes, and a kitchen cupboard—along with some roughly made chairs, a table, and a bed topped with a handmade quilt. "Women did all the washing, cooking, spinning, gardening, and childcare, and also helped out in the fields when needed," says the interpreter.

BLENDED BREED
Several breeds of pigs, including Poland, China, Irish grazier, Byfield, and Berkshire, were cross-bred in the 1870's in southwestern Ohio to produce the distinctive Poland China, below.

DIARIES TELL TALES	The staff is able to give an authentic picture of day-to-day life on the farms in large part because of the museum's col-

lection of diaries written by the early pioneers (not on display to visitors). For example, one diary entry, written by Elisabeth Koren, a frontier minister's wife in northeastern Iowa in 1854, reads, "When we get our own house, one of the first things will be a fence about it so that I may escape this business of having the cows wash the windows for me with their muzzles." Thomas M. Terrill, an Iowa farmer writing at the end of the 18th century, left 42 volumes of his diaries, most of them giving terse accounts of family and farm life such as this one about an afternoon's work. "Otis was home from school. He and I plowed the evergreen patch A.M.

I drove to Sam Ammerman's and back. After which we planted potatoes and sweet corn west of grove. It was wet. Cool and cloudy. N.E. wind. I am 50 years old today and feel like it too."

THE 1900 FARM

As visitors leave the frontier site and walk to the next farm, interpretive signs along the path provide reminders of the passage of time and the significant changes that have taken place: "1862: Homestead Act: Free 160 Acres"; "1872: Montgomery Ward began its mail orders"; "Labor Needed Per Acre of Corn: 1850—32 hours; 1890—15 hours." Then, on the other side of the hill, a familiar Midwestern scene comes into view: a 1900 homestead with a big red barn and a white frame farmhouse, a tall windmill, and a half-dozen outbuildings. The tremendous impact the Industrial Revolution had on rural Iowa is keenly felt at this site. The 120-acre farm is three times the size of its 1850 counterpart, and the introduction of a wide variety of cast-iron and steel tools and equipment has changed the farm's daily routines. A burr grinder cracks the corn for animal

feed, machines plow and harvest the fields, and a wooden windmill pumps water.

A tour of the barn and outbuildings reveals other ways that farming methods have changed. Percheron horses now work the fields of corn, oats, and hay, moving at a faster clip than the plodding oxen. The barn's loft is filled with sweet-smelling hay, lifted into the building by a fork-and-pulley system powered by horses. The hogs are leaner than those on the frontier farm and are penned in instead of being allowed to roam freely. Duck and goose have been added to the family's diet.

Even greater change has been wrought inside the house, which is heated by a big wood-burning stove and filled with all the latest mail-order furniture, cooking utensils, tableware, and other manufactured goods. Women still worked hard to feed and clothe their families, though by then the treadle sewing machine had replaced stitching by hand.

Although the turn-of-the-century farm boasts labor-saving devices, much of the workload is the same as in 1850. The family spent most of its time raising livestock and processing and preserving food. The women of the household maintained a

large garden and orchard, and did all their baking and cooking over a wood-burning stove. Daily chores—such as washing clothes, ironing, and canning food—were highly labor-intensive.

GOLDEN AGE OF FARMING

As visitors enter the house, the farm wife pauses from her ironing to point out that 1900 is sometimes called the golden age of farming. Running the farm had become easier and less backbreaking, farm prices had risen, and the national economy had weathered the financial panics of the late 19th century. This more prosperous era is familiar to many visitors at Living History Farms. "My mother had a sewing machine just like this one," says a woman as the memories rush back. Another visitor laughs as she tries her hand at ironing using a heavy flatiron heated on the stove. "I remember my grandmother talking about having to iron for hours as a girl," she recalls, "and getting burned by the hot stove."

After leaving the 1900 site, visitors complete their tour of the western side of Living History Farms with a final stop at the Wallace Crop Center. The center was named after Henry A. Wallace, a native Iowan who served as vice president under Pres. Franklin D. Roosevelt. The permanent exhibit is housed in an unusual domed structure covered with soil and planted with Iowa prairie grasses. Inside visitors can view a multimedia show titled "Since Yesterday: Agriculture in the Twentieth Century." The presentation begins with strains of a Depression-era song, "How You Gonna Keep 'Em Down on the Farm?", and picks up the timeline of Iowa agriculture where the 1900 farm leaves off. A presentation highlights the effects that two world wars, the Great Depression, and other events such as the mid-1970's Soviet grain embargo

MERCHANDISE FOR SALE
Visitors can take a peek at the groceries and housewares section of the Greteman General Store, above, which provided local farmers with coffee, tea, chocolate, spices, sugar, rice, and other goods that they could not produce themselves.

WORKING FARM
Outbuildings, left, such as the corncrib in the foreground, and the hog house in the background, are in use at the 1900 Farm.

have had on agriculture. Visitors also learn about the impact on farming of innovations such as new machinery, pesticides, fertilizers, computers, and genetic engineering.

The tractor-drawn cart pulls up to the last stop on the trip through the Living History Farms, the 1875 town of Walnut Hill. This town is a re-creation of a central supply depot for farmers in the surround-

ing region. Here several craftsmen, such as a blacksmith, potter, broommaker, and carpenter, have set up shop. Other buildings include a schoolhouse, doctor's office, bank, law office, millinery shop, and veterinary clinic. A Victorian mansion, once owned by a young immigrant from Ireland named Martin Flynn, dominates the hill. Flynn was almost penniless when he came to this country and—in a classic tale of rags to riches—became a millionaire by the time he was 21 through railroad speculation. The mansion and adjoining white barn

were built in 1870 and are listed on the National Register of Historic Places.

Visitors to Walnut Hill need only open a shop door to step into another world. Inside the general store the owner shows off his vast array of patent medicines that claim to cure every ill known to humankind. Across the street in a small printing enterprise, a typesetter with ink-stained hands displays a copy of the town paper, filled with news items on national affairs, commodity prices of crops and livestock, local social events, and household hints. At the cabinetmaker's shop, a carpenter explains that coffins make up a large part of his business, particularly children's coffins, because in 1875 two out of every three children died of diseases such as cholera and influenza. At the law office, the town's attorney corrects misconceptions about 19th-century frontier justice. "People often think of 1875 as an era when disputes were settled

LIVING IN STYLE
A tour of the Flynn Mansion, left, includes the elegant front hall where callers presented their cards; the front parlor, which was reserved for honored guests, weddings, funerals, and holiday celebrations; and the back parlor, where the mistress of the house entertained friends.

with gunfights, but in reality people were suing each other constantly," he says.

At the end of Walnut Hill's Main Street is the interfaith Church of the Land, a simple wooden structure erected on the site where Pope John Paul II addressed a quarter of a million people on October 4, 1979. Here he spoke to the people of America's heartland, calling them "stewards of some of the most important resources God has given to the world," and exhorted them to conserve the land. Nearby is the New Hope Cemetery. Although no one is buried in the cemetery, some authentic 19th-century headstones were donated to the site. Every aspect of frontier life, including death, is told here.

CHANGE AND CONTINUITY

The church is a fitting place to end this journey and to stop and reflect. Although much has changed in Iowa since the days when Native peoples tilled the soil and settlers built their homesteads and raised crops, the rhythms of rural life remain constant: the ceaseless round of seasons, the routines of planting and harvesting, the cycle of birth and death—all of them have meanings that resonate through the eras presented at Living History Farms.

Ephraim Fairchild, a young tenant farmer originally from New Jersey, provides a final glimpse into the lives of the men, women, and children who eked out a living in Iowa during the 1850's.

He wrote home to his parents: "You said in your letter that Mother wants to know whether I think I can make a better living here than I did in Jersey or not. Well Mother, that is a hard question for me to answer yet for a certainty for I cannot tell about it until fall when I get my crops gathered, but one thing is certain, I don't have to work as hard here as I did in Jersey to get in my crops. The wheat looks first rate. It is up about half-leg high . . . and is growing very fast."

VICTORIAN SPLENDOR
The dining room table in the Flynn Mansion, above, is set for a traditional Christmas dinner. In the late 1800's meals were formal affairs, and children ate their dinner in the kitchen under the supervision of their governess, until they learned proper table manners.

A bedroom in the small cottage at the Herbert Hoover National Historic Site, above, displays some of the original modest furnishings.

NEARBY SITES & ATTRACTIONS

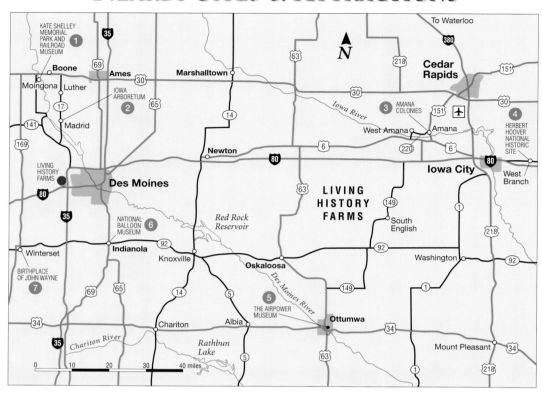

1 KATE SHELLEY MEMORIAL PARK AND RAILROAD MUSEUM

During a ferocious rainstorm on July 6, 1881, a locomotive plunged off a railroad trestle and into Honey Creek, near the town of Boone. A witness to the train wreck, 15-year-old Kate Shelley set out immediately for the North Western depot in nearby Moingona to warn railway officials to stop a passenger train that was scheduled to ride on the same stretch of track. On the way Shelley crawled across a 600-foot railway bridge. After notifying officials, she led a rescue party to Honey Creek, and they saved two injured survivors of the accident. Kate Shelley's bravery is commemorated at the museum that bears her name. It is located at the site of the old North

Western depot. Antique items on display include a ticket window, potbellied stove, waiting room bench, telegraph, and a hand-cranked telephone. A Rock Island Rocket passenger train adjacent to the museum has been transformed into a theater where visitors can watch a video presentation that tells Kate Shelley's story. Located in Moingona.

2 IOWA ARBORETUM

The arboretum showcases the plants that thrive in the Iowa climate and soil. Sparkling streams flow swiftly through deep ravines in this 378-acre garden where hundreds of species of trees, flowers, and

John Wayne was born on May 26, 1907, in this unpretentious frame house, right. He and his family lived in the house until 1910, when they moved to Earlham, Iowa.

shrubs grow. The Library Trail winds through the 40-acre western section of the arboretum. On display are thousands of plants, including dwarf conifers, nut trees, wetland trees, flowering trees, herbs, and perennial flowers. Within the larger eastern section, 338 acres of timberland can be explored via four self-guided nature trails. The Walnut Trail is a good place to spot the flitting forms of colorful butterflies and birds. Located in Madrid.

3 AMANA COLONIES

Seven villages, encompassing 475 mid-19th-century historical sites and buildings, have earned this location National Historic Landmark status. The original villages were established in 1855 by the 1,200 members of the Community of True Inspiration, a religious society that was fleeing persecution in Germany. The members constructed their villages in the Old World style. Barns, factories, and workshops were built at each end of a main thoroughfare. Each village planted gardens, orchards, and vineyards, and had its own post office, bakery, general store, and church in the village center. Modern visitors walk the village roads, stopping to look into an open-hearth bakery, cooper's shop, and a woolen mill. There are five museums within the Amana Colonies, including the Museum of Amana History, which displays 19th-century artifacts, a schoolhouse, and a typical home. Located in Amana.

4 HERBERT HOOVER NATIONAL HISTORIC SITE

Born on August 10, 1874, to a Quaker family living on the Iowa plain, Herbert Hoover became the 31st president of the United States. The small cottage in which he was born, the Hoover Library, and his gravesite are located at this 186-acre historic site. In contrast to the well-manicured lawns and colorful flowerbeds on the cottage grounds, a large expanse of restored prairie land gently undulates in the park as the tall grass bends in the wind. Guides conduct tours of the two-room cottage, where Hoover's baby cradle and other pieces of original furniture are on display. The Hoover Library includes documents and some 20,000 books. The visitor center offers a slide show that covers much of Hoover's career. Other buildings at the site include a Quaker meetinghouse and a reconstructed blacksmith's shop. Located at the junction of Parkside Dr. and Main St. in West Branch.

5 THE AIRPOWER MUSEUM

Vintage aircraft and flight memorabilia bring to life the spirit of the early days of flight. An exhibit titled "Lighter Than Air" displays an early hot-air balloon and its wicker basket gondola. An exhibit on American aviation innovators takes a look at the breakthroughs made by the Wright brothers with the 1903 *Flyer I* and the aeronautic advances made by subsequent inventors up to 1914. Both world wars are represented in exhibits that focus on glider pilots and on various units of the Air Force. Also on display is a Link trainer, the world's first flight simulator, which was used by Allied air forces during World War II. More than 20,000 square feet are filled with airplane models, photographs, engines, propellers, and actual aircraft built between the 1920's and the 1940's. Among them is a 1942 Culver, made almost entirely of wood, and a 1925 Anderson Model 2 biplane, the oldest aircraft in the museum. Located at 22001 Bluegrass Rd. in Ottumwa.

6 NATIONAL BALLOON MUSEUM

Housed in a structure that resembles two upside down hot-air balloons, this museum celebrates 200 years of ballooning history. On display are gondolas, deflated balloons, and the equipment used to inflate them. There are also photographs, trophies, and a collection of pins that were awarded for scientific, competitive, and record-setting balloon flights. Located on Hwy. 65/69 in Indianola.

7 BIRTHPLACE OF JOHN WAYNE

Born Marion Robert Morrison in 1907, John Wayne first reached Hollywood stardom with his role as the Ringo Kid in *Stagecoach* (1939). Over the next 40 years, he acted in more than 80 movies, usually as a warmhearted, somewhat laconic gunfighter or lawman. Wayne's early childhood home has been restored to its original 1907 appearance. Two of the four rooms contain rare photographs and memorabilia from his days as an actor, including letters from fellow movie stars and the black eye patch he wore in *True Grit* (1969). Other rooms display period furnishings, such as a potbellied stove and a rocking chair in the family parlor, and an ice box, kerosene stove, and trundle bed in the kitchen. Located at 216 South Second St. in Winterset.

A communal kitchen in Middle Amana, above, is equipped with a wood-burning stove and various cooking utensils. Although families lived in separate dwellings, the kitchen served as a community center where they cooked and ate their meals together.

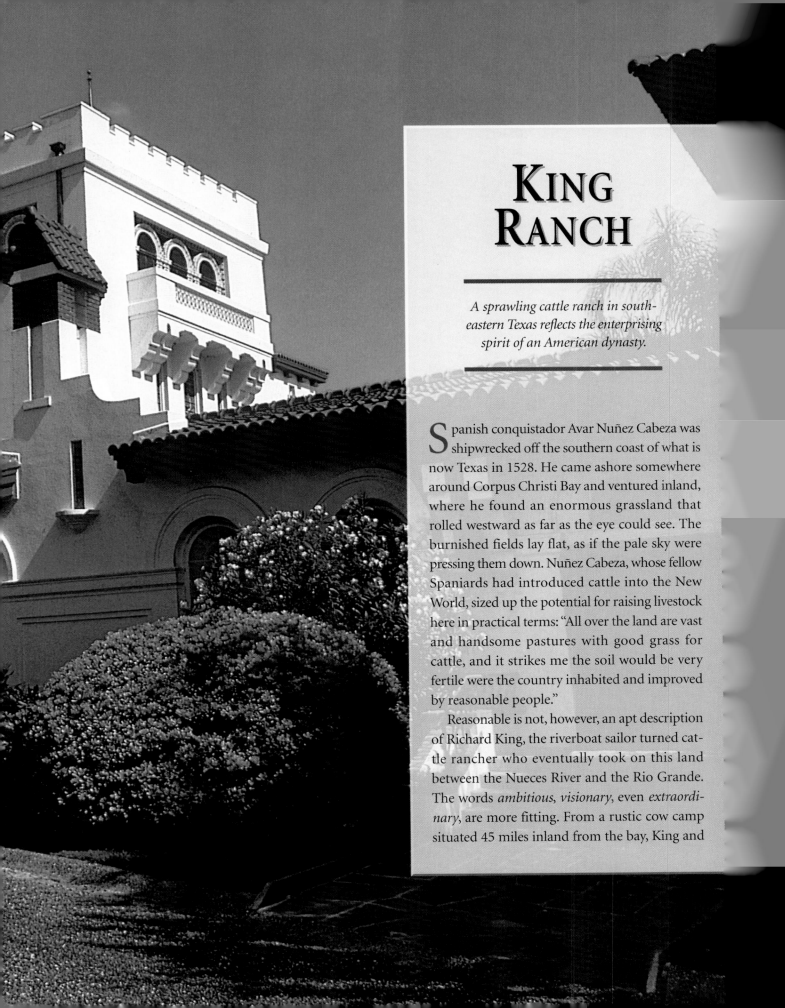

KING RANCH

A sprawling cattle ranch in south-eastern Texas reflects the enterprising spirit of an American dynasty.

Spanish conquistador Avar Nuñez Cabeza was shipwrecked off the southern coast of what is now Texas in 1528. He came ashore somewhere around Corpus Christi Bay and ventured inland, where he found an enormous grassland that rolled westward as far as the eye could see. The burnished fields lay flat, as if the pale sky were pressing them down. Nuñez Cabeza, whose fellow Spaniards had introduced cattle into the New World, sized up the potential for raising livestock here in practical terms: "All over the land are vast and handsome pastures with good grass for cattle, and it strikes me the soil would be very fertile were the country inhabited and improved by reasonable people."

Reasonable is not, however, an apt description of Richard King, the riverboat sailor turned cattle rancher who eventually took on this land between the Nueces River and the Rio Grande. The words *ambitious*, *visionary*, even *extraordinary*, are more fitting. From a rustic cow camp situated 45 miles inland from the bay, King and

TEXAS MANSION
Overleaf: The King Ranch's main house was designed in the mission style by Adams & Adams of San Antonio and Tiffany Studios of New York City. The house was built between 1912 and 1915 for Richard's wife, Henrietta, after the family's original home was destroyed by fire.

TWO TONS OF BEEF
The imposing Santa Gertrudis bull, below, is a cross between the Brahman and the British Shorthorn. Santa Gertrudis thrive in the sweltering Texas heat and in some cases reach 2,000 pounds by the age of three.

his descendants developed a ranching operation that today extends for some 1,300 square miles—an area larger than Rhode Island.

More than 50,000 people visit King Ranch each year. They come to see cowboys round up cattle and watch rambunctious yearling colts cavorting in the green pastures. They linger in the King Ranch Saddle Shop, with its sweet, leathery scent, and uncover the past in the King Ranch Museum.

ENTERPRISING ADVENTURER

The museum is a tribute to persistence and ingenuity, two qualities that King possessed in abundance. Although he lacked formal schooling—young Richard ran away from his New York home at age 11, stowed away on a ship, and was piloting riverboats by age 19—he was a shrewd businessman. He built a thriving cargo business on the Rio Grande during the Mexican War by designing a shallow-drafted steamboat that could better negotiate the fast currents and sharp bends of the channel. He applied the same thinking to his ranching enterprise and bred cattle specifically for prairie conditions.

It took a person with imagination to see the promise of this land. To the Mexicans who had once owned it, the seemingly boundless and untamable coastal plain was known as El Desierto de los Muertos, Desert of the Dead. The Texans, who claimed the region as part of the spoils after

A RANCHING EMPIRE
Richard King, far right, his wife, Henrietta, center, and their children pose for a family portrait in 1870, above. The husband and wife team built one of the most successful cattle empires in the nation. Today King Ranch is run by fifth- and sixth-generation descendants of the couple.

INFORMATION FOR VISITORS

King Ranch Visitor Center is located off Hwy. 141, 3 miles west of Kingsville. From San Antonio take Hwy. 281 south to Hwy. 141 east. From Corpus Christi take Hwy. 44 west to Hwy. 77, then travel south to Kingsville. Take Santa Gertrudis Ave. through Kingsville to the King Ranch gate. Regular bus tours are available. Customized tours to view cattle and horses must be booked in advance. Bird-watching and guided wildlife observation tours vary in length from about three hours to four-day retreats. The nearest airport is about 40 miles east of Kingsville in Corpus Christi. Lodging can be found in Kingsville, which has a variety of motels and bed-and-breakfast establishments. For more information: King Ranch Visitor Center, P.O. Box 1090, Kingsville, TX 78364-1090; 512-592-8055.

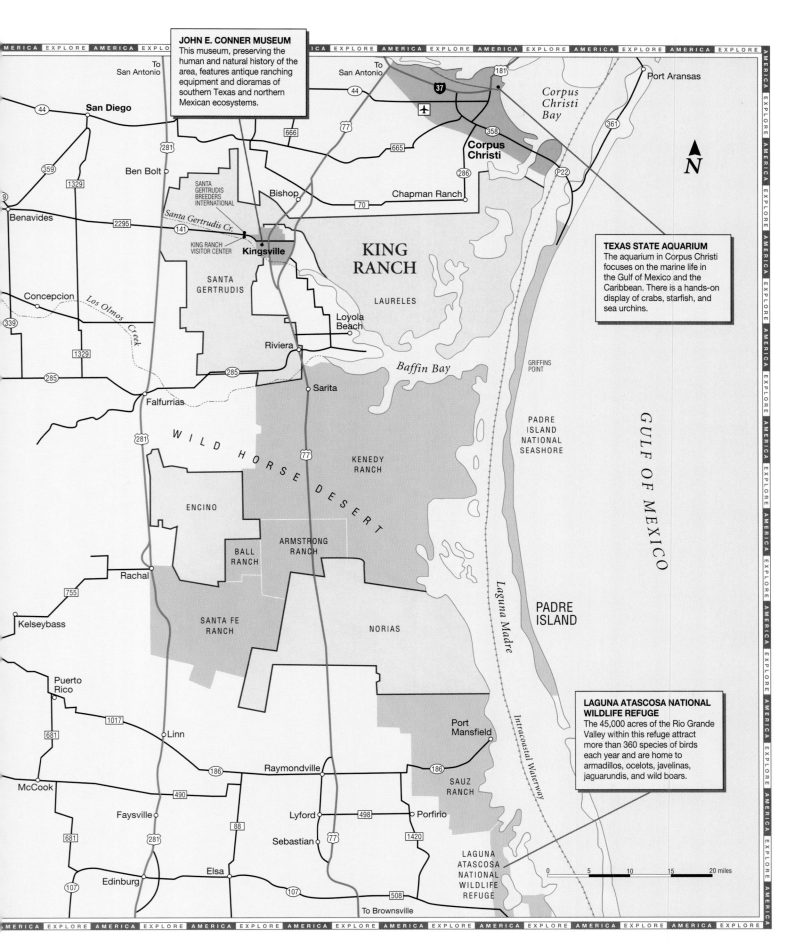

JOHN E. CONNER MUSEUM
This museum, preserving the human and natural history of the area, features antique ranching equipment and dioramas of southern Texas and northern Mexican ecosystems.

TEXAS STATE AQUARIUM
The aquarium in Corpus Christi focuses on the marine life in the Gulf of Mexico and the Caribbean. There is a hands-on display of crabs, starfish, and sea urchins.

LAGUNA ATASCOSA NATIONAL WILDLIFE REFUGE
The 45,000 acres of the Rio Grande Valley within this refuge attract more than 360 species of birds each year and are home to armadillos, ocelots, javelinas, jaguarundis, and wild boars.

To San Antonio
San Diego
To San Antonio
Port Aransas
Corpus Christi Bay
Corpus Christi
Ben Bolt
SANTA GERTRUDIS BREEDERS INTERNATIONAL
Bishop
Chapman Ranch
Benavides
Santa Gertrudis Cr.
KING RANCH VISITOR CENTER
Kingsville
KING RANCH
LAURELES
Concepcion
Los Olmos Creek
SANTA GERTRUDIS
Loyola Beach
Riviera
Baffin Bay
GRIFFINS POINT
Sarita
Falfurrias
PADRE ISLAND NATIONAL SEASHORE
GULF OF MEXICO
W I L D   H O R S E   D E S E R T
KENEDY RANCH
ENCINO
Laguna Madre
Kelseybass
BALL RANCH
ARMSTRONG RANCH
Rachal
PADRE ISLAND
SANTA FE RANCH
NORIAS
Intracoastal Waterway
Puerto Rico
Linn
Port Mansfield
Raymondville
SAUZ RANCH
McCook
Faysville
Lyford
Porfirio
Sebastian
LAGUNA ATASCOSA NATIONAL WILDLIFE REFUGE
Elsa
Edinburg
To Brownsville

0   5   10   15   20 miles

their war for independence from Mexico, gave it the name Wild Horse Desert. By any name, the land was inhospitable and unforgiving.

For much of the 19th century, the desert was a perilous territory. The Mexicans, who bought tracts of land through Spanish grants, and the white settlers who came later were terrorized by renegades, thieves, and looters from both sides of the border. Settlers also feared marauding bands of Comanche Indians and the dreaded Karankawa, a coastal tribe of cannibals possibly of Caribbean origin.

A HARSH LAND

The desert was the domain of wild turkeys, javelinas, and deer. Stray cattle became as feral as the pumas that preyed on them. The grass that covered the desert turned out to be not quite what Nuñez Cabeza had imagined. During periods of drought, which were frequent, the creeks ran dry and the lush prairie turned yellow and brittle. At other times, heavy rains transformed the lowlands into marsh, and winds from the sea sheared the plant life off the knolls and dunes near the coast. Hurricanes were an all too familiar phenomenon. And the area's oppressive heat caused one young cavalry officer, riding

through the Wild Horse Desert during the war with Mexico, to compare the landscape to hell. If he owned both places, the officer said, he would rather live in hell and rent out the desert.

Yet this is the land that Richard King would turn into a cattle ranch. He saw it in 1852 as he traveled from Brownsville to Corpus Christi for what was billed as the first state fair of Texas. It took him four days to travel 165 miles through Wild Horse Desert, where the grasses reached up to his horse's belly, matted clusters of palmetto and mesquite broke through the surface, and sentrylike rows of live oaks marched across the skyline. The dusty road took him across parched arroyos to the battlefield near Palo Alto, where the army had routed

Mexican forces in 1846, and past makeshift huts long abandoned by Mexican settlers.

King had spent most of his life on the water and he understood the vicissitudes of the seafaring life. "Boats," he once said, "have a way of wrecking, decaying, falling apart, decreasing in value and increasing in cost of operation." On the other hand, ranching held greater promise, King told his riverboat partner, Mifflin Kenedy: "Land and livestock have a way of increasing in value."

Within a few months of his ride through the Wild Horse Desert, King established a small ranch on Santa Gertrudis Creek. It consisted of a corral to hold a few horses and cattle and a rude shelter for the vaqueros. Visitors touring King Ranch can see

where the camp once stood. A guide describes how King expanded his investment by buying land from the scattered heirs of the original grantees, requiring him to make the most of the Mexican contacts he had established during his eight years of hauling cargo on the Rio Grande.

King paid $300 for the 15,500-acre Rincon de Santa Gertrudis tract, which became the nucleus of King Ranch. He began to carve out an empire, taking to heart the advice given to him by Lt. Col. Robert E. Lee, who befriended the rancher while on a mission to the Rio Grande. "Buy land," the future general had said, "and never sell."

As Richard King added parcel after parcel of land to the property, the lowly job of cowboy on the ranch was elevated to something approaching a profession. Until then, few ranchers had joined the stream of farmers, mountainmen, prospectors, and speculators in the move west. And certainly none of those who did knew the difficulty involved in husbanding huge herds on vast tracts of land with only the branding iron to mark ownership and methods borrowed from the Spaniards. King understood that if one were seriously interested in making money, it would require rethinking the hacienda system. He also realized that while the Longhorns of Mexico were sturdy enough both to survive the prairie without too much oversight and to make the 1,000-mile drives north to market, they lacked the heft of a good slaughter animal. So

ALL CREATURES GREAT AND SMALL
A massive Longhorn steer, left, eyes an intruder warily. Richard King's first herd was formed from the wild Longhorns that roamed freely throughout the region. The purple-and-yellow flower of a sensitive brier, below, adds a vibrant touch of color to the grasslands.

Prickly pear cactus and net wire fencing act as barriers against wayward cattle, right. Richard King, who was the first of the large Western landowners to fence in his land, using pine planks and cypress posts. In 1931 his descendant, Robert Kleberg Jr., designed a net-wire galvanized fencing that had the double advantage of keeping cattle in while allowing other animals to pass over or through the mesh.

THE MARK OF SUCCESS
A quarter horse's saddle blanket bears the famous Running W, above. Richard King began branding his cattle with this insignia in 1869.

King experimented with crossbreeding, blending Hereford, Shorthorn, and Brahman cattle with his Longhorn stock. He also fenced in the open range and worked to develop sturdier grasses that could withstand the frequent droughts and heavy rains of the area.

INVALUABLE PARTNERSHIP By the time of his death in 1885, King had purchased more than 614,000 acres of the Wild Horse Desert. Ownership of the ranch passed to his widow, Henrietta, a shrewd woman who saw in Robert Justice Kleberg, one of the ranch's lawyers, the kind of man her family—and the ranch—needed now. Kleberg married Henrietta's daughter, Alice, in 1886 and over the next 15 years, Kleberg and Mrs. King increased the ranch to more than 1.1 million acres. Kleberg's son, Robert Kleberg Jr., extended his family's empire to other parts of the world, buying up more than 11 million acres in seven countries. King

Ranch has remained in Kleberg hands ever since Mrs. King's death in 1925. The impact of the two families on Texas is apparent from a map of the state: The town of Kingsville was established in 1904 within the boundaries of the original Santa Gertrudis tract and eight years later it became the government seat of Kleberg County.

Pieces of the property have been sold off in the last 80 years, and the South Texas spread now stands at 825,000 acres. The ranch has 60,000 head of cattle, stables prize thoroughbred and quarter horses, and includes 60,000 acres of cotton and milo fields. The descendants of the Kings and the Klebergs have proved as tenacious and creative as Richard King was in ensuring the continued prosperity of the ranch.

In the 1890's mesquite and shin oak had begun to overtake the prairie, choking the grass and growing in such dense thickets that cattle, and sometimes even rabbits, had trouble moving through them. Plows, mammoth tractors, and other equip-

tions often had to build roads 30 miles long over productive grassland in order to move equipment in and oil out. After heavy rains the dry lowlands become small lakes three feet deep, and some locations were reachable only by marsh buggy or amphibious vehicle. Rigs might be 100 miles apart, and the traffic to supply them could easily have turned the ranch into a wasteland of tire ruts.

Instead the Kleberg family enforced a strict code of land preservation on all oil field development by the industry. The restrictions worked, as author Tom Lea observed in his 1957 history of the King Ranch: "The small evidences of human kind on the immense pastures, whether they be fence or petroleum installations, are made unobtrusive; they blend with unmarred landscape. . . . The air of an untouched and untrammeled original world envelopes these efficient and highly productive pastures." These qualities described by Lea persist to this day.

From the ranch headquarters visitors ride on a tour bus through stands of ebony and date palm

ment and methods have been designed and developed at the ranch to rid it of destructive brush. Visitors can see the machines that are on the front lines of this struggle with nature.

HORSES AND OIL RIGS

King's descendants have continued his practice of breeding fine horses and, consequently, have produced America's first registered quarter horse. Buyers come from all over the world to purchase King Ranch animals, and visitors can watch ranch hands working the stock in corrals and paddocks near the Main House.

In 1933 the Kleberg family leased out some of the land for oil exploration, and in 1939 oil was discovered. Limiting damage to the land caused by drilling presented new challenges, in part because of the land's size and in part because of the varying terrain and soil types. Fertile black farmland meets rolling prairie and dunes, which yield in turn to salt marshes and freshwater lakes. Drilling opera-

to the feeders and pens where a cowboy describes how cattle are vaccinated, branded, and raised. The tour continues through pastures and oak mottes inhabited by javelinas, sandhill cranes, and deer and where bobcats and coyotes still prowl. Next visitors arrive at the horse barns and at the arena that is used for rodeos and where the King Annual Auction was held from 1950 to 1988. Nearby stands the Main House, a Spanish-style *casa grande* that served as the family seat and is an important part of the King legacy. The past has never faded from memory in these prairies. It is kept alive by images of roaming herds, swaying grasses, and by the men and women whose lives are spent in the saddle. King Ranch is a working ranch—still everything Richard King intended it to be.

EQUINE MARVELS

Sorrel quarter horses, above, are just some of the 300 horses stabled at the ranch. The most famous horse raised on King Ranch was Assault, a thoroughbred who won racing's Triple Crown in 1946.

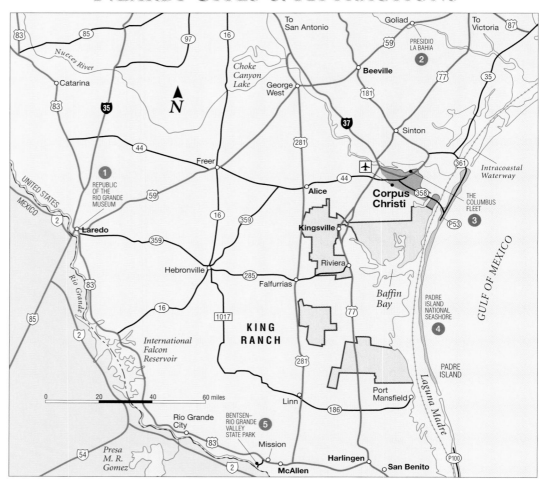

1 REPUBLIC OF THE RIO GRANDE MUSEUM

When three northern Mexico states declared independence in 1840, the home of a prominent sympathizer, Laredo rancher Don Bartolomé García, became their capitol building. Today the limestone-and-sandstone home, erected in the 1830's, houses a museum devoted to the Republic of the Rio Grande, which lasted 283 days before it was suppressed by Mexican forces. Several rooms contain period furnishings. In the kitchen are a hand-made cradle and a pie safe; a foot-powered sewing machine and a rope-strung bed frame sit in the bedroom; and the ranching office contains a rolltop desk, saddles, barbwire, and a safe. A fourth room is used for changing exhibits. Located in Laredo.

Sea oats anchor the windswept dunes along Padre Island National Seashore, right. The golden plumed grass sends an intricate network of roots into the sand, securing the dunes and creating a more hospitable environment for other plant life, such as beach croton and beach morning glory.

2 PRESIDIO LA BAHIA

The presidio was built in 1721 near Lavaca Bay on the site of the French Fort St. Louis to secure Spanish territories in Texas against the French. It was moved twice and ended up 28 years later in Goliad. The strategically positioned fort changed hands no less than six times and has flown nine different flags. Spanish troops stationed at the fort assisted American colonists in defeating the British in several battles during the American Revolution. The fort was also the site of three unsuccessful battles against Spanish rule, which took place in 1812, 1817, and 1821. In 1812 it was captured by Spanish and American rebels and besieged by the Spanish Army for four months. In 1836, after Texas had declared itself a republic, the presidio was the scene of the infamous Goliad Massacre when 342 Texas rebels were executed after surrendering to Mexican forces at nearby Coleto. The fort was restored in 1967, and the barracks, guardhouse, bastions, and officers' quarters remain intact. A museum displays artifacts and mass continues to be held at Our Lady of Loreto Chapel. Located in Goliad.

3 THE COLUMBUS FLEET

In commemoration of the 500th anniversary of Christopher Columbus' 1492 voyage to the New World, the government of Spain built life-size replicas of his ships, the *Niña*, the *Pinta*, and the *Santa María*. The vessels were built using 15th-century techniques and supplies such as hand-forged nails and hemp to caulk the keels. Oak and pine from the same region in Spain that provided the lumber for the original ships were employed in the replicas. After they crossed the Atlantic, the ships were presented as a gift to the city of Corpus Christi. On board, costumed interpreters demonstrate 15th-century cooking methods, sailhandling, and other navigational skills. They also describe Columbus' perilous journey—the food shortage and the near mutiny of the crew. The *Santa María* and the *Pinta* are in dry dock as part of a re-created 15th-century shipyard; the *Niña* is moored in Corpus Christi Harbor. Located in Columbus Plaza in Corpus Christi.

4 PADRE ISLAND NATIONAL SEASHORE

This 113-mile-long coastal barrier island, the longest in the world, separates the Gulf of Mexico from Laguna Madre and the Texas mainland. Swimming, beachcombing, camping, and hiking are popular activities with visitors. The Gulf side of the island is dominated by sandy beaches, backed by rolling coastal dunes. Red snapper, marlin, mackerel, and sand trout are found in these waters, along with three species of dolphin. The Laguna Madre has an average depth of two to three feet, and the water is extremely salty. The coastal area is composed of grasslands backed by marshy tidal flats and tide pools, which support 20 species of crabs. The short distance between the island and the mainland and the shallow water allow many animals to traverse the Laguna Madre. Padre Island is home to 32 species of snakes, including the Mexican milk snake and the western coachwhip, as well as 5 species of sea turtles, coyotes, and raccoons. Located 20 miles south of Corpus Christi on Hwy. 358.

5 BENTSEN–RIO GRANDE VALLEY STATE PARK

Situated along the Rio Grande, this 588-acre park protects the northernmost range of many subtropical plants and animals native to Mexico. The riparian and thorn scrub environment attracts a great diversity of flora and fauna. Chachalacas, great blue herons, and green jays along with 6 species of owls and 16 species of ducks are among the 270 species of birds that can be spotted. The park is home to coyotes, nine-banded armadillos, endangered ocelots and jaguarundis, and seven species of bats. The Texas indigo snake and bull snake are among 12 species of reptiles found here; the Rio Grande leopard frog and the Rio Grande siren are unique to the area. Vegetation ranges from Texas ebony, desert olive, manzanita, and rare guayacan trees to willows and cattails. Many plants and birds can be seen along the Singing Chaparral Nature Trail and the Rio Grande Hiking Trail. Located 5 miles southwest of Mission off Hwy. 374.

Replicas of Christopher Columbus' fleet for his historic journey from Spain to the New World in 1492, are seen at left entering Corpus Christi Harbor for the quincentennial. The ships, which are on loan from Spain, will remain in Texas for 50 years then make their return voyage across the Atlantic Ocean.

On December 20, 1835, Our Lady of Loreto in Presidio La Bahia, above, was the setting for the signing of Texas' declaration of independence from Mexico.

TAOS

New Mexico's Indian, Hispanic, and Anglo cultural heritage endures in the Taos Valley.

It was the Rio Grande and its tributaries that first attracted people to the Taos Valley. They dug trenches that ushered life-giving water to their crops and mixed the water with clay and straw to make adobe, the material that defines the character of the architecture in Taos. At Kit Carson's home, located just off Taos Plaza, a corner of a 30-inch wall has been exposed to reveal stages of construction dating back to 1825. The successive layers of adobe and plaster are much like the history of the valley itself, a history that consists of tiers of different cultures, languages, and interests—including Native Americans, Spanish priests and settlers, American trappers, merchants, soldiers, and an exotic collection of early 20th-century artists and their patrons.

The town of Taos grew up on a grand sweep of land painted silver green with sagebrush in northern New Mexico. The tree-covered Sangre de Cristo Mountains form a backdrop to the north and east, and the great river of the Rio Grande flows to the west, cutting a deep gash through dark basalt cliffs. To speak of Taos is to speak of three different communities: Taos Pueblo, the

DRY BONES
Overleaf: The sun-bleached skulls of steers, on a door of the Featherstone Trading Company in Ranchos de Taos, evoke the mysticism of the region.

home of Native Americans; Ranchos de Taos, a center of Spanish farming and site of one of the oldest Catholic churches in New Mexico; and Don Fernando de Taos, the formal name for the historic center of Taos.

Taos Indians belonging to the Tiwa group have lived continuously in this pueblo for more than 600 years. The village consists of two house groups divided by Red Willow Creek, a precious water source referred to as Rio Pueblo de Taos: the five-story North House and the smaller South House. The adobe houses—with their smooth tan walls,

and buffalo hides for food, pottery, and rabbit fur blankets. They also exchanged slaves.

Visitors to the pueblo today will be struck by the simultaneous persistence of tradition and adaptation to outside influences. Each morning women bake bread, mixing the dough and shaping the round loaves as their mothers and grandmothers have for generations. They place the loaves in outdoor beehive-shaped ovens called *hornos*, and slip them out, perfectly browned and ready to eat, on long-handled paddles. Seasonal ceremonies—featuring Buffalo, Corn, and Deer dances—are

ADOBE FORTRESS
Heavy wooden doors guard the entrance to the imposing home of Don Antonio Severino Martínez, above. The wealthy merchant bought the land in 1803 and began building the next year. By his death in 1827 he had expanded it to 21 rooms. Its massive adobe walls offered refuge to neighbors and livestock during Comanche and Apache raids.

characteristic turquoise door frames, small windows, and flat roofs supported by large *vigas* (wood beams)—are a study in harmony. Taos Pueblo was originally built without windows or doors; entry was by ladders to hatchways in the roofs. Such fortification was necessary in earlier days as a defense against potential attacks by Ute, Comanche, and Apache Plains Indians.

In peaceful times these neighboring tribes were also trading partners. Taos Pueblo's location, where the Plains and the southern Rocky Mountains intersect, had made it a prominent site for trade in the Southwest by the 1500's. During the summers Pueblo and Plains Indians used to gather here for trade fairs in which they bartered exotic shells

held, but at the same time residents worship at the Catholic chapel of San Gerónimo, at the entrance to the pueblo. Farmers still plant their fields with white and blue corn in May, and at the end of September villagers mark the harvest with a feast honoring San Gerónimo (St. Jerome), the pueblo's patron saint. Traditional underground chambers, or kivas, are used for ceremonies. They are reached by ladders to the roofs and are off limits not only to outsiders, but also to uninitiated members of the tribe. And still the villagers look each day to Taos Mountain, a sacred place for ceremonial rituals, which rises before them to more than 12,200 feet. It is home to the freshwater Blue Lake, the source of Red Willow Creek.

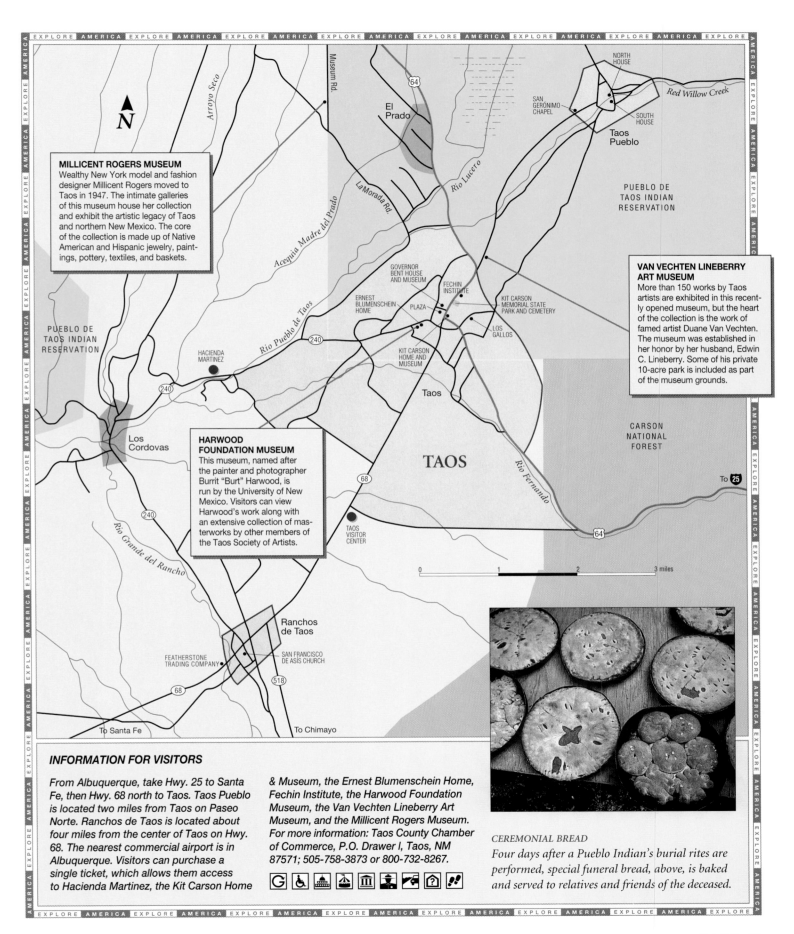

N

NORTH HOUSE

El Prado

Red Willow Creek

SAN GERÓNIMO CHAPEL

SOUTH HOUSE

Taos Pueblo

Museum Rd.

64

Arroyo Seco

La Morada Rd.

Rio Lucero

PUEBLO DE TAOS INDIAN RESERVATION

MILLICENT ROGERS MUSEUM
Wealthy New York model and fashion designer Millicent Rogers moved to Taos in 1947. The intimate galleries of this museum house her collection and exhibit the artistic legacy of Taos and northern New Mexico. The core of the collection is made up of Native American and Hispanic jewelry, paintings, pottery, textiles, and baskets.

Acequia Madre del Prado

GOVERNOR BENT HOUSE AND MUSEUM

FECHIN INSTITUTE

ERNEST BLUMENSCHEIN HOME

PLAZA

KIT CARSON MEMORIAL STATE PARK AND CEMETERY

VAN VECHTEN LINEBERRY ART MUSEUM
More than 150 works by Taos artists are exhibited in this recently opened museum, but the heart of the collection is the work of famed artist Duane Van Vechten. The museum was established in her honor by her husband, Edwin C. Lineberry. Some of his private 10-acre park is included as part of the museum grounds.

Rio Pueblo de Taos

PUEBLO DE TAOS INDIAN RESERVATION

HACIENDA MARTINEZ

240

LOS GALLOS

KIT CARSON HOME AND MUSEUM

Taos

CARSON NATIONAL FOREST

Los Cordovas

HARWOOD FOUNDATION MUSEUM
This museum, named after the painter and photographer Burrit "Burt" Harwood, is run by the University of New Mexico. Visitors can view Harwood's work along with an extensive collection of masterworks by other members of the Taos Society of Artists.

TAOS

Rio Fernando

To 25

240

68

Rio Grande del Rancho

TAOS VISITOR CENTER

64

0   1   2   3 miles

Ranchos de Taos

FEATHERSTONE TRADING COMPANY

SAN FRANCISCO DE ASÍS CHURCH

518

68

To Santa Fe

To Chimayo

INFORMATION FOR VISITORS

From Albuquerque, take Hwy. 25 to Santa Fe, then Hwy. 68 north to Taos. Taos Pueblo is located two miles from Taos on Paseo Norte. Ranchos de Taos is located about four miles from the center of Taos on Hwy. 68. The nearest commercial airport is in Albuquerque. Visitors can purchase a single ticket, which allows them access to Hacienda Martinez, the Kit Carson Home *& Museum, the Ernest Blumenschein Home, Fechin Institute, the Harwood Foundation Museum, the Van Vechten Lineberry Art Museum, and the Millicent Rogers Museum. For more information: Taos County Chamber of Commerce, P.O. Drawer I, Taos, NM 87571; 505-758-3873 or 800-732-8267.*

CEREMONIAL BREAD
Four days after a Pueblo Indian's burial rites are performed, special funeral bread, above, is baked and served to relatives and friends of the deceased.

EXPLORE AMERICA EXPLORE AMERICA EXPLORE AMERICA EXPLORE AMERICA EXPLORE AMERICA EXPLORE AMERICA EXPLORE AMERICA EXPLORE AMERICA EXPLORE

TAOS 87

CHILE RISTRA
Green chilies, tied in bundles and hung out in the sun, right, turn a deep red and are called chile ristras. Their fiery taste flavors traditional New Mexican dishes.

SNOWY SLUMBER
San Francisco de Asís Church, below, in Ranchos de Taos has been the subject of works by many painters and photographers, including the likes of Georgia O'Keeffe, Ansel Adams, and Alfred Stieglitz.

In 1540 Hernando de Alvarado, sent to the region from Mexico by the Spanish explorer Francisco Vásquez de Coronado, became the first European to encounter Taos Pueblo. Coronado and his soldiers were seeking fabled cities of gold, but all they found gleaming under the hot New Mexico sun were adobe pueblos.

Catholicism and commerce spurred the early Spanish explorers to invade this arid region. They traveled the Camino Real, or Royal Road, between Mexico City and Taos in caravans bearing much coveted metals, such as iron, and tools, linen, silk, and chocolate, which they exchanged for local salt, woolen products, and animal hides. At the same time, Franciscan monks were establishing missions to minister to the Native peoples. Although almost all the Taos Indians were converted to Christianity, most were discontented with Spanish rule, which imposed forced labor and outlawed Pueblo religious rites and ceremonies. The coexistence between the two cultures erupted into violence on more than one occasion.

In 1680 the pueblos along the Rio Grande planned a revolt. One of their leaders, a San Juan Indian named Popé, set up headquarters in Taos Pueblo. But two days before the uprising was to take place, the Spanish uncovered the plot.

When Popé learned that his plan was known, he moved at once, staging an attack on the morning of August 10. The Pueblos massacred some 400 Spaniards—21 of them priests. The Spaniards retaliated, executing 300 Indians; but by August 21 Santa Fe had been surrendered to the Indians, and 1,000 Spanish settlers fled the area and returned to Mexico.

The lure of commerce remained strong when 12 years later the Spanish reconquered the area, and traffic resumed along the Camino Real. From then on, the Spanish became a permanent presence in northern New Mexico.

More than a century later, the Camino Real was still a busy trade route. One of the Spaniards whose mules plodded the road between Chihuahua and Taos was Antonio Severino Martínez. By 1803 Don Antonio was a rich man and he bought some land south of Taos on the banks of the Rio Pueblo de Taos. The next year he began construction on his home, enlarging it from time to time to accommodate his growing family. Hacienda Martínez is one of the few remaining haciendas in the northern New Mexico–Spanish Colonial style open to the public. Solid walls of warm brown adobe lend it a fortresslike appearance. They surround two *placitas,* or courtyards, and enclose various rooms, including the *sala,* or living room, and the larger *gran sala,* where parties and political meetings were hosted. The *gran sala,* unlike the other mud-floored rooms, has a wood floor, an indication of the family's wealth and status. The sparse pine furniture in the house was entirely handmade. Wheat, barley, and corn for both people and livestock were stored in three large bins in the granary. Community members came here to the chapel to be baptized, to pray, and to be married. And in the trade room local people bargained for the goods that Don Antonio brought from Old Mexico and via the Santa Fe Trail.

| LARGER THAN LIFE | Antonio Severino Martínez's son, Antonio José, attended a seminary in Mexico, then returned to Taos where he was |

ordained in 1822. In addition to serving as a priest, Martínez became a state legislator, started a school, and ran a printing press. He was an outspoken critic of the local bishop, Jean Baptiste Lamy, whose mission was to modernize the almost medieval way that Roman Catholicism was practiced in New Mexico. Padre Martínez was much loved by his parishioners for challenging Lamy's attempts to tithe them. He was ultimately excommunicated for his rebellious stance. His reputation endures through a character modeled after him in Willa Cather's book *Death Comes for the Archbishop.*

The Taos suburb of Ranchos de Taos, which flourished in the 17th century, is the site of the Church of San Francisco de Asís, an outstanding example of Spanish Colonial mission architecture. Its golden adobe exterior, winglike buttresses, and twin bell towers topped by white crosses give it balance and harmony. The building is 108 feet long and, as with most Catholic churches, is built in the shape of a cross. Inside, red votive candles cast a soft light and the altars are backed by *retablos,* colorfully rendered religious scenes painted on wood.

No one knows exactly when San Francisco de Asís was built, but most authorities date it to the mid-1700's. The church is not included, however, in the records of a Fray Domínguez who visited

SPRINGTIME GLORY
A riot of spring wildflowers blooms in the green meadows that surround Taos, above.

ABIDING PARTNERS
At the Kit Carson Memorial State Park and Cemetery, above, Carson and Josefa, his beloved wife of 25 years, are buried side by side. Josefa died in April 1868, after giving birth to their eighth child. Kit died a month later.

northern New Mexico in 1776—an odd omission given that he was there to give an accounting of all the churches in the area. It is known that in 1813 a license was granted to build a church in Ranchos de Taos, and records indicate that a finished church existed there two years later.

The church building is a tangible symbol of the timeless power of faith. Enormous timbers supporting the church roof were carried down one by one from the mountains, and tens of thousands of adobe bricks were made and laid for the walls. When attempts were made to preserve the walls years later by putting a layer of cement over them, there was an outcry from people who felt that concrete was no substitute for adobe; unfortunately, the cement was applied and sealed in moisture. Then, in 1979 the 1,200 families belonging to the church parish raised the necessary money to undertake an ambitious reconstruction. They shored up the buttresses and replastered the entire exterior using traditional techniques.

In the parish hall of San Francisco de Asís hangs the 1896 oil painting of Christ by the French-Canadian painter Henri Ault. It has been given the name *The Shadow of the Cross*, because when the lights are turned off, the background of the painting takes on a strange luminescence, and Christ appears to be carrying a cross. Some people see a halo over his head, others the bow of a ship behind him. No one is able to explain the unusual effect.

By the late 18th century most people who went to Taos were more interested in trade than they were in saving souls. French-Canadian fur trappers arrived in 1739, followed by their American counterparts, including a legendary character who once traded his entire winter's catch for new clothes and a barrel of Taos Lightning, stiff whiskey brewed at the local Turley's Mill distillery. When Mexico won independence from Spain in 1821, New Mexico's borders were opened to Americans, and a brief period of trapping and trading followed that lasted until the beavers were almost wiped out.

One of the best-known figures around Taos Plaza in those prosperous days was fur trader Charles Bent, a partner in the prominent Bent, St. Vrain & Company store located on the south side of the plaza. He and his family lived in an adobe home near the plaza, which still stands. Bent was named the first civil governor of New Mexico after the United States seized the territory in 1846. Early on the morning of January 19, 1847, a group of Mexican rebels and Native Americans dramatically demonstrated their refusal to bow to American rule by seizing the Bent home. His five-year-old daughter, Teresina, wrote an account of the events: "Father step to the porch asking them what they wanted and they answered him we want your head gringo, we do not want for any of you gringos to govern us, as we have come to kill you." Bent, his wife and children managed to escape to another room in the house through a small hole they dug in the wall. But the mob found them, and scalped, then killed, Charles Bent. The hole in the wall can be seen in the Governor Bent House and Museum.

One of Bent's hunters was a man who became famous as a roughriding, hard-fighting frontier trailblazer. At 17 years of age, Christopher Houston "Kit" Carson had run away from an apprenticeship with a Missouri saddlemaker, and headed west along the Santa Fe Trail. He arrived in Taos in 1826, where he worked as a rancher, hunter and trapper, Indian agent, and colonel for the Union forces during the Civil War, when the Confederates tried to capture a fort in New Mexico.

In 1842 Carson served as guide for John Charles Frémont on a cross-country expedition to the Pacific Ocean that charted the route of the Oregon Trail. A year later he settled down and, after converting to Catholicism, married 14-year-old Josefa Jaramillo. They moved into an adobe house that

TRADITION SURVIVES
Dancers, wearing colorful traditional dress, left, prepare for a ceremonial dance during a Taos powwow.

PLACE OF WORSHIP
The chapel of San Gerónimo, below, stands at the gate to the Taos Pueblo. Most of the residents of the pueblo are Roman Catholics, who also continue to adhere to their traditional religion.

now serves as the Kit Carson Home and Museum. In 1860 a reporter for *Frank Leslie's Illustrated Newspaper* wrote: "His residence in the city of Taos is a popular place of resort for travellers passing through the country, and one often meets there a motley array of Americans, Mexicans, and Indians." The reporter's description of Carson conflicted with his public image: he said Kit was short and stout with straight brown hair, mild eyes, and a "round, kindly face." Indeed, he was a modest man who seldom spoke of his adventures.

MAGICAL LIGHT

At the turn of the century, this rustic town nestled in the high valley was discovered by a group of artists who decided to establish a colony here. Taos is almost 8,000 feet above sea level. The air is clean and dry, and the light has an unusual, almost magical, clarity to it. One of the first artists to remark on the beauty of the region was Joseph Sharp, a young painter from New York, who in 1895 praised Taos and its inhabitants to two fellow artists, Bert Phillips and Ernest Blumenschein. Three years later the two men took a trip from Denver to Mexico to sketch and see the Southwest for themselves. Blumenschein and Phillips outfitted a surrey, which was pulled by two broncos. They loaded the surrey with camping gear and painting supplies, and watched local cowboys for tips on how to handle and harness horses.

Their journey southward went off without a hitch until, about 20 miles from Taos, the surrey slid into a rut and broke a wheel. A flip of a coin sent Blumenschein off to find a blacksmith to repair the wheel. As he descended a hill and got his first glimpse of Taos Valley, he stopped in his tracks. "No artist," he later wrote, "had ever recorded the New Mexico I was now seeing. No writer had ever written down the smell of this air or the feel of the morning's sky. I was receiving, under rather painful circumstances, the first great unforgettable inspiration of my life." And so Blumenschein and Phillips decided to stay.

Blumenschein and his wife, artist Mary Shepherd Greene, purchased part of a Spanish-style adobe house, portions of which dated back to 1797, where they spent a few summers before becoming permanent residents. In 1912 Blumenschein, Phillips, and Sharp founded the Taos Society of Artists, which counted many well-known painters and sculptors among its charter members. The Ernest Blumenschein Home is a low-ceilinged, dark house with antiques and art culled from the artists' world travels. The large main room was Blumenschein's studio; the kitchen features a refrigerator made of adobe called a California Cooler; and each room is heated by a fireplace, which kept the house warm

through many long, cold Taos winters until gas and electricity were installed in 1938.

Among the artists who turned Taos into a vibrant colony was the Russian sculptor Nicolai Fechin, who arrived in 1927 after making his name in New York City. Fechin's Russian-style carvings distinguish his house in town: the building's doors, windows, and furniture were all crafted by the artist. A fine collection of the work of other renowned artists is also on view.

Every art colony has a patron. For Taos, this role was amply filled by the heiress Mabel Dodge. She arrived in Taos in 1918 with her third husband, the artist Maurice Sterne, and fell in love with the area. She also took up with her chauffeur, a Pueblo man named Tony Luhan. Unconcerned with the scandal she would inevitably cause, Mabel divorced Sterne and married Luhan. At Los Gallos, her home built in a mix of hacienda and Italian villa styles, Mabel hosted an endless round of dinners and parties attended by artists and celebrities. Among her guests were writers Willa Cather, Thomas Wolfe, Aldous Huxley, and D. H. Lawrence, author of many works, including *Lady Chatterley's Lover*. Lawrence and his wife, Frieda, stayed a while on Mabel's ranch about 15 miles north of town. It is now the site of a memorial to Lawrence.

The history of Taos is long and rich, steeped in the sweet scent of piñon smoke. The stories of the people who made it—Native American, Spanish, and Anglo-American, farmer, adventurer, and artist—bring its multifaceted past to life.

PAINTER'S DREAM
Afternoon sunlight creates a chiaroscuro of light and shadow on the snowswept landscape around Taos.

PUEBLO BAKING
A Taos Pueblo woman removes some bread from one of the dome-shaped ovens called hornos, *left.*

NEARBY SITES & ATTRACTIONS

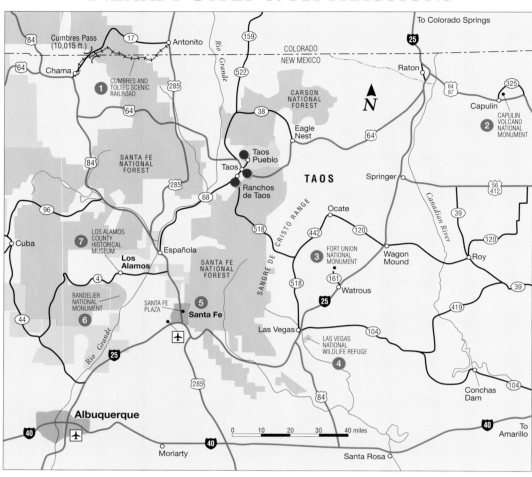

Clusters of volcanic rocks lie at the feet of Capulin Volcano, above. The volcano last erupted about 10,000 years ago.

1 CUMBRES AND TOLTEC SCENIC RAILROAD, COLORADO/NEW MEXICO

This railroad, built in 1880 to link the mining camps in the San Juan Mountains, takes visitors on a 64-mile excursion. Antique steam engines haul the vintage cars between Antonito, Colorado, and Chama, New Mexico—the longest and highest narrow-gauge railroad line in North America. The train climbs to 10,015 feet and crosses the Continental Divide at Cumbres Pass, a gap in the mountains once used by Native peoples and Spanish explorers. Located in Chama on Hwy. 17 and in Antonito on Hwy. 285.

2 CAPULIN VOLCANO NATIONAL MONUMENT, NEW MEXICO

Active a relatively recent 62,000 years ago, the conical form of Capulin Volcano rises more than 1,000 feet above the surrounding plain. A two-mile road spirals to the summit, where visitors can follow a self-guiding trail around the rim or descend to the crater's vent. Covered with junipers, piñons, and ponderosa pines, the extinct volcano is home to mule deer, porcupines, and a variety of birds. Located on Hwy. 325.

③ FORT UNION NATIONAL MONUMENT, NEW MEXICO

The largest military installation west of the Mississippi River in the 19th century, Fort Union also served as a major supply depot. In the 1870's the fort counted more than 50 buildings and housed soldiers and civilians who worked at the supply depot. Today the once-bustling fort can be seen by a self-guided trail that leads visitors past the remains of foundations, walls, chimneys, and fireplaces. Artifacts on display at the visitor center include a cavalry dress jacket and cattle brands. Located 8 miles northwest of Watrous on Hwy. 161.

④ LAS VEGAS NATIONAL WILDLIFE REFUGE, NEW MEXICO

Situated at the foot of the Sangre de Cristo range, the Las Vegas National Wildlife Refuge is a popular destination for bird-watchers. Sandhill cranes, snow geese, a variety of ducks and birds of prey, including prairie falcons, kestrels, sharp-shinned hawks, and bald and golden eagles, are attracted by the refuge's 8,672 acres of grasslands and juniper forest. Visitors can tour the refuge by car or on foot, following a nature trail that winds between sandstone and granite bluffs. Located 6 miles southeast of Las Vegas off Hwy. 25.

⑤ SANTA FE, NEW MEXICO

Established as the capital of the new Spanish colony in 1610, Santa Fe was captured by Native Americans during the 1680 Pueblo Revolt and restored to Spanish rule by Don Diego de Vargas 12 years later.

Historic Santa Fe Plaza, a picturesque square, is situated in the center of the old city. The Palace of the Governors just north of the plaza is the nation's oldest continuously occupied public building. The palace served as a seat of government for Pueblo Indians, Spaniards, Mexicans, and Americans. It is now a museum dedicated to the history of the Southwest. Located on Hwy. 84.

⑥ BANDELIER NATIONAL MONUMENT, NEW MEXICO

Jutting above the Pajarito Plateau, the pockmarked cliffs at the center of this 50-square-mile national monument house the ruins of hundreds of prehistoric Native American pueblos. A 45-minute hike takes visitors to the main ruins, which include a ceremonial chamber. A network of longer trails leads through the rugged backcountry to the Painted Cave, decorated with ancient petroglyphs, and Tsankawi, a prehistoric village perched atop a high mesa. Located 46 miles west of Santa Fe on Hwy. 4.

⑦ LOS ALAMOS COUNTY HISTORICAL MUSEUM, NEW MEXICO

Although this museum contains exhibits on local geology and anthropology, the most fascinating section focuses on the atom bomb that was developed in secret here as part of the Manhattan Project. Newspaper articles, photographs, and military uniforms are on display. There are also exhibits pertaining to homesteading and ranching. Located at 1921 Juniper St. in Los Alamos.

A colorful collection of gourds and pumpkins, above, brightens the back of a pickup truck in Santa Fe.

Prairie grass grows where soldiers once marched at Fort Union, below. The fort was an important stop along the Santa Fe Trail.

COLUMBIA STATE HISTORIC PARK

The Gem of the Southern Mines is California's best-preserved gold country settlement.

A grizzled old-timer beams a crooked grin as he hands over the big, shallow pan full of dark sand. He points to the creek sparkling in the morning light a dozen paces away. Oaks and manzanitas frame the gulch, where the water tumbles clear and cold down a channel fringed with buttercups and poppies. At first the earth in the bottom of the pan looks black, but a generous dip in the stream brings out its luster. A gentle swirling motion sloshes grains against the rim, and a ray of sunlight catches a tiny yellow fleck, glimmering brightly and unmistakably. The hollows resound with the cry of "Gold! Gold!"

The era of California's Gold Rush still echoes through the streets of Columbia in the Sierra Nevada. During its heyday in the 1850's, it was a boomtown of 6,000 permanent residents. A decade later the gold and the fever it set off were fast disappearing, and the population shrank rapidly.

It doesn't take long for the visitor to feel right at home on Main Street. A promenade meanders between covered wooden sidewalks and narrow red-brick buildings with ornate iron balconies. The still air is broken by the clank of hammer on anvil as a blacksmith demonstrates the proper way to make a horseshoe. The rich smell of tanned hides floats across the street from a leather shop that has been in operation since 1853. Elegant antique coaches sit in the livery, and old-fashioned sweets are on display at Nelson's Candy Kitchen.

Farther up Main Street, the William Cavalier Museum occupies a prominent place in the center of town. During the Gold Rush, this solid brick building housed Sewell Knapp's Miners Supply Store, probably the busiest address for miles around. Even today the wood floor is dulled by the dust of dry gulches, the oil from lanterns, and the nicks of pickaxes and shovels. The

A NIGHT ON THE TOWN
Overleaf: The Fallon Hotel Theater was built after Columbia's fire of 1857 and is still open for business. Touring performers, small theatrical troupes, choral societies, and bands came here to entertain the weary miners.

TREASURES OF ANOTHER KIND
A celestial scene, below, painted by James Fallon in the mid-1800's, adorns the altar of St. Anne's Church, where weddings are performed regularly.

display cases burst with memorabilia and the goods Knapp sold to prospectors in exchange for gold dust, standard currency in gold country. Park personnel, sometimes in period costume, recount the story of those rip-roaring days.

SUTTER'S DISCOVERY	James Marshall is credited with discovering gold on January 24, 1848, at Coloma on the American River, about 80 miles

north of Columbia. While building a sawmill for his partner, Swiss landowner John Sutter, Marshall noticed a gleaming nugget in the structure's tailrace. He searched further and found more nuggets along the river bank. Several days later Marshall went to Sutter's Fort, and told Sutter of his discovery. The two men tried to keep the find a secret, but before long word got out, and thousands of fortune seekers from up and down the West Coast were tramping through Sutter's property in the foothills of the Sierra Nevada. They found gold in such abundance that keeping the bonanza to themselves was nearly impossible.

Tales spread that the Mother Lode had been located in the Sierra Nevada. Farmhands abandoned their fields. Sailors jumped ship, leaving their vessels at anchor in San Francisco Bay, and the territory's only significant settlement was virtually deserted. Gold fever had taken hold.

The "forty-eighters" who mined that first year panned the sedimentary deposits in the riverbeds,

STOCKING UP
A wooden sign, above, outside one of the town's dry goods shops, advertises the wares typically sold by such a store in the 1850's.

INFORMATION FOR VISITORS

The town of Columbia is located within Columbia State Historic Park less than one mile off Hwy. 49. To reach Hwy. 49 from San Francisco, take I-80 east; from Sacramento, take Hwy. 50 east; from Stockton, take Hwy. 4 east; from Reno, Nevada, take I-80 west. The nearest airports are in San Francisco, Sacramento, Reno, and Columbia. There is also bus service to the nearby towns of Placerville and Grass Valley. The state park is open daily throughout the year except Thanksgiving and Christmas. Automobiles are prohibited in a six-square-block section of town. Special events are scheduled throughout the year, including Columbia Diggin's, held May 30 to June 2, and Miner's Christmas in December. On these occasions interpreters in period dress faithfully re-create the era of the Gold Rush. For more information: Columbia Chamber of Commerce, P.O. Box 1824, Columbia, CA 95310; 209-536-1672.

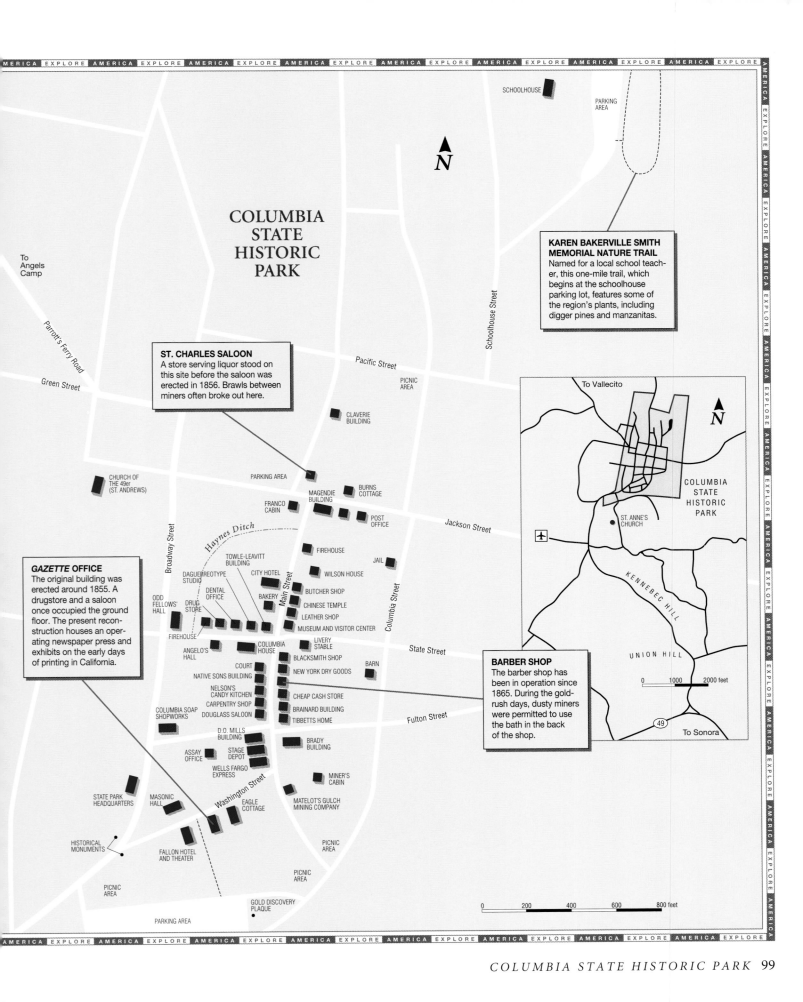

COLUMBIA
STATE
HISTORIC
PARK

To
Angels
Camp

N

Parrott's Ferry Road

Green Street

Schoolhouse Street

SCHOOLHOUSE

PARKING
AREA

KAREN BAKERVILLE SMITH MEMORIAL NATURE TRAIL
Named for a local school teacher, this one-mile trail, which begins at the schoolhouse parking lot, features some of the region's plants, including digger pines and manzanitas.

ST. CHARLES SALOON
A store serving liquor stood on this site before the saloon was erected in 1856. Brawls between miners often broke out here.

Pacific Street

PICNIC
AREA

CLAVERIE
BUILDING

CHURCH OF
THE 49er
(ST. ANDREWS)

PARKING AREA

BURNS
COTTAGE

MAGENDIE
BUILDING

FRANCO
CABIN

POST
OFFICE

Jackson Street

Broadway Street

Haynes Ditch

TOWLE-LEAVITT
BUILDING

FIREHOUSE

DAGUERREOTYPE
STUDIO

WILSON HOUSE

JAIL

CITY HOTEL

Main Street

Columbia Street

GAZETTE OFFICE
The original building was erected around 1855. A drugstore and a saloon once occupied the ground floor. The present reconstruction houses an operating newspaper press and exhibits on the early days of printing in California.

DENTAL
OFFICE

BUTCHER SHOP

ODD
FELLOWS'
HALL

DRUG
STORE

BAKERY

CHINESE TEMPLE

LEATHER SHOP

FIREHOUSE

MUSEUM AND VISITOR CENTER

ANGELO'S
HALL

COLUMBIA
HOUSE

LIVERY
STABLE

State Street

BLACKSMITH SHOP

COURT

NEW YORK DRY GOODS

BARN

BARBER SHOP
The barber shop has been in operation since 1865. During the gold-rush days, dusty miners were permitted to use the bath in the back of the shop.

NATIVE SONS BUILDING

NELSON'S
CANDY KITCHEN

CHEAP CASH STORE

CARPENTRY SHOP

BRAINARD BUILDING

COLUMBIA SOAP
SHOPWORKS

DOUGLASS SALOON

TIBBETTS HOME

Fulton Street

D.O. MILLS
BUILDING

BRADY
BUILDING

ASSAY
OFFICE

STAGE
DEPOT

WELLS FARGO
EXPRESS

MINER'S
CABIN

STATE PARK
HEADQUARTERS

MASONIC
HALL

EAGLE
COTTAGE

Washington Street

MATELOT'S GULCH
MINING COMPANY

HISTORICAL
MONUMENTS

FALLON HOTEL
AND THEATER

PICNIC
AREA

PICNIC
AREA

PICNIC
AREA

PARKING AREA

GOLD DISCOVERY
PLAQUE

0   200   400   600   800 feet

To Vallecito

N

COLUMBIA
STATE
HISTORIC
PARK

ST. ANNE'S
CHURCH

KENNEBEC HILL

UNION HILL

0   1000   2000 feet

49

To Sonora

and eventually gouged it from veins in granite boulders with pocketknives. It is estimated that anywhere from $250,000 to $2.5 million worth of the precious metal was taken out of the mines that year—enough to set imaginations reeling across the country. The United States government, which only two years before had annexed the rugged frontier known as California during the war with Mexico, began to realize the value of what it had won. On December 5, 1848, Pres. James Polk told Congress of the magnitude of the gold strike, and two days later a government courier arrived in Washington bearing a tea caddy full of freshly mined California gold.

LURE OF THE LODE

Landowners, sometimes working with amateur geologists, noted the sites where gold was found and looked for similar topography on their own haciendas. It was not difficult. The gold was created deep underground millions of years ago and percolated and rose to the surface during the seismic activity that created the Sierra Nevada. Gold ore crystallized with quartz rock, and weathering caused small flecks of gold to fall into the riverbeds as placer. The gold that was locked within the rock became known as the Mother Lode. The forty-niners washed, picked,

and blasted gold along a 200-mile strip of drainages that stretched from Vintin to Oakhurst.

Prospectors arrived by the tens of thousands in 1849. Easterners chartered ships and rounded the tip of South America in voyages that lasted months, if they survived the icy seas and howling winds. Others came by way of the isthmus in what is now Panama, where some fell victim to bandits or cholera. Some were stranded in Central America because there weren't enough ships available to take them to San Francisco. They came in wagon companies from the heartland after crossing the Great Plains, deserts, and mountains of the West. Often they arrived with nothing but the clothes on their backs—and visions of striking it rich.

These dreams were often shattered. The diggings were overcrowded and hitting pay-dirt was not a sure thing. Miners worked elbow to elbow and were sometimes lucky to scrape up enough gold to cover the cost of food and supplies.

HILDRETH'S DIGGINGS

Some of the most skilled diggers working in the California gold fields had mined in the Andes of Chile and the Sierra Madre of Mexico. Their humble camps were scattered across the Sierra Nevada. One prospector to the area was Dr. Thaddeus Hildreth of Maine, who with his American party had been mining in the Calaveras region with little success. He decided to try his luck on the other side of the Calaveras River. Hildreth's initial dig was unsuccessful, but as so often happened in these mountains, good luck followed on the heels of failure, and on the morning of March 27, 1850, Hildreth struck gold. Within a month the finds, known variously as Hildreth's Diggings and American Camp, had attracted some 2,000 to 3,000 men. The gulch earned the official name of Columbia.

In the euphoria of those early days, gold-rush prospectors tended to be short-sighted, even naive, and there was no shortage of people waiting to capitalize on their free-spending ways. Saloons and gambling houses opened wherever the miners worked. Of its estimated 150 businesses, Columbia counted 30 saloons and an equal number of card parlors where the miners spent much of their spare time. The stakes were high and many a fortune was squandered in a single reckless night of gambling. Visitors can relive the lamplit glamor of the roaring 50's during Casino Night in Tent Town, as would-be hustlers challenge cardsharps at games of monte, faro, and heironymus, and dance hall girls entertain patrons seated at the bar, a rough plank laid across two kegs of whiskey.

But card hustlers and dance hall girls weren't the only people looking to separate a man from his hard-won gold. Legendary highwaymen like Black Bart and Joaquin Murietta prowled gold country, ready to waylay stages or miners on horseback as they left the diggings with their fortunes.

The initial frenzy caused by some truly spectacular finds—one lump weighed in at 72 pounds and was valued at $14,000—came up against some hard realities by that first July. The creek dried up in the heat, making it impossible for miners to use their pans to sift through the soil and find the placer. Things were so bad that Mexican and Chilean miners resorted to tossing the earth up in the air,

allowing gravity to separate the heavier gold particles from the dirt, and catching the precious metal in sheets. Most of the American miners gave up and decided to try their luck again in the fall when the creeks would be running again. By late summer the population had shrunk to less than 100, but Columbia was too rich a deposit to ignore. By the following year, miners were hired by a local water company to dig a ditch to Five Mile Creek that delivered enough water for prospectors to work the placers at Columbia again. This was the first of a network of ditches, flumes, and aqueducts that tapped the Stanislaus River and provided Columbia with an uninterrupted flow of water.

A permanent water source created a permanent settlement. The miners began constructing sturdy dwellings for year-round living, and the cabin at Matelot's Gulch Mining Supply was stockpiled then as now with the tools of the trade. New

BRICK SCHOOLHOUSE
Restored in 1960, the schoolhouse, above, was built 100 years earlier at a cost of $5,000. It is equipped with a bell tower, pump organ, and potbellied stoves.

methods were developed for sifting large quantities of dirt more efficiently. The use of a rocker or cradle enabled miners to process shovelfuls of earth at a time. The Long Tom, a trough set up by a river for rinsing soil for gold, took this technique one step further by extending a sluice lined with ribs to catch heavy nuggets. Once the miners had exhausted the placers, they moved to higher ground and broke quartz rocks with pickaxes and the arrastre, a mule- or ox-driven grinding wheel. More gold was washed from the Columbia gravels than from any other comparably sized area in the western hemisphere, amounting to $87 million from just 640 acres. By 1853 some estimates had Columbia shipping as much as $100,000 of gold a day to the newly constructed mint in San Francisco.

Main Street became a busy thoroughfare flanked by brick buildings, many of which still stand. With

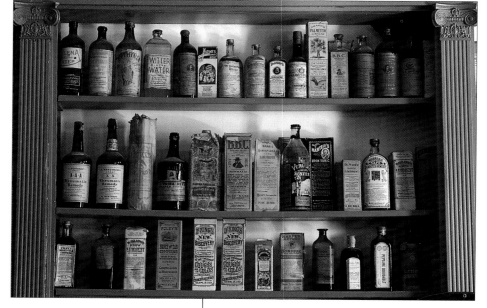

bars. Matelot's Gulch Mining Supply still sells pans to tenderfoot miners—complete with "pay dirt." The Cheap Cash Store went up in 1854, and the New York Dry Goods store the next year. Time has not dulled the blades at one of the oldest barber shops in California, which has operated on Main Street since 1865. At the Carpentry Shop, today's do-it-yourselfers will be interested in the collection of 19th-century tools, such as planes and mallets that were sold to people accustomed to building things by hand.

GOLD-RUSH SOCIETY

When Mark Twain visited gold country in the 1860's, he said that the Gold Rush's multinational society "was the only population of the kind that the world has ever seen gathered together, and it is not likely that the world will ever see its like again." Columbia's was a tiny universe, peopled by miners from France, Mexico, Germany, China, Italy, Spain, Australia, Peru, and other countries around the world. The Chinese were among the earliest and the most successful prospectors. They persevered despite hardships and incidents of bigotry. Their contribution is honored in several places in Columbia State Historic Park. The herbal shop on Main Street contains a battery of traditional Chinese remedies used to treat frontier ills.

Although outbreaks of violence against foreign miners, shoot-outs, and even a lynching marred Columbia's history, most of the time the town was an energetic, friendly place. And for the people

such prosperity, doctors' and dentists' offices, stores, hotels, banks, laundries, breweries, and syrup mills opened to serve the miners' needs. The boom created a market that no enterprising Yankee could help but exploit. Many of the men who had come to Columbia to dig found robbing the spendthrift miners more lucrative than mining, and some of the biggest gold-rush fortunes were built on charging prospectors astronomical prices for goods: $20 for a shovel, $5 a pound for pork, $1 for a candle. Saloons changed from nothing more than tents offering swigs from barrels of whiskey to the brick buildings with swinging doors and brass rails made famous in movie Westerns. Among the finest and best preserved watering holes are the Jack Douglass and the St. Charles saloons on Main Street, where visitors can sip sarsaparilla at the long polished

who lived there, nothing could beat a good dance. Any pretext sufficed—a holiday, a birthday, even the opening of a new boardinghouse. With so few women around, the men made do—by dancing with one another. Men who sought the company of fast women could find them at fandango halls, where libations flowed to the beat of Spanish music, and figures danced seductively amid the gauzy veil of smoke and dim lamplight.

WOMEN AT COLUMBIA Although a handful of women were a part of life in the mines from the outset, it was not until more respectable businesses arrived in Columbia that they became a common sight. The first women to come to the area made a deep impression in a world of bachelors and they were often followed around on their daily errands by droves of curious and adoring miners. Gradually families settled in Columbia, and life there grew as

rich socially as it had economically. Fraternal orders were established in buildings such as the Masonic Hall on Washington Street and the Oddfellows on State Street. Priests and parsons, who at first had led services under the trees, now presided over proper congregations in churches such as St. Anne's, possibly the first brick church in California, located just outside the park.

Yet for all the civilizing influences, this was still gold country. The city's cemetery had to be moved in 1855 after desperate prospectors began digging there in the frenzied search for gold. Once the departed had been removed to higher ground, the cemetery was mined with gusto.

The Fallon House Theater opened in 1857 to enthusiastic audiences. When the actors took their curtain calls, they were rewarded by a cascade of clapping, hollering, and weeping, and bags of gold dust flew onto the stage. The miners, swept up in an adventure of epic proportions, appreciated the

MAIN STREET
Early morning light filters through the trees along Main Street, above. Wooden barrels stand outside the Towle & Leavitt Shop, which was built in 1857.

stagings of grand melodrama and low comedy that mirrored their own experience. Plays depicted hardship overcome, faithful heroines awaiting the return of heroic men, and sudden reversals of fortune. These were the themes that charmed and moved the miners. Though the men's taste ran toward the sentimental, they were also a highly critical audience, and the unprofessional dared not tread the boards in the Sierra Nevada. Columbia's demanding audiences attracted everyone from the famous Shakespearean thespian Edwin Booth to a singing and dancing child performer named Lotta Crabtree, who stole hearts in the gold camps before going on to conquer New York, London, and Paris. Today Fallon House Theater's stage is home to the Columbia Actors' Repertory, which offers everything from family fare to Broadway musicals throughout the year, keeping alive an important Columbia tradition.

DECLINE AND REBIRTH The occasional ringing from State Street's red bell tower serves as a reminder that real-life drama was never far from the miner's mind. During hot summers wildfires driven by gusty winds sometimes swept through the foothills without warning, wiping out entire towns in a matter of minutes. Fire ravaged Columbia twice—in 1854 and 1857. Undaunted, the people rebuilt using brick instead of wood.

At the annual Firemen's Muster held on the first weekend in May, buckets of water slip and slosh from hand to hand down the line, and competitions put the pumping skills of locals and visitors to the test on antique fire engines, such as one called Papeete. This jaunty little engine, built on the East Coast for delivery to Tahiti, sat in San Francisco awaiting its ship when it caught the eye of a delegation from Columbia, and they quickly snapped it up for their own community.

The Papeete's arrival in town was cause for much celebration. The engine's only rival in the public affections was Monumental, a big four-pumper that was too heavy for the firemen to pull up the steep hills of San Francisco, making it often more dangerous than the fires it fought. So Monumental also ended up in Columbia, the proud responsibility of Engine Company No. 2. There was more than pride riding on the rivalry between the two volunteer crews because the first to arrive at the scene of a fire received a financial reward. Today's annual Firemen's Muster renews the contest of old and revives the spirit of cooperation that more than once saved Columbia from ruin.

By the late 1850's Columbia was washed out as a gold town, and most of the miners had moved on. Related mining businesses deserted town and

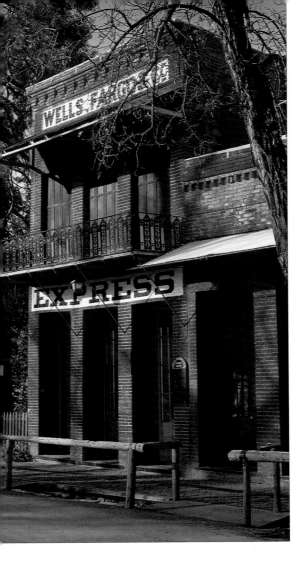

and Volcano. The spirit of the early days lives on in the picturesque building facades of these towns, and in their well-preserved houses and museums displaying local lore. There is Rough And Ready, a town that seceded from the United States in 1850 over a mining tax and didn't rejoin the Union for a century; Growlersburg, which produced nuggets so big they growled in miners' pans; and Jackass Hill, known for the braying of recalcitrant mules at a pack station. Numerous events bring the mining days to life, such as May's Calaveras County Fair in Angel's Camp and a celebrated Jumping Frog Jubilee inspired by a Mark Twain yarn. Malakoff Diggings, the Empire Mine at Grass Valley, and Sutter's Mill in Coloma—all state parks—preserve the history of the gold-rush years. Anyone who feels the urge to dig strongly enough may pull off the highway and, where allowed, pan for pay dirt.

On the hillside above Columbia is the town's enduring pride and joy, a red-brick schoolhouse that served the local population from 1860 until 1937. In 1960 schoolchildren from all over the state raised more than $50,000 toward the building's restoration. Today thousands of children visit the school and sit at the old desks, listen to the pump organ, feel the warmth of the potbellied stoves, and learn how their predecessors were taught the "three R's." Doubtless those earlier students also gazed dreamily out the big windows and traced the trails of clouds across the sky.

In Columbia State Historic Park visitors learn to appreciate the realities of a time often obscured by the tall tales of the era. And as long as the waters stream down the foothills of the Sierra Nevada, gold will continue to lure people to the creekbeds of California's Mother Lode.

followed the boom elsewhere, setting up shop near still thriving gold enterprises or returning home. As buildings fell into disrepair, diehard prospectors tore them down and mined their foundations for any last scraps of ore.

California was transformed by the Gold Rush. It brought untold wealth and an influx of young and energetic entrepreneurs to what had been an untamed wilderness. San Francisco and Sacramento grew in size and spread to areas where cattle had grazed only a season or two before. With an output of more than $2 billion in gold, California became one of the richest states in the nation.

PRIDE AND JOY

In 1945 the state of California began purchasing buildings in Columbia with the intention of starting a state historic park as a way of paying homage to California's gold-rush origins. Columbia joins other towns in gold country in welcoming the traveler with restorations, reenactments, and samplings of real gold dust. Highway 49 and its offshoots reach into the oak-fringed hills and dales, linking such renowned and notorious haunts as Placerville, Angel's Camp,

STOCKING UP, WEIGHING IN
Early prospectors took their gold to an assayer set up in a tent. Later, business was conducted in such cramped little offices as the one presently located behind the Wells Fargo Express building on Main Street, left. Here, miners waited anxiously as an agent balanced gold dust on scales sensitive enough to detect the extra weight of a signature on a piece of paper. Mining supplies could be purchased at several establishments in town, like the one shown on the opposite page.

STAGECOACH RIDES
During the summer months, vintage vehicles, below, depart every quarter-hour from the stage depot for rides through the surrounding countryside. Passengers have the option of sitting inside the coach, or riding "shotgun" beside the driver.

NEARBY SITES & ATTRACTIONS

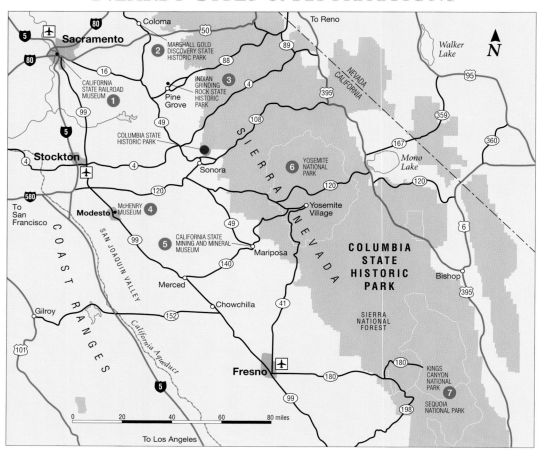

The slopes of the Sierra Nevada in Kings Canyon National Park shelter glaciers—remnants of the powerful ice flows that carved the mountains and valleys of the park.

At Marshall Gold Discovery State Historic Park, a single barred cell is all that remains of the old stone jail, below, built in 1857.

1 CALIFORNIA STATE RAILROAD MUSEUM

Railroad buffs from all over the country are drawn to this museum in Old Sacramento. The reconstructed 1876 Central Pacific Railroad Passenger Station depicts waiting areas, the baggage room, and numerous locomotives and railroad cars. It also serves as a depot for the museum's steam excursion train, which operates throughout the year. The reconstructed Big Four Building houses an 1855 hardware store, changing exhibit gallery, and the museum's railroad history library. The main museum displays toy trains, 21 restored locomotives and cars, an 1888 railroad bridge, and numerous other interpretive displays and dioramas that trace the history of the railroad in California and the West. Located at 2nd and I streets in Old Sacramento.

2 MARSHALL GOLD DISCOVERY STATE HISTORIC PARK

When James Marshall discovered gold in 1848 at the site of John Sutter's sawmill on the American River, he quickly put California on the world map. Unfortunately neither Marshall nor Sutter was able to establish a legitimate claim to the land surrounding the mill, and Marshall died a pauper. In 1851 Sutter and his wife moved to the East Coast where he attempted to regain ownership of the land, but was unsuccessful. The park shows films about the history of gold mining in the area and displays wooden beams from the original sawmill, mining equipment, household articles, and horse-drawn vehicles. Visitors can see how a 19th-century sawmill was operated, and in the Wah Hop Store, items used by Chinese miners are on view. A bronze statue of Marshall stands on a hilltop overlooking the town. Located in Coloma.

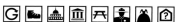

3 INDIAN GRINDING ROCK STATE HISTORIC PARK

For thousands of years Miwok Indians used the limestone slabs of this area to grind acorns and other seeds into meal. These ancient grindstones, one of which is pierced by 1,185 mortar holes, are situated in a 135-acre park, which also includes a restored Miwok village, ceremonial roundhouse, and a museum. Petroglyph carvings in the shape of circles, spoked wheels, and animal tracks are inscribed in the rock. At the Chow'Se Regional Indian Museum visitors can learn about the technology and crafts of the Miwok and other Sierra Nevada Indians from a display of their tools, jewelry, arrow points, and baskets. Two trails wind through the park meadows and stands of oaks, providing visitors a glimpse of native birds and 130 species of plants. Located 2.5 miles north of the town of Pine Grove off Hwy. 88.

4 McHENRY MUSEUM

Housed in what was once a library, the McHenry Museum, named after the building's original owner, is devoted to the cultural history of Stanislaus County. Exhibits include the interiors of a doctor's office, a general store, and a re-created blacksmith's shop, built with the wood and square nails from another 19th-century building. Cattle brands, period firefighting equipment, a collection of guns, and gold-rush memorabilia make up other exhibits. Located at 1402 I St. in Modesto.

5 CALIFORNIA STATE MINING AND MINERAL MUSEUM

Gold in many forms—crystallized, nuggets, gold leaf, and wire gold—is on display in the museum. Exhibits include a working model of a five-stamp quartz mill and an underground mining tunnel with life-size figures of miners at work. Stones such as diamonds and benitoite—the state gemstone—are on permanent display as are 19th-century mining artifacts. Temporary exhibits feature unusual mineral specimens from other museums and private collections. Located 2 miles south of Mariposa on Hwy. 49.

6 YOSEMITE NATIONAL PARK

This 1,200-square-mile park is world famous for its waterfalls, mountains, canyons, and granite domes. The most popular area of the park is the 3,000-foot-deep Yosemite Valley. Upper Yosemite Fall, Lower Yosemite Fall, and Middle Cascade together drop a total of 2,425 feet. Upper Yosemite alone tumbles 1,430 feet, making it one of the highest waterfalls in the world. Other sights include the 7,569-foot-high monolith of El Capitan and 13,114-foot-high Mount Lyell, site of the park's largest glacier. Hikers and horseback riders can explore 840 miles of trails that wind through groves of 3,000-year-old sequoia trees. Yosemite is home to some 80 species of mammals and 247 species of birds. Located 36 miles northeast of Mariposa on Hwy. 140.

El Capitan in Yosemite National Park, above, is one of the world's largest exposed granite monoliths. Its sheer walls prove irresistible to experienced rock climbers.

7 SEQUOIA AND KINGS CANYON NATIONAL PARKS

Ancient groves of sequoia trees, mountain peaks, meadows, and canyons draw visitors to these contiguous parks, which together measure 66 miles long and 36 miles at their widest point. A network of scenic roads and hiking trails cuts through the lower terrain and Redwood Mountain Grove—the world's largest stand of sequoias. More than 3,000 of these trees measure 10 feet in diameter or more and two of them—the General Sherman tree and the General Grant tree—are the largest in the world. The Giant Forest of Sequoias is home to the General Sherman tree. Believed to be as old as 4,000 years, it measures 275 feet high and 101 feet in circumference, making it the largest living thing on earth. In the General Grant Grove, the General Grant tree rises to a height of 267 feet. The high country is dominated by the 12,000- to over 14,000-foot peaks of the Sierra Nevada. Experienced mountaineers can meet the challenge of Mount Whitney, which at 14,495 feet is the highest peak in the United States south of Alaska. In winter the parks offer opportunities for cross-country skiing and snowshoeing. Located 40 miles east of Visalia on Hwy. 198.

FORT CLATSOP

A fort in the wilderness conjures up the spirit of the explorers who spearheaded the opening of the West.

Along the storm-tossed Oregon coast a dense mist drifts through bracken and fir, and glosses the hollows in a satiny drizzle. Trickles turn into rivulets, and rivulets into streams that slide over moss-lined rocks and cascade in gentle waterfalls. In a small clearing, set back about a hundred yards from the bank of the Lewis and Clark River, stands a log stockade, its front gates swung open wide. Water beads on hand-hewn timbers and drips from shingled eaves. Smoke curls skyward from a crude chimney, and out of the fort comes the merry trill of a frontier fiddle, incongruous in the gloom. Figures clad in buckskin clothing and carrying long rifles emerge from the shadows cast by the lofty evergreen trees that overhang the stockade.

The dark forests of the Pacific Northwest play many tricks with the imagination, but these figures are not apparitions. They are interpreters at Fort Clatsop National Memorial, located near Astoria, Oregon. The men reenact the days of Meriwether Lewis and William Clark, the

Overleaf: Fort Clatsop is set amid a dense forest of towering trees. At the end of November 1805, Meriwether Lewis and a small party of men set out to look for a safe site for a winter fort. They found one after canoeing along the Columbia River, around the peninsula where Astoria is located, and into a small river called Netul. Though the explorers were some four miles east of the Pacific Ocean, they could hear the roar of the surf.

WILDERNESS STUDY

A costumed interpreter, above, demonstrates some of the activities of William Clark, who, during the winter of 1805–06, spent countless hours poring over his notes. Clark executed the first map of the land between North Dakota and the Oregon coast.

explorers who ended their search for a route to the Pacific Ocean here. The fort is a faithful re-creation of the original structure erected by members of the Lewis and Clark expedition during the winter of 1805–06. It offered a refuge from intemperate weather and lifted their sinking spirits.

The 125-acre national memorial also includes a comprehensive visitor center that features artifacts, films, and informative displays relating to the winter the explorers spent at Fort Clatsop. On select days during the summer, interpretive programs and demonstrations immerse visitors in life at the camp. Living quarters within the fort are set up much as they were in the explorers' day, giving the magic of time travel a helpful nudge. The interpreters have mastered many frontier skills. They scrape, tan, and sew swaths of hide for their own costumes, and occasionally hew canoes from the trunks of red cedar trees. Rangers lead discovery walks in the forest now and then and explain the many uses of native plants. Visitors may learn how to care for, load, and fire a replica of an 1803 Harpers Ferry muzzle-loading rifle—a firearm designed especially for the expedition. They may be shown how to make candles from tallow, rendered animal fat, or how to light a fire using flint and steel. By participating in some of the explorers' daily tasks, visitors step back almost 200 years to an age when the nation was still in its infancy.

LOUISIANA PURCHASE

In 1800 the great expanse of the Pacific Northwest territory was virtually unknown to anyone other than the Native peoples who inhabited the area. Many Americans were eager to find a riverine Northwest Passage across the continent. When, in 1803, the young American Republic negotiated the Louisiana Purchase with the French, it obtained sovereignty over a vast tract of land extending from the bayous of the Mississippi Delta to the glacial peaks of the northern Rocky Mountains.

No one knew precisely how large the Louisiana Purchase was or what natural treasures it might contain. Determined to ascertain the country's dimensions and its commercial possibilities, Pres. Thomas Jefferson created the Corps of Discovery, placing it under the command of his secretary, Meriwether Lewis. Lewis was a young officer with considerable wilderness experience, sound judgment, and a remarkable gift of observation. Jefferson instructed Lewis to explore the Missouri River and other water routes to the Pacific Ocean and to establish "the most direct and practicable water communication across this continent for the purposes of commerce"—a Northwest Passage.

Lewis selected as co-captain his former military commander, William Clark, an Army veteran and resourceful woodsman. The leaders recruited a team of several dozen able-bodied frontiersmen and rivermen harking primarily from outposts along the Ohio Valley. On May 14, 1804, following months of training and preparation, the team set forth from outside St. Louis on their journey up the Missouri, and into the pages of legend.

Throughout 1804 and 1805, the Corps of Discovery pursued Jefferson's objectives, charting the headwaters of the Missouri, Clearwater, Snake, and Columbia rivers with the aid of the latest navigational instruments. En route they won the respect and friendship of tribes such as the Mandan and Nez Percé, and learned about Native American laws, religions, and customs. The 4,000-mile journey by canoe, on foot, and on horseback was rife with unanticipated challenges. Time and again, the entire enterprise was put at risk by severe weather and other untimely crises. The Corps was harassed by Teton Sioux warriors on the High Plains; an early snow in Idaho's Bitterroot Mountains forced them to slaughter their colts for food as the supply dwindled; and they lost a canoe shooting the churning rapids of the Columbia River.

The agony subsided once the explorers felt the tidal surge beneath their dugouts. On November 7, 1805, they landed 20 miles upriver from present-day Ilwaco, Washington, and William Clark wrote in his journal: "Ocian in view! O! the joy."

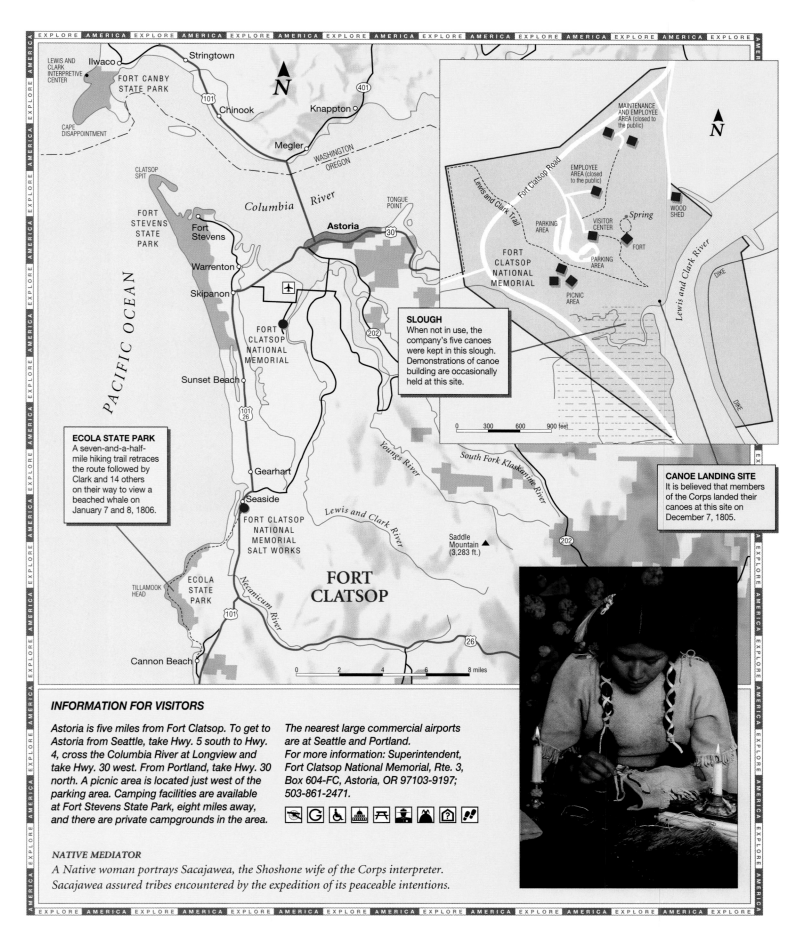

LEWIS AND CLARK INTERPRETIVE CENTER

Ilwaco

Stringtown

FORT CANBY STATE PARK

CAPE DISAPPOINTMENT

Chinook

Knappton

101

401

Megler

WASHINGTON
OREGON

TONGUE POINT

Columbia River

N

CLATSOP SPIT

FORT STEVENS STATE PARK

Fort Stevens

Astoria

30

Warrenton

Skipanon

202

FORT CLATSOP NATIONAL MEMORIAL

PACIFIC OCEAN

Sunset Beach

101 26

Youngs River

South Fork Klaskanine River

ECOLA STATE PARK
A seven-and-a-half-mile hiking trail retraces the route followed by Clark and 14 others on their way to view a beached whale on January 7 and 8, 1806.

Gearhart

Seaside

Lewis and Clark River

FORT CLATSOP NATIONAL MEMORIAL SALT WORKS

Necanicum River

TILLAMOOK HEAD

ECOLA STATE PARK

101

FORT CLATSOP

Saddle Mountain (3,283 ft.)

202

0   2   4   6   8 miles

Cannon Beach

26

Detail map (upper right)

MAINTENANCE AND EMPLOYEE AREA (closed to the public)

Fort Clatsop Road

Lewis and Clark Trail

EMPLOYEE AREA (closed to the public)

WOOD SHED

Spring

PARKING AREA

VISITOR CENTER

FORT

FORT CLATSOP NATIONAL MEMORIAL

PARKING AREA

PICNIC AREA

Lewis and Clark River

DIKE

DIKE

N

0   300   600   900 feet

SLOUGH
When not in use, the company's five canoes were kept in this slough. Demonstrations of canoe building are occasionally held at this site.

CANOE LANDING SITE
It is believed that members of the Corps landed their canoes at this site on December 7, 1805.

INFORMATION FOR VISITORS

Astoria is five miles from Fort Clatsop. To get to Astoria from Seattle, take Hwy. 5 south to Hwy. 4, cross the Columbia River at Longview and take Hwy. 30 west. From Portland, take Hwy. 30 north. A picnic area is located just west of the parking area. Camping facilities are available at Fort Stevens State Park, eight miles away, and there are private campgrounds in the area.

The nearest large commercial airports are at Seattle and Portland.
For more information: Superintendent, Fort Clatsop National Memorial, Rte. 3, Box 604-FC, Astoria, OR 97103-9197; 503-861-2471.

NATIVE MEDIATOR
A Native woman portrays Sacajawea, the Shoshone wife of the Corps interpreter. Sacajawea assured tribes encountered by the expedition of its peaceable intentions.

Clark's joy was short-lived. The Corps was unprepared for winter on the Northwest Coast and could not find adequate shelter from incessant rain, wind, and the high tides of the Columbia estuary. The camp was swamped by crashing breakers, the men became "as wet as water could make them," and their leather clothes rotted in the damp. Logs adrift on the river smashed their canoes, and swarms of fleas infested their bedding, robbing them of sleep. Some fell ill. Unable to hunt because of the bad weather, the Corps divided the last morsels of dried fish it had acquired from Indians living upriver.

Lewis hoped that an American or English vessel might put into the Columbia estuary and replenish their goods and supplies so they could trade with Indians, but he now learned from the Chinooks that ships wouldn't call before spring arrived. As the rain poured on, the explorers faced the dismal prospect of a long and hungry winter on a wet, inhospitable coast.

It was clear to them as soon as they arrived at this remote outpost that, in order to survive, they needed the assistance of their neighbors, the Chinook Indians. As seasoned veterans of the fur trade, the Chinook tribes had become important

drank at the freshwater spring that burst from the dappled glades. The explorers immediately set about erecting a shelter and stocking food. Lewis ordered trees felled for a fort and dispatched his men to hunt elk. Soon axes clove deep into the thick trunks, and the crisp report of flintlocks sounded across the bogs.

WELCOME REST Meanwhile, Clark and a small group of men hacked their way through thickets and brambles toward the ocean, where they hoped to find a suitable place for making salt. The salt would improve the taste of game and preserve meat. After several soggy nights in the bush, they came upon a Clatsop village, whose chief, Cuscular, welcomed Clark with "extrordeannary friendship" and served up a banquet of smoked salmon, berry syrup, and cockle soup. For the first time some of the men enjoyed a brief respite from the bitter fight for survival, and joined their Clatsop neighbors in games and song.

When the scouting party returned to the hilltop encampment, they found the others hard at work cutting down trees to build a fort. Gradually the 50-foot-square log structure took shape in the clearing. The captains' quarters were built first, followed by a smoke room for the meat. Across the parade ground, a row of three bunkhouses was erected to house the enlisted men, and then a cabin for the group's indispensable cook and guide, Toussaint Charbonneau, his Shoshone wife, Sacajawea, and infant son, Jean Baptiste. The Charbonneaus had joined the Corps the winter before at Fort Mandan on the Missouri. Sacajawea played an essential role on several occasions in allaying the fears of the tribes they met along the way, as Native American war parties never traveled with women. Acting as both interpreter and diplomat, Sacajawea was instrumental in securing horses from the Shoshones, enabling the expedition to continue its voyage across the Rocky Mountains.

The Fort Clatsop National Memorial is a faithful reconstruction based on a sketch that Clark laboriously etched into the elk-skin cover of his field notes. The reconstructed fort, built by residents and skilled Finnish carpenters, has a more finished appearance than the original, which was built by exhausted men in a matter of just 17 days.

On December 25, 1805, the Corps of Discovery moved into their winter home, which Lewis named Fort Clatsop in honor of the local Indians whose help had been so important. That Christmas Day, though "showery wet and disagreeable" according to Clark's journal, found the group in good spirits. They exchanged gifts, received Indian visitors, and celebrated their good fortune with a festive

links in the economy of the West, exchanging the metals, tobacco, and fabrics of American and British traders for beaver and sea otter pelts bound for Europe and China, where fur hats fetched high prices. Having thus learned the virtues of the hard bargain, the Chinooks were not about to part with scarce food and valuable furs for the beads and trinkets in Lewis and Clark's depleted inventory.

Fortunately, at the end of November, the beleaguered explorers learned from the Clatsops—a Chinook people that lived in villages along the Columbia's southern bank—that there was better protection from the weather and more game on that shore. After making a perilous crossing of the turbulent Columbia River, Lewis and a small scouting party set out to explore the marshes and forests of the coastal lowlands. A week later, they returned with news of "a Most eligible Situation"—a low hill above the Netul River (now known as Lewis and Clark River). On December 7 the Corps of Discovery arrived at the site of the present-day Fort Clatsop National Memorial.

At that time, western hemlock, Sitka spruce, and western red cedar towered above a dense understory of ferns and huckleberries. Black-tailed deer

TANNING PELTS
An interpreter stretching a beaver pelt, above, sports buckskin clothing made from elk and deer. George Drouillard, who trapped beavers and otters along the creeks near the fort, was touted as the most skilled hunter in the Corps. The skins were transported back east as examples of the region's riches.

Fed by the moist climate of the West Coast, lush growths of berries and shrubs surround Fort Clatsop. The succulent red elderberries, right, are a favorite of birds and animals of the region.

WILD SHORES

The Pacific Ocean rolls into a cove on Oregon's northwestern coast, below. When the Lewis and Clark expedition finally arrived at these shores, the seas were so rough that Clark quipped he could not call them Pacific, "for I have not Seen one pacific day Since my arrival in its vicinity."

dinner. Though the meal was barely palatable—the elk meat was so spoiled that they ate it "thro mear necessity"—the expedition retired happily to snug lodgings for the first time in almost a year.

Clatsop delegations, often led by Chief Coboway, frequented the camp that winter. While they no doubt found the Corps unequal trading partners, they soon recognized the real needs and finances of the camp and brought them baskets of fish, berry cakes, and wappatoo, a starchy root that William Clark considered "equal to the Irish potato and . . . a tolerable substitute for bread."

Visitors to Fort Clatsop can well imagine the natural bounty once offered by the region. But during that winter of 1806, the cold damp land gave sustenance grudgingly. Fishing was difficult that time of year, and the men were not experienced anglers. Hunters ventured many miles on a grueling slog through morasses to find elk, and then hauled the carcasses back to camp. The meat spoiled quickly, often before it could be eaten. Once the meat was stored in the fort, it had to be checked regularly for spoilage. Visitors can take a look inside the reconstructed shack located just outside the door to the meat room and the captain's quarters. A sergeant of the guard was always posted here to protect the meat from theft and check it for signs of spoilage every few hours.

Nothing was easy for the explorers that winter. Three months of enforced residence at Fort Clatsop proved to be nearly as daunting as the rigors of the trail. The rain never let up, and the men complained of a multitude of aches and pains. Combating their own low morale, the captains ministered to their men's flagging spirits as well, and to their declining health. On January 1, 1806, Lewis established a

strict set of regulations for life at the fort, including tasks such as standing sentry, hauling water, and keeping the fires stoked. The rules ensured that basic needs were met and reminded everyone that the expedition shared a common goal. On January 5 the men established a salt works on a beach some 15 miles south of the fort, in present-day Seaside. For the next two months, a small team lived next to this kiln, and collected and boiled down seawater for salt to sustain the expedition both at Fort Clatsop and on the long trip home. The reconstructed salt works, now located along the town boardwalk, are maintained as part of the Fort Clatsop National Memorial.

SCHOLARLY PURSUITS For Meriwether Lewis and William Clark, the long winter at Fort Clatsop provided them with the time to turn their attentions to the more scholarly pursuits of exploration. They committed to writing the information encapsulated in countless notes scribbled during the adventures of the previous months. A respected botanist, Lewis investigated the woods around the fort, describing and drawing plants and taking many specimens. In all, his observations during the voyage added more than 120 new species to science. He was especially taken by the imposing conifers, the largest trees he had ever seen, but his interest extended to the smallest of plants, berries, and native species of moss.

Following Jefferson's instructions, Lewis paid particular attention to the practical uses made of these plants by local Indians. He tasted thistle and fern roots roasted over an open fire, watched Indians pound salal berries into paste for baking, and noted the water-repellent qualities of cloth made from woven cedar bark and bear grass, providing the first wide-ranging observations of Native subsistence economy.

Animals fascinated Lewis as well, and his journal soon numbered page after page of sketches and descriptions of elk, sea otters, steelhead trout, badgers, cormorants, and dozens of other creatures. Many species, such as the whistling swan, white sturgeon, and Oregon bobcat, were new to science.

Lewis and Clark also got an intimate glimpse of the Clatsops, a Native American culture largely unknown to other Americans. While noting the ravages of smallpox, Lewis observed that the Clatsops were a flourishing people living a typical north coast life. The cedar-plank longhouses, the ingenious dugout canoes, and the penchant for haggling with traders were hallmarks of the tribes from Oregon that had migrated up the coast to Canada. The two worlds were mutually admiring. The explorers remarked on local seafaring skills

and were astonished at how much say Clatsop women had in daily affairs, especially in matters of trade. The Clatsops were impressed by Clark's marksmanship and by Yankee metal tools. Scarcely 20 years later, malaria would devastate the thriving nation, and white migration and settlement would further reduce their hold on the land. Little did

Lewis and Clark know that their notes on the Clatsops would so soon become epitaphs for a vanished way of life.

For his part William Clark turned his attention to the maps that represented the goal of the expedition and a vital part of its legacy. Using notations of latitude and longitude recorded on the outbound voyage, Clark provided the first reliable measure of the breadth of the North American continent. His maps revealed more than mileage or even topography to his contemporaries. These renderings of the northern Plains and Pacific Northwest revealed a varied landscape quilted with Native

RAISING A FORT
Interpreters hoist a log, above, in a demonstration of how the fort was built. The expedition's carpenter, Sergeant Gass, praised the timber, which could "be split 10 feet long and 2 broad, not more than an inch and a half thick."

The gnarled branches of giant Sitka spruces, right, create eerie forms in the forests of northwestern Oregon, where Lewis and Clark blazed a trail.

TEDIOUS WORK

Fifteen miles southwest of Fort Clatsop, above, where the seawater has a high salt content, members of the Corps worked day and night for weeks to distill salt for the return voyage. They boiled about 1,400 gallons of seawater in five brass kettles, producing less than four bushels of salt that was pronounced "excellent, white and fine" by Captain Clark.

civilizations. The maps were filled with information provided by the Native American tribes they had encountered and bore witness to the diplomatic finesse of the explorers, who followed President Jefferson's admonition to treat all Native peoples with fairness and respect.

The maps also turned the explorers' thoughts to home and, by incorporating Native American knowledge of unexplored rivers, revealed shorter routes back. April 1, 1806, had been chosen as a departure date, but as March advanced and the spring rains fell, the explorers began to consider leaving even earlier. For one thing, their food supply was dwindling: the elk were migrating to higher ground, and the spring runs of salmon were slow to materialize. In addition, there were worrisome reports of inclement weather upriver. Lewis feared that if the Corps waited much longer, they would be unable to secure adequate provisions for the return journey.

On March 23, in a drizzling rain, Lewis and Clark formally handed over Fort Clatsop to their good friend and ally Chief Coboway, and boarded canoes for the long trip home. The expedition took Fort Clatsop with them in the form of barrels of salt, a store of jerked meat, a cache of candlefish, 358 pairs of moccasins, and a handsome wardrobe of new elk-hide clothes.

It took the explorers six months to get to St. Louis, their accomplishments setting a standard for subsequent expeditions by John C. Frémont, Lt. George Montague Wheeler, Nathaniel P. Langford, Henry D. Washburn, and others. The wanderings of mountain men such as Jedediah Smith and Jim Bridger filled in the remaining blanks in the map of North America. The information pouring in from the frontier inspired the American imagination, and immigrants soon followed the routes blazed by explorers through the Rockies and into the fertile valleys of the West. By the middle of the 19th century, Texas, California, and the Oregon territories had been absorbed by the burgeoning United States.

At the same time, Fort Clatsop, which had played such a crucial role in the drama of discovery, receded into the mists of memory, and the brooding forests that had so bewitched Lewis and Clark reclaimed the fort. Fifty years later, homesteaders cleared and burned the fort's rotting remains.

In 1900 the Oregon Historical Society undertook to establish the exact site of the fort. They were helped by homesteaders who had moved to the area in the 1850's, some of whom had seen the remains of the fort's foundation. In 1901 the society bought the three-acre hillock above the Netul River where the fort once stood. Fifty-four years later the Clatsop County Historical Society and Astoria Junior Chamber of Commerce marshaled the financial support and manpower to build a reconstruction of the fort according to Clark's original plan. A dedication ceremony was held in August 1955, and three years later Fort Clatsop was designated a national memorial.

CLARK'S POINT OF VIEW

Fort Clatsop is the main attraction on the Lewis and Clark National Historic Trail, which includes about 80 landmarks, reconstructions, and interpretive centers at stations along the explorers' route. The saga of the voyage continues in nearby places of related interest, such as the site west of Ilwaco, Washington, where Clark first saw the Pacific Ocean; Fort Canby, and its Lewis and Clark Interpretive Center, which tells the story of the expedition in a multimedia montage; and Astoria, where the company made camp after crossing the Columbia. Visitors can take a walk along a nature trail that leads to the densely forested bluff of Tillamook Head, where Clark stopped on his way to purchase whale blubber from the Tillamook Indians. On the morning of January 8, 1806, Clark looked out on the breathtaking scenery that awes visitors today: waves crashing 1,000 feet below, and the coastline falling away to the south in an endless series of serrated headlands. Clark opened his heart and mind to the wild beauty of the western shore, writing later, "I beheld the grandest and most pleasing prospect which my eyes ever surveyed." Two days later he dubbed the vista Clark's Point of View.

A visit to Fort Clatsop nurtures the explorer in everyone. To listen to the call of herons, spot the flash of coho salmon as they battle their way upstream to spawn, or survey the boundless sea from a windblown crag is to see the West as it appeared to the Corps of Discovery long ago.

PEACEFUL SETTING
Cow parsnips bloom along the bank of a quiet tributary of the Lewis and Clark River, below.

The Columbia, below, the last seagoing lighthouse to serve on the West Coast, is on display at the Columbia River Maritime Museum.

The Hudson's Bay Company stewards of Fort Vancouver prepared food in the kitchen, right, for the chief factor, John McLoughlin, who dined in the well-appointed Mess Hall upstairs. The dishes on display are reproductions of English Spode ware by Copeland and Garrett.

① CAPE MEARES STATE PARK, OREGON

Named after the 18th-century seafarer John Meares, this 232-acre coastal state park is highlighted by a 38-foot-tall lighthouse that offers spectacular views of the Pacific Ocean. Perched atop a 217-foot promontory, the lighthouse guided mariners through treacherous waters from 1890 until 1963. Today visitors armed with binoculars use the beacon as an ideal vantage point from which to scan the water for glimpses of Steller sea lions migrating along the coast on their way to Alaska. Easily spotted offshore are several rock island bird sanctuaries, such as the Three Arch Rocks, a nesting colony for over 200,000 sea birds—including common murres, cormorants, and puffins. A two-and-a-half-mile trail runs along the edge of the sheer cliffs and winds through stands of towering Sitka spruces. One of these trees is named the Octopus Tree because its massive trunk and branches lie close to the ground, giving it the appearance of a giant sea creature. Located 10 miles west of Tillamook off Hwy. 101.

② THE COLUMBIA RIVER MARITIME MUSEUM, OREGON

The rich maritime heritage of the Columbia River is brought to life at this fascinating museum. Its seven galleries house artifacts, documents, photographs, and model ships. The Fur Trade and Exploration

Gallery focuses on the history of the region's Native Americans, British exploration of the river, and the founding of Astoria. Visitors can examine the keel of the British ship *Raccoon*. The boat sank in 1813 and its keel washed ashore in 1973. Harpoons and other tools of the whaling trade are exhibited in the Fishing, Canneries, and Whaling Gallery, along with scrimshaw—the intricate carvings made by sailors during long voyages on whaling ships. The evolution of shipping technology is documented with displays ranging from wooden vessels and steam-powered ships to the actual bridge of the USS *Knapp*, a destroyer that served in both World War II and the Korean conflict. Visitors can also walk the deck of the lightship *Columbia*, which served from 1950 to 1979 as a floating lighthouse. Located in Astoria.

③ RIDGEFIELD NATIONAL WILDLIFE REFUGE, WASHINGTON

Fed by the nutrient-rich Columbia River, this 5,200-acre refuge attracts tens of thousands of nesting and migratory waterfowl each year. The refuge is divided into two sections and serves as the winter destination for more than 20,000 ducks, including mallards, widgeons, gadwalls, and cinnamon teals. Some 12,000 Canada geese spend the winter here after nesting in Alaska's Copper River Delta over the summer. Cottonwood and Oregon white oaks, with their huge trunks and high canopies, make excellent watchtowers for raptors, such as red-tailed hawks and bald eagles, to survey their surroundings for prey. Visitors can meander down the two-mile-long Oaks to Wetlands Wildlife Foot Trail, which winds through oak groves and past ponds, offering views of sandhill cranes, tundra swans, and chestnut-backed chickadees. The headquarters of the refuge is located in Ridgefield.

④ FORT VANCOUVER NATIONAL HISTORIC SITE, WASHINGTON

The American Northwest, known as the Oregon Territory, was coveted by the United States and Britain in the early 19th century. The British-owned Hudson's Bay Company built Fort Vancouver in 1825 in an effort to force American traders from the area and to protect British claims to the region. It was run by John McLoughlin, whose gray hair earned him the Native American name White-Headed Eagle. The fort once employed up to 500 people, making it the most important fur trading post in the region. Eight of the fort's original 23 buildings have been reconstructed, including a blacksmith's shop, Indian trade store, fur warehouse, and McLoughlin's residence. The buildings are enclosed by a 15-foot-high wooden palisade. The visitor center presents a video on the history of the fort, and a museum displays numerous artifacts uncovered during archeological digs. Located in Vancouver.

⑤ AMERICAN ADVERTISING MUSEUM, OREGON

Visitors to this unique museum are invited to explore how advertising introduced a new world of products and ideas to Americans. The only museum of its kind

One of only two octagonal lighthouses in the nation, the Cape Meares Lighthouse, left, was built of brick and sheet iron in 1889. The small building attached to the lighthouse serves as a gift shop and information center for visitors.

in the world, it is founded on the idea that advertisements are cultural artifacts, the study of which is essential to the assessment of a society. Many of the ads on display have become the currency of modern American culture. The section on print advertising runs from 1704 to the present and includes a poster made by Paul Revere to promote his services as a dentist, silversmith, and printer. Turn-of-the-century ad campaigns for Ivory soap, Coca-Cola, and Quaker oats are also on exhibit. Radio and television commercials occupy a large section of the museum, providing a glimpse of the changing styles of advertising in those media, including the gradual slimming down of models for Campbell Soup advertisements. The museum is housed in the historic New Market Theater Building, which is listed in the National Register of Historic Places. Located in Portland.

⑥ MISSION MILL VILLAGE, OREGON

This five-acre village of restored 19th-century buildings captures the flavor of pioneer life in Oregon as interpreters go about their daily tasks. Architectural highlights include the Jason Lee House, the oldest frame house in the Pacific Northwest, constructed in 1841. Exhibits in the Pleasant Grove Presbyterian Church, built in 1858, demonstrate the important role religion played in the lives of immigrants as they moved west and settled the frontier. Period lamp posts line the herb-and-dye garden, situated beside the old mill stream. Exhibits at the red-brick Thomas Kay Woolen Mill demonstrate how simple turn-of-the-century technology was used to create wool products. A water-powered turbine, similar in design to the one that originally operated here, is still in use. Located in Salem.

Sunrise bathes Bent's Old Fort, Colorado.

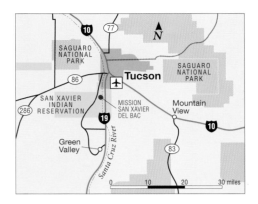

The resplendent white towers and domes of Mission San Xavier del Bac, above, seen through the arches of the inner courtyard, are set off by the blue of a cloudless Arizona sky.

Located some nine miles southwest of Tucson on the San Xavier Indian Reservation, home of the Tohonó O'odham Indians, the twin towers of Mission San Xavier del Bac reach for the heavens. Catholic missionary efforts in the area date back to 1700, when the Jesuit Eusebio Francisco Kino laid the foundation stones for a church near the present mission. The energetic and charismatic priest went on to found some 21 missions in southern Arizona and Mexico but never completed the mission here.

About 40 years after Kino's death in 1711, a simple adobe church was built by Father Alonso Espinosa, but by then the Jesuits' days as Christianity's chief proselytizers among Native Americans were numbered. In 1767 all Jesuits were expelled from Spanish territories in the New World by the Spanish crown who feared the Jesuits' power. The following year, the Franciscan order took over their missions, including the Mission San Xavier del Bac. The monks and their O'odham converts began working on a new building in the early 1780's.

Their architect was Ignacio Gaona, a talented maestro *albañil*, or master mason, from Mexico. He used fired adobe bricks plastered over with white stucco, which gives the structure an almost luminescent glow and earned it the name White Dove of the Desert. A shortage of materials and money hampered construction, but after 14 years present-day Mission San Xavier del Bac was completed. It has been holding religious services for the O'odhams ever since.

ARCHITECTURAL MARVEL

An outstanding example of Mexican ultra-baroque architecture, Mission San Xavier del Bac gracefully blends a wealth of architectural features, including flying buttresses, domes, carved arches, round parapets, and towers, one of which remains unfinished—probably due to a lack of funds. Visitors to the mission are immediately struck by the elaborately carved brick-and-plaster portal in front, which includes four niches, each occupied by a different female saint.

Inside the church, visitors can listen to a recording that gives the history of the mission and identifies some of the saints who figure in the vivid frescoes and paintings that adorn its interior. At the head of the church, within the chancel, stands the altar, which appears to be made of marble. Closer inspection reveals that the altar is made of brick and plaster, ingeniously

painted to create the illusion of marble. Even more stunning is the carved *retablo* behind the altar; it represents a gorgeous vision of heaven, a host of angels and saints and is dominated by a statue of God. Guarding the chancel is a pair of wooden lions that have been affixed to the communion rail. Visitors may photograph the workmanship in the church when services are not in progress.

In the mission's small museum there are exhibits of the architectural plans for the church, religious art, and some original vestments and furnishings. The replica of the Grotto of Lourdes, on a small hill nearby, was built in 1908 at the request of Henri Granjon, the bishop of Tucson, who thought the small cave bore a resemblance to the holy site in France.

Native American culture is evident in and around the mission. At the gift shop, Hopi, O'odham, Navajo, and Zuni crafts are on sale, and outside, food stalls offer visitors a tantalizing taste of Native American cuisine. Visitors can attend the O'odham powwow, which is held in March.

For more than 300 years Mission San Xavier del Bac has served as a place of worship for the Tohonó O'odhams people. Today, it draws modern pilgrims who appreciate its singular majesty.

FOR MORE INFORMATION:
Franciscan Friars, 1950 W. San Xavier Rd., Tucson, AZ 85746; 602-294-2624.

The detailed reliefs carved on the exterior of the Mission San Xavier del Bac, left, are painted in subtle shades of pink, red, and beige.

P acking his belongings and heading to the San Pedro Valley to seek his fortune in March of 1877, Edward Schieffelin was warned that the only thing he would find in this inhospitable "Apache-infested" part of the world was his own tombstone. Instead, the plucky prospector found silver and struck it rich.

On the spot where he staked his first claim, Schieffelin established a mining town that

Tenacious weeds and shrubs poke through the ruins of the century-old Tombstone Mining and Milling Company headquarters, left.

he called Tombstone—a tongue-in-cheek reference to the dire predictions of the nay-sayers. News of the discovery traveled fast, and by 1884 some 10,000 treasure hunters had set up camp in Tombstone. Estimates of gold and silver extracted from the parched desert terrain during the boom years range from $38 to $80 million. With the mining boom came gunfighters, cattle rustlers, cowboys, con men, high rollers, women of ill repute, and adventurers—a population that helped make Tombstone a notorious frontier town.

Reveling in their infamy, Tombstone's hard-bitten inhabitants boasted "a dead man for breakfast every morning." The local newspaper, aptly named the *Epitaph*, ran a standing headline, "Death's Doings," above grisly descriptions of the latest shootout, lynching, or murder. Still in business, the *Epitaph* is the oldest continuously published newspaper in Arizona.

The headline of an October 1881 issue of the *Epitaph* read: "Three Men Hurled into Eternity in the Duration of a Moment." This was the first report of Tombstone's infamous shootout at OK Corral, an incident that has become part of American folklore. At the corner of Third and Fremont streets, visitors can stand on the exact spot where the Earp brothers and their friend Doc Holliday faced off against the Clanton and McLaury brothers. In OK Corral, life-sized mannequins authentically dressed as the gunslingers re-create the gun battle. The restored studio and home of Camillus Fly, located near the corral, house an exhibit of his work. Fly was an established Western photographer in the late 1880's, and his moody black-and-white photographs capture the flavor of the town during this period.

HISTORIC STROLL

Another way to soak up the atmosphere is to take a walk through the center of town. The streets are lined with historic buildings, including the Bird Cage Theater—a one-story adobe building that was once the most raucous nightspot in town. Schieffelin Hall, which once served as the theatrical and civic center, is reputed to be one of the largest adobe buildings in the West, and the Crystal Palace Saloon once enjoyed the reputation of being one of the most opulent watering holes in the region.

Residents regularly don the garb of gun-slingers, dancehall girls, and cowboys to

stage simulated gunfights and barroom brawls throughout the year, making many visitors head for cover. Various annual festivals also help re-create the town's heyday. The largest is Helldorado Days, held the third weekend of October, which features parades, dances, and mock shootouts.

Tombstone has several other attractions that continue to attract visitors. St. Paul's Episcopal Church, erected in 1881, is the oldest Protestant church in Arizona, and the Rose Tree Inn Museum is built on a site that claims to be the world's largest rose-bush. The bush, which was started with a cutting sent from Scotland more than 100 years ago, now covers an area more than 8,000 feet square.

The Tombstone Courthouse State Historic Park looks much as it did when it administered frontier justice. The judge's bench and prisoner's dock are original, and a reconstruction of the gallows stands in the courtyard. Built in 1882, the courthouse was the site of many trials. In 1884 John Heath, charged with robbery and murder in the nearby town of Bisbee, was lynched by an angry mob. A coroner's jury later recorded that Heath had suffered from emphysema of the lungs, "which might have been caused by strangulation, self-inflicted or otherwise."

Heath was buried in Boot Hill Cemetery, which overlooks the mountains. Boot Hill is the final resting place for more than 250 people, and the crude grave markers give terse accounts of how life was lived—and lost—in Tombstone. "Here lies Lester Moore, Four Slugs From A .44, No Les No More" reads one epitaph, showing how gallows humor was sometimes used to leaven these violent episodes. Tom and Frank McLaury and Billy Clanton, shot during the gunfight at OK Corral, are also buried here.

Tombstone survived gunfights, lawless-ness, and a devastating 1880 fire that burned down a third of the business district after a barrel of bad whiskey was ignited by a bartender's cigar. The boomtown even outlasted the flooding that inundated the mines, labor problems, and drop in silver prices that befell it during the next few years. But it never really recovered from an 1886 fire that destroyed the pumps in the Grand Central mine. By 1910, Tombstone's days of silver mining were over.

FOR MORE INFORMATION:
Tombstone Chamber of Commerce, P.O. Box 995, Tombstone, AZ 85638; 520-457-3929.

A pair of paddlewheelers, left, are docked at Old Sacramento's waterfront. Travelers can take a tour up the Sacramento River aboard these picturesque old boats.

I
n a twist of fate, Sacramento grew from a dusty trading post into a bustling mining town, while its most prominent citizen plummeted into poverty.

The area's first landowner was Swiss immigrant Capt. John Sutter, who arrived on the banks of the Sacramento River in 1839 with visions of civilizing California's Central Valley. He built an adobe trading post on the fork of the American and Sacramento rivers and two years later he acquired 48,000 acres of land from the Mexican government. As his fortunes grew, so did the population of his fort. He soon diversified into agriculture and manufacturing and decided to construct a sawmill on the American River. But a millwright named James Marshall discovered tiny flecks of gold in the sawmill trace, and the orderly world of John Sutter was shattered.

Despite their attempts to keep the discovery of gold a secret, word spread, unleashing a stream of prospectors in the region. As gold fever mounted, Sutter's

workers abandoned the mill for the mines. Crops withered in the fields, miners had to slaughter livestock for food, and squatters overtook the land. Sutter was ruined.

Sacramento, on the other hand, boomed. New businesses sprang up to cater to the needs of fortune seekers. By the 1850's the city's population had doubled, and in 1854 it was named the state capital. In 1856 the first railroad line was built in California, linking Sacramento to the interior. The burgeoning city soon became the western terminus for both the famed Pony Express and the first Transcontinental Railroad.

EXPLORING THE PAST

Old Sacramento, a 28-acre national historic site sandwiched between the Sacramento River and Interstate 5, harkens back to that bygone era. Visitors can explore more than 100 structures built between 1860 and 1890 that have been lovingly restored to their original splendor. Shops and restaurants are tucked among these architectural monuments to the past. Visitors can acquaint themselves with this pioneer town by wandering along the boardwalk, taking a horse-drawn carriage ride, or walking on a self-guided tour.

Pony Express riders took a well-earned rest at the B. F. Hastings Building at 2nd and J streets before completing their mail runs in 1860–61. One such run, a 2,000-mile journey from Sacramento to St. Joseph, Missouri, took 80 riders 10 days to complete. The riders shared these quarters with Wells Fargo employees. Today the building houses a museum with exhibits on the Pony Express, Wells Fargo & Company, and the transcontinental telegraph.

The California State Railroad Museum—the country's largest interpretive railroad museum—is located a block from the B. F. Hastings Building. The museum brings to life the early years of the railroad. There are 21 authentically restored locomotives and railway cars on display, and more than 40 exhibits document the story of railroading in America. Visitors can sit in authentically refurbished rail cars or take a seven-mile steam locomotive ride from the Central Pacific Freight Depot on Front Street.

The reconstructed Sutter's Fort is situated 15 blocks away from the state capitol. Costumed interpreters dressed as pioneers, and a re-created blacksmith's shop and trade store capture the spirit of California's first inland settlement and bring to life an immigrant's experiences in the New World.

FOR MORE INFORMATION:
Sacramento Convention and Visitors Bureau, 1421 K St., Sacramento, CA 95814; 916-264-7777.

A wrought-iron balcony and colorful wooden shutters, left, are reminders of the elegance of a bygone era in Old Sacramento.

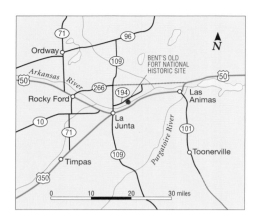

A cat surveys the plaza at Bent's Old Fort, right. At the fort's height, hundreds of people thronged the plaza to trade for merchandise brought by caravan from Independence, Missouri.

Massive beams support the ceiling of the blacksmith's shop in Bent's Old Fort, above, which displays the cast-iron tools of the trade.

Described by a traveler in 1839 as "an air-built castle," the former trading post known as Bent's Old Fort, rises from the desert and glows red in the Colorado sun. An oasis of commerce for mountain men, French-Canadian trappers, trailblazers, Plains Indians, and Mexican traders, this quadrangular fort was the brainchild of brothers Charles and William Bent and the French nobleman Ceran St. Vrain. They built it in 1833 on the north side of the Arkansas River, which was then the boundary between the United States and Mexico, and the fort soon became one of the most important outposts along the fabled Santa Fe Trail. Its success

was attributable in part to William Bent's good relations with the Plains tribes. He married a Cheyenne woman and lived on and off in her village. An adept negotiator, he persuaded warring tribes to set aside their differences and trade at the fort.

For 17 years Bent's Fort remained the crucial trading link between Independence, Missouri, and Santa Fe, New Mexico. It was near enough to the Rockies to draw trappers and to Native American hunting grounds to attract the Cheyenne, Arapaho, Kiowa, and other Plains tribes. The unifying forces of economics and necessity made the fort a place where differences in color, culture, and religion were sometimes overlooked. No questions were asked and bargains were sealed with a handshake and a shot of trading-post whiskey.

The Bent brothers and St. Vrain controlled a huge commercial empire and for years their fortunes grew rapidly. However, in time all this changed. The Mexican War broke out in 1846, and the US Army began storing military supplies at the post. Their livestock stripped the land. In 1847, Charles Bent, who was named the first American civil governor of New Mexico, was killed in an uprising of Pueblo Indians and New Mexicans in Taos. A stream of settlers and gold seekers disrupted the carefully nurtured relations with the Native Americans, and a cholera epidemic finally killed trade. In 1849 William moved to a new fort on the Arkansas River. Shortly afterward Bent's Old Fort was damaged by fire. Legend has it that in a fit of anger at the army's refusal to purchase the fort from him William deliberately set it aflame.

HISTORY'S FOOTSTEPS

Visitors can experience frontier life on America's Great Plains at this national historic site. Bent's Old Fort has been carefully restored to its 1840's appearance. The 15-foot-high, 2-foot-thick walls of this old adobe outpost are imposing with their musket loopholes and two large round corner bastions for cannons. Beyond the threshold is an open plaza, or *placita*, surrounded by living quarters, warehouses, workshops—even a billiard room—all of which have been furnished with reproductions that are faithful to historical detail. Volunteer interpreters, clad in buckskin and sombreros, add a further touch of authenticity to the fort. Other park staff,

dressed as trappers, demonstrate daily tasks such as tanning and trading. Sometimes Native Americans participate, offering insight into the impact the fort had on their traditional way of life.

Visitors can wander into the council room where terms of trade were negotiated and peace talks between various Native American Indian tribes were conducted. The trade room next door was used by entrepreneurs of all backgrounds to hammer out deals. Here French-Canadian and American trappers and Plains Indians traded buffalo robes and beaver pelts for luxury items such as coffee and Hudson's Bay blankets brought in from the East by caravan along the Santa Fe Trail. Trading goods were stored over the winter in the warehouses on the other side of the plaza.

Most trappers, laborers, and craftsmen cooked in their own quarters. However, the Bent brothers and St. Vrain entertained guests in the dining room—the fort's largest room. As tales of explorers, Indians, and rawboned mountain men filtered back East, their table filled with travelers drawn by the fort's unique character and vitality. Today those stories continue to lure visitors from all over to the fort's sunlit plaza and shadowy rooms.

FOR MORE INFORMATION:
Superintendent, Bent's Old Fort National Historic Site, 35110 Hwy. 194 E., La Junta, CO 81050-9523; 719-384-2596.

Although not as famous as the White House, which is one block away, the Octagon has enjoyed a colorful history, including a brief stand-in as the famed executive mansion.

At the close of the 18th century, Washington, D.C., was a city of unpaved streets and open fields—an unlikely place to build a town house, let alone a mansion. But, legend has it that at the urging of his good friend George Washington, wealthy Virginia plantation owner Col. John Tayloe III decided to construct a palatial home in the young nation's capital. He bought a parcel of land at the corner of New York Avenue and 18th Street and chose Dr. William Thornton, winner of the competition for the design of the United States Capitol, to plan his new residence. Challenged by the odd-shaped lot, Thornton designed an irregular octagon, broken along the facade by a semicircular bay. The residence was later dubbed the Octagon by the Tayloe family.

After its completion in 1801, the Octagon became the hub of Washington society, drawing many notable guests, including presidential neighbors Thomas Jefferson, James Madison, James Monroe, John Adams, and Andrew Jackson.

In the War of 1812, when much of Washington was razed, the Octagon was spared. The fact that Tayloe had loaned the house to French ambassador Louis Serurier, who was living there at the time, may have deterred the British from destroying it. However, the White House was gutted in August 1814, and that September President Madison and First Lady Dolley Madison moved into the Octagon at the Tayloes' invitation. On February 17, 1815, in the upstairs parlor, James Madison signed the Treaty of Ghent, thus ending the war with Great Britain.

After the death of Ann Tayloe in 1855 the Tayloes moved away and the Octagon fell on hard times. Fortunately in 1902 it was rescued by the American Institute of Architects. A series of restorations has returned the building to much of its former glory. Now administered by the American Architectural Foundation, the Octagon houses America's oldest museum devoted to architecture.

LAYERS OF PAINT AND TIME

Visitors will be struck by the bold colors used to repaint the Octagon's interior. After stripping away some 26 layers of paint, restorers have achieved what they believe to be the color scheme of the era. Corals, light blues, yellows, and apple greens adorn the walls. Before the days of electricity, rooms were illuminated with the help of bright colors, which reflect sunlight by day and candlelight by night.

The revival of the ideal of classical forms, which distinguishes Federal period architecture, can be seen in the refined simplicity of the Octagon's overall plan, its Ionic columns and cornices, its graceful curves, such as in the circular entry hall, diagonally placed rooms, and the magnificent oval staircase that curls its way gracefully up to the third floor. The hall for the staircase is furnished with original Tayloe pieces, which include a settee and armchairs shipped from London in the early 1800's.

The dining room, where Dolley Madison entertained heads of state during the Madisons' six-month stay in 1814, contains period furnishings. During state dinners, the table was laid with delicate Chinese porcelain and English silver and glassware. Elaborate English Coade stone mantels, made in 1799 from artificial cast stone, grace the dining and drawing rooms. In the Treaty Room on the second floor is the original circular rent table upon which it is believed President Madison signed the Treaty of Ghent. Nearby rooms display exhibitions on architecture, design, and early Washington history. After nearly two centuries, the Octagon remains a hallmark of elegance in American design.

FOR MORE INFORMATION:

The Octagon, The Museum of the American Architectural Foundation, 1799 New York Ave., NW, Washington, DC 20006-5292; 202-638-3221.

The front portico of the Octagon, left, leads to a large circular entry hall, still with its original gray-and-white marble floor.

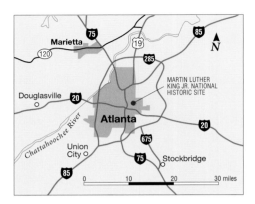

Although he was only 39 years old when he was killed by an assassin's bullet on April 4, 1968, Martin Luther King Jr. accomplished more in his brief life than most people dream of. An ordained minister, the holder of three degrees, including a Ph.D. in systematic theology, and the author of six books, Dr. King is best remembered as the founder and spiritual leader of the American Civil Rights movement. As the eloquent and impassioned voice of social change through nonviolent means, he was awarded both the Congressional Medal of Honor and the Nobel Peace Prize for his heroic efforts to promote racial equality.

Dr. King's remarkable life is celebrated at the Martin Luther King Jr. National Historic Site in Atlanta. The historic site encompasses a two-block section of the downtown Sweet Auburn district, the neighborhood where M. L., his nickname as a boy, was born and raised.

Visitors should begin their tour at the Martin Luther King Jr. Birth Home. It was here, in the upper bedroom of 501 Auburn Avenue, that Alberta King gave birth to her second child on January 15, 1929. The two-story Queen Anne–style home, purchased in 1909 by Dr. King's maternal grandfather, Rev. A. D. Williams, contains family memorabilia, furniture from the 1930's, and an icebox in the kitchen. The family resided in this house until 1941 when they moved a few blocks away.

The Ebenezer Baptist Church, located just down the street, played a pivotal role in the lives of the King family. Dr. King followed in the footsteps of a long line of pastors that included his grandfather, father, and uncle. He preached his first sermon here at the age of 17 and became an ordained minister in 1948. Beginning with Reverend Williams

The bronze Behold Monument *was inspired by an African baptism scene in the TV series* Roots. *It stands outside the visitor center.*

in 1894, the church was presided over by a member of the King family for more than 80 years. Dr. Martin Luther King Jr. served as copastor from 1960 to 1968. The church is haunted by two tragic events. In 1968 Dr. King's body lay in state here as huge crowds of mourners filed past to pay their final respects. And in 1974 his mother, Alberta, was fatally shot here by Marcus Shenault as she sat at the church organ.

A GREAT MAN
The focal point of the historic site is the Freedom Hall Complex, situated between Dr. King's Birth Home and the church. A walk through the King Center gives visitors who only knew Dr. King as a political activist a unique glimpse of the private man. His minister's robe and Bible are on display, as are the original leather workboots and the blue jeans he wore in 1965 when he led the famous civil rights march from Selma to Montgomery, Alabama.

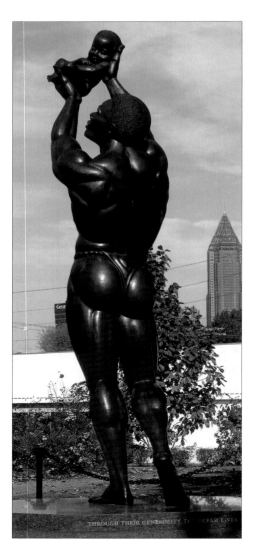

Some items are poignant reminders of the great personal risk posed by Dr. King's crusade, including the suit he wore when he was stabbed in New York in 1958 and the key to the Memphis hotel room on the balcony of which he was brutally murdered.

Dr. King's tomb is also located on the grounds of the complex. The large Georgian marble crypt rests atop a huge circular disc, and an eternal flame burns nearby, symbolizing his dream of a global community. Each year thousands of visitors are moved by its simple inscription: "Free at last! Free at last! Thank God Almighty I am free at last."

To better understand the vital community that fostered Dr. King's inspirational vision, visitors should tour the neighborhood in which he grew up. Sweet Auburn's thriving commercial district supported hundreds of African-American–owned or –operated businesses, including banks, jewelers, doctors' and lawyers' offices, law firms, and libraries.

The Herndon Building was named for its builder, Alonzo Herndon, an ex-slave who became a prominent local businessman and founded the Atlanta Life Insurance Company—the nation's second-largest black-owned insurance company. The building that served as company headquarters from 1920 to 1980 is also located down the street. Right next door to the Atlanta Life Insurance Company headquarters is the Rucker Building, Atlanta's first black office building. It was constructed by Henry A. Rucker, an influential businessman and successful local politician, and completed in 1904.

The Odd Fellows Building and Auditorium provided a venue for civic meetings. In its heyday from 1922 to 1948, the Top Hat Club attracted such legendary performers as Cab Calloway and Louis Armstrong. The Atlanta Municipal Market, erected in 1923, served both black and white customers during the years of legal segregation in Georgia.

A strong sense of pride and a yearning for justice permeate the district. Inspired by the examples that surrounded him, Dr. King strode into the world and made it better. An example of the impact of his quest for equality can be found in his hometown: In 1973 Atlanta became the first major city in the South to elect a black mayor to office.

FOR MORE INFORMATION:
Martin Luther King Jr. National Historic Site, 450 Auburn Ave. NE, Atlanta, GA 30312; 404-331-5190.

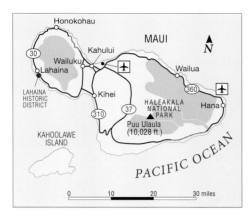

Towering over Lahaina Harbor, the masts of the Carthaginian II, *above, pierce the sky. In one section of this floating museum, the recorded songs of humpback whales can be heard.*

Crowning the palm-fringed coast of western Maui, the town of Lahaina, a Hawaiian word that means "merciless sun," has seen many changes through the centuries. Up until 1850 Lahaina was Maui's royal seat, home to the warrior-king Kahekili. Then, with the arrival of the first American whaling ships in 1819, Lahaina soon became a major port and a prosperous center of commerce. Industrious Christian missionaries from New England soon followed and built Lahaina's first school and Hawaii's first printing press. Preaching moderation and morality, the missionaries often found themselves at odds with the itinerant free-spirited sailors. The tension between the groups deteriorated to the point that angry seamen fired a cannon at the mission house in 1825.

While Lahaina is tamer now than it was back then, much of its colorful history has been preserved. Lahaina's ties to the whaling industry are commemorated in the floating museum *Carthaginian II*, a replica of the brigs that carried the first Americans

Foundation bricks made from hardened mud, above, were used for the Brick Palace, commissioned by Kamehameha I in 1801.

to Hawaii. The boat now houses displays on whales and the whaling trade, with artifacts dating from the early 19th century. The ship was restored in 1978 using handcrafted masts, spars, yards, and iron fittings—a project that took two years to complete.

DOCTOR AND MISSIONARY
The Baldwin Home, situated on Lahaina's town square and owned by New England missionary and physician Dwight Baldwin, was used to entertain members of the Hawaiian royal court, ship captains, and an assortment of world travelers. Baldwin also treated patients at the house and his fees are still posted. Prices ranged from $3 for a diagnosis to $50 for treatment of a "very big" sickness. The first missionary doctor in Hawaii, Baldwin contained a smallpox epidemic that raged on Oahu in 1853 by forbidding anyone on that island access to Maui, Molokai, and Lanai. He witnessed the great change that swept the region, from the creation of a constitutional monarchy to the growing literacy of the Hawaiian people. The two-foot-thick walls of Baldwin's house are made from cut coral and lava bricks and a mortar of crushed coral. The roof and window and door frames were supported by beams of hand-hewn timber. The house has been faithfully restored and much of the original furniture has been preserved, including a Steinway piano built in 1859.

Farther west on Front Street is the Wo Hing Museum devoted to Hawaii's Chinese heritage. Chinese immigrants came to Maui after Captain Cook's discovery of the

Hawaiian Islands in 1778 but long before the whalers and missionaries arrived. Chinese immigrants helped construct the island's irrigation system, which still exists.

The Wo Hing Temple, now housing the museum, was built in 1912 by the Wo Hing Society, a fraternal society with chapters throughout the world. A Buddhist shrine is maintained on the upper floor of the building, which also houses artifacts and antiques. Visitors can also view films of the islands made in 1898 and 1906 by Thomas Edison.

Built on a mountaintop overlooking Lahaina, Hale Pai housed the Lahainaluna school and the press shop, where Hawaii's first newspaper, the *Ka Lama Hawaii,* and its first paper currency were printed. A white stucco structure with a wood-shake roof reminiscent of New England architecture, Hale Pai now serves as a museum preserving the history of the oral, written, and printed word in Hawaii. Visitors can operate a replica of the original press and print a souvenir copy of the first Hawaiian school primer.

As the palm trees that line Lahaina's boulevards sway in a balmy breeze, it is easy to feel the attraction the town held for so many throughout its rich history.

FOR MORE INFORMATION:
Maui Visitors Bureau, P.O. Box 580, 1727 Wili Pa Loop, Wailuku, HI 96793; 808-244-3530 or 800-525-MAUI.

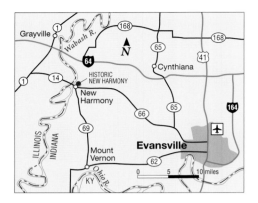

L ocated on the banks of Indiana's Wabash River, this sleepy little town was the site of two utopian experiments in communal living in the 19th century. The first was established in 1814 by a group of German Lutheran separatists, called the Harmony Society, led by the charismatic George Rapp.

In preparation for the second coming of Jesus Christ, the Harmonists rose each morning to the sound of a French horn, calling them to clear the land, work the fields, and construct new buildings for the settlement they named Harmonie. Rapp's followers built a town of more than 150 houses and shops. Some of these houses are still occupied today.

As the Harmonists grew more prosperous, Rapp decided that the community needed to move closer to the eastern markets that bought their grain, lumber, beer and whiskey, and woolen and cotton goods.

He sold the Harmonie land and moved the settlement back to Pennsylvania, where he and his followers established a community they named Economy.

The man who bought Harmonie was Robert Owen, a famous Scottish industrialist and social theorist. New Harmony, as he named it, was established to provide its inhabitants with intellectual freedom, equal rights for women, the abolition of class distinctions, and the pursuit of scientific knowledge. News of Owen's radical ideas reached the shores of Europe and, before long, hordes of intellectuals, revolutionaries, socialites, and the curious flocked to New Harmony. In 1825 a distinguished group of scientists, geologists, and educators arrived in New Harmony with the intention of joining the enlightened community. They traveled in the *Philanthropist*, nicknamed the Boatload of Knowledge.

Owen's utopian dream settlement dissolved within two years and he returned to Britain. His partner, the geologist William Maclure, and a group of the town's citizens rescued it from collapse and turned Owen's idealistic experiment into a permanent town.

A LASTING IMPRESSION

The grand visions of Father Rapp and Robert Owen have made a lasting impression on both the physical and intellectual landscape of New Harmony. The careful workmanship and planning of the early Harmonists are seen today in such structures as the Granary. A fortresslike building,

it stored grain, which according to Harmonist beliefs would be used by the community at the time of the second coming of Jesus Christ.

A short distance from the granary, visitors come upon the largest residence built by the Harmonists, known as Dormitory #2. Originally constructed to house unmarried Harmonists, this three-story brick building was converted into a school during the Owen period and later became the print shop for a local newspaper.

Both Owen and Maclure were responsible for the introduction of kindergarten, vocational training, and other innovations in education. The settlement's intellectual interests are highlighted at the George Keppler House, named after the Harmonist who once lived here. The restored residence now displays important examples of early American surveying, including hand-drawn maps from geological surveys conducted by William Maclure and one of Robert's four sons, David Dale Owen, who went on to become the state geologist. He later became a founding member of the Smithsonian Institution.

During the 1830's Prince Maximilian of Wied-Neuwied and Swiss artist Karl Bodmer visited New Harmony to consult with the town's noted naturalists before their 1832–33 expedition to the American West. An impressive collection of Bodmer's work, including spectacular prints depicting Native American life, hang in the Lichtenberger Building on the town's Main Street. Performance art is presented today on the 1820's stage of Thrall's Opera House, formerly Dormitory #4.

The creative spirit and independence of mind characteristic of the town's founders are visible in the bold architectural design of the New Harmony Atheneum—the most modern building in New Harmony. Its visitor center displays artifacts, biographical memorabilia, and a scale model of the Harmonist Brick Church of 1822, providing visitors a glimpse into an interesting social experiment of the past.

FOR MORE INFORMATION:
Historic New Harmony, P.O. Box 579, 506½ Main St., New Harmony, IN 47631; 812-682-4488 or 812-682-3271.

The David Lenz House, left, 1 of 11 historic buildings in New Harmony, has been restored and furnished with period pieces dating from the Harmonist period.

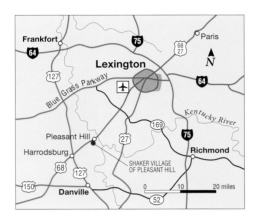

In August 1805, a small group called the Society of Believers in Christ's Second Appearing converged on Elisha Thomas' 140-acre farm. Atop a pleasant plateau overlooking the bubbling Shawnee Run Creek, they founded the colony of Pleasant Hill. Their religion was based on the beliefs of the sect's founder and spiritual leader, Mother Ann Lee, some of the tenets of the Church of England, and Quaker theology. They acquired the name Shakers for the twirling, dancing, and stomping they did during religious ceremonies to physically shake away their sins.

The Shakers followed the teachings of Mother Lee who said, "Do all your work as though you had a thousand years to live and as you would if you knew you must die tomorrow." Whether harvesting crops, finishing carpets, or building and repairing homes, the group was famous for its industriousness. Unlike other closed religious communities such as the Amish, whose members shunned innovation, the Shakers reveled in it and were responsible for many important inventions, including the apple peeler and corer, the clothespin, a Shaker washing machine, and the circular saw.

PRESERVING THE PAST

The restored Shaker Village of Pleasant Hill in this land of steep ravines, ancient oaks, and thick morning mist captures the essence of these spiritual people. Many of the 33 restored buildings inside the fieldstone fence around Pleasant Hill are the handiwork of a young Shaker architect, Micajah Burnett, who worked here in the 1830's. These dignified edifices stand among 2,700 acres of rolling hills covered with bluegrass, and are a reflection of the Shakers' reverence for simplicity. This is an attitude shared by the caretakers who now maintain the Shaker land, and faithfully preserve the character of the buildings down to the traditional trim around the windows and doors.

Travelers to the village can tour rooms rimmed with the traditional Shaker pegboards on which everything from chairs to candleholders were hung. One of the most beautiful examples of Shaker design is found in the Trustee's Office, once the hub of business for the bustling village. Twin spiral staircases flanked by cherry-wood railings wind gracefully to the upper story. The Trustee's dining room now offers visitors typical Shaker meals consisting of corn pudding, fried chicken, and biscuits, served by attendants clad in bonnets and long dresses.

In the Meeting House original Shaker music is performed regularly by costumed interpreters. A tour of the two craft stores within Shaker Village offers visitors the opportunity to purchase a variety of handmade products. The famed Shaker broom, oval wooden boxes with sparrow-tail joints that have become hallmarks of these master woodworkers, and various furniture reproductions all display the purity of style and the firm clean lines of Shaker craftsmanship.

FOR MORE INFORMATION:

Shaker Village of Pleasant Hill, 3501 Lexington Rd., Harrodsburg, KY 40330-8846; 606-734-5411.

A maple tree ablaze with the colors of fall stands by a sturdy frame house, above, that exhibits the symmetry typical of Shaker architecture.

The elegant lines of a Pleasant Hill Shaker table, below, attest to the simplicity in design and the skills of these master carpenters.

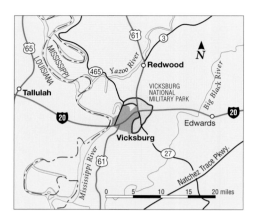

The broad crescent of peaceful meadows and soft woodlands that curves around the city of Vicksburg belies its bloody heritage. In 1863 this strip of land was the scene of a crucial Civil War confrontation, which pitted Union troops against one of the last major Confederate bastions on the Mississippi River.

During the first years of the war, Confederate supplies from Texas and Louisiana were shipped by river to Vicksburg, then sent to other points by rail. The heavily fortified town was also a base for the Confederate batteries that blocked the river. If the North captured Vicksburg, Union troops would have access to the South and the tightly knit Confederacy would unravel.

After he had launched amphibious attacks against Vicksburg for seven months without success, Gen. Ulysses S. Grant decided to cross the river in the spring of 1863 well below Vicksburg and then mount a land assault from the south. Grant's soldiers crossed the river at Bruinsburg and swiftly overcame Confederate resistance at Port Gibson, Raymond, Jackson, Champion Hill, and Big Black River Bridge. But they were repulsed twice at Vicksburg.

Admiral David D. Porter's Union gunboats moved into position on the Mississippi and tightened the noose around the embattled town. Cut off from supplies and bombarded for 47 days, Vicksburg finally surrendered on July 4, 1863.

Today visitors can imagine this bloody siege by touring the 1,800-acre Vicksburg National Military Park, which features reconstructed Union siege lines, nine major Confederate forts, elaborate earthworks, and many monuments. Visitors can drive, cycle, or hike along a 16-mile paved road that loops past sites with markers that

Rows of grave markers at the Vicksburg National Cemetery, right, are lined up with military precision.

130

describe the tactics used in waging the siege. Hovey's Approach demonstrates how Union troops evaded the Confederate line of fire by digging trenches in zigzag patterns. At Thayer's Approach, Northern forces burrowed a six-foot-deep tunnel to avoid crossing a ridge that would expose the soldiers to heavy fire.

Visitors can also explore Third Louisiana Redan and Great Redoubt, Confederate fortifications that guarded the Jackson Road approach to Vicksburg. Grant's troops detonated underground mines at the redan and fired artillery at the redoubt but both proved impervious to Union attack.

Shirley House is the only wartime building that still stands in the park. Dubbed "the white house," this two-story structure served as the headquarters for the 45th Illinois Infantry which built hundreds of bombproof shelters around it in the event of a Rebel attack.

The Illinois Memorial, a stately monument modeled after the Pantheon in Rome, honors the Illinois soldiers who fought in the Vicksburg operations with bronze tablets engraved with their names.

RECOVERED GUNBOAT
Situated to the left of Confederate lines, Fort Hill was so well armed that Union forces never ventured to attack the Rebel stronghold. Gunners stationed here combined forces with Confederate batteries and sank the Federal gunboat *Cincinnati* on May 27, 1863.

An early Union gunboat, the ironclad USS *Cairo*, was raised in 1964 from the bottom of the Yazoo River, where it was sunk by an electronically detonated mine in 1862. The only surviving vessel of her type,

The Illinois Memorial, above, honors the 36,000 soldiers from that Union regiment who fought valiantly at Vicksburg.

the partially restored gunboat is the showpiece of the USS *Cairo* Museum. Artifacts recovered from the wreck include naval stores, armaments, and the personal gear of the crew.

Nearly 17,000 Union troops are buried in Vicksburg National Cemetery adjacent to the museum. Confederate soldiers rest in Vicksburg City Cemetery, whose neat rows of white headstones stand as eloquent reminders of the devastating price exacted by this confrontation.

FOR MORE INFORMATION:
Vicksburg National Military Park, 3201 Clay St., Vicksburg, MS 39180; 601-636-0583.

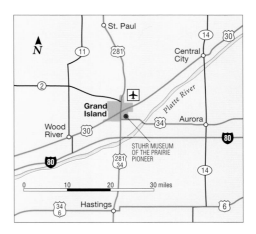

Two of the restored farm buildings at the Stuhr Museum's Railroad Town, above, re-create a typical American prairie community at the end of the 19th century.

When trains began to chug their way through Nebraska in the mid-19th century, early pioneers began to inhabit the small towns that the railway companies established along the tracks. The settlements were laid out in T-shaped plans, with the depot building located at one end of town and the village green at the other. The railway was the lifeline of these communities, transporting much needed goods and supplies from the East. By the end of the century, residents were able to order articles from the Sears Roebuck catalog.

Located at Grand Island, the Stuhr Museum of the Prairie Pioneer is a tribute to these early railroad towns. The 200-acre complex was named for Leo B. Stuhr, a prominent Grand Island businessman and history buff who donated the initial land and the funds for the project.

The museum's settlements are comprised of old buildings transported here from other locations in Nebraska. Many of the buildings contain machinery, home furnishings, and pioneer mementos that offer realistic glimpses of frontier life in these turn-of-the-century communities.

A seven-acre railyard exhibit traces the history of steam railroading in Nebraska. Visitors can also admire a 1901 standard-gauge locomotive, examine standard- and narrow-gauge equipment, and visit the 1890's depot on the eastern edge of Railroad Town.

In Railroad Town, costumed interpreters play the roles of blacksmith, marshal, housewives, merchants, and other townspeople, and recount tales of the frontier. This prairie community is typical of 19th-century railroad towns in Nebraska. Sixty authentic pioneer structures border the carefully laid-out streets. The Nebraska Midland Railroad Depot, built in 1895, was moved here from Oconto in 1966. Other structures include a bank, general store,

church, barber shop, doctor's office, hotel, and a farmstead, all equipped with period furnishings. In the residential area, travelers can visit the actual cottage where Academy Award–winning actor Henry Fonda was born in 1905. The house, which originally stood in Grand Island, was donated and moved to the museum by the Fonda family.

West of the village, broad walkways to the Main Building meander through an arboretum enhanced by flower gardens, shrubs, and picnic areas. A windmill whirls beside a small lake in the sylvan setting.

Designed by renowned architect Edward Durell Stone, the Main Building displays items dating from 1860 to 1910. The collections range from clothing and tools to household articles and photographs of frontier life. An auditorium on the first floor features "Land of the Prairie Pioneer," a short film narrated by Henry Fonda.

CONTRASTING CULTURES
The Gus Fonner Memorial Rotunda explores the contrasts between Native American and Old West cultures. Displays of Plains Indian artifacts alongside objects associated with the cattle industry include guns and ranching equipment.

At Runelsburg, visitors get a glimpse of daily life in the small towns built far from other settlements and the railroad. Founded on the hope that the railway line would one day connect the community to the rest of the world, this spartan little inland town

features a charming country school and an 1888 Danish Lutheran church with a wooden steeple painted white and neatly trimmed in jade green.

In nearby Pioneer Settlement, visitors can explore eight buildings dating from 1857 to 1867 that represent a typical road ranch. The community sold provisions, offered overnight accommodation, and serviced the wagons of weary travelers heading West.

A 200-piece exhibit on the east grounds displays early steam engines, an 1880 threshing machine, tractors, and a variety of horse-drawn farm equipment and vintage automobiles, such as a 1909 Model T, a 1913 Overland, and a 1903 American.

Summertime at the Stuhr Museum ushers in all kinds of festivals and activities celebrating traditions that evolved with the growth of the frontier communities. A blacksmith, a tinsmith, and a man at the planing mill demonstrate their trades, and special celebrations mark Memorial Day and the Fourth of July. Civil War re-enactments of infantry and artillery drills and mock battles rekindle the patriotic fervor of the small-town pioneers.

FOR MORE INFORMATION:
Stuhr Museum of the Prairie Pioneer, 3133 W. Hwy. 34, Grand Island, NE 68801; 308-385-5316.

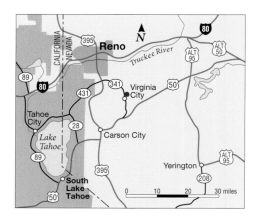

In 1859 Virginia City, a small town clinging to a mountainside in the Sierra Nevada, suddenly became a mining mecca when gold and silver in the Comstock Lode were discovered. Suddenly, prospectors and merchants thronged the town, and vice became as pervasive as the silver that flowed into bankers' coffers. A second larger boom came in 1873 when the Consolidated Virginia Mine dug 1,200 feet below downtown Virginia City and struck the Big Bonanza—a body of ore estimated at a gross value of more than $200 million.

Legend has it that the town was given its name after a whiskey-loving miner, James Finnemore, known as Old Virginny Finney. The burgeoning town reached its zenith in the mid-1870's, when it boasted 110 saloons, 4 major banks, and 7 churches. Elegant residences sprang up, and Mount Davidson was pumping out seemingly endless supplies of high-grade silver ore.

While its glory days lasted a mere 20 years, the recent revival of Virginia City has sparked an influx of travelers, drawn by its illustrious history, sumptuous mansions, and colorful mining lore.

Visitors can grasp the extent of the boomtown's bounty at the Castle, dubbed the House of the Silver Doorknobs. Built in 1868 by Robert Graves, who was the superintendent of the Empire Mine at the time, the fabulous 16-room mansion is exquisitely furnished with pieces shipped from all over Europe. Several of them exhibit outstanding workmanship, including 200-year-old Czechoslovakian crystal chandeliers, fireplaces made of Italian Carrara marble, hand-painted Dutch vases, Belgian lace, and a 600-year-old walnut sideboard from Heidelberg, Germany.

Other buildings served as both mining headquarters and residences. The 1860's Mackay Mansion, which housed the offices of the Gould and Curry Mine, had the added advantage of being the perfect spot to observe nearby mining operations. The

stately house was occupied by John Mackay, the Bonanza King and owner of the Consolidated Virginia Mine. Scattered among its 10 rooms are original furnishings and pieces from Mrs. Mackay's extensive silver collection.

The Fourth Ward School, located nearby, is another monument to the town's prosperity. Built in 1876, the trim three-story building featured innovations such as indoor drinking fountains and the latest in heating and ventilating systems. It accommodated more than 1,000 students in its heyday; the last class graduated in 1936.

Profits from the mines were put into rebuilding the town after 33 blocks of Virginia City were destroyed by a fire in 1875. As flames consumed Saint Mary's Catholic Church, Mackay promised to resurrect it if the townspeople would help him save his mine. They did, and the Gothic Revival–style Saint Mary's in the Mountains boasts 100-foot vaulted ceilings, remarkable stained glass, and two huge pipe organs.

Like the mythical phoenix, Piper's Opera House rose from the ashes of the Great Fire. It was faithfully reconstructed in 1885. The opera's unique design includes acoustic-enhancing canvas wallcoverings and chandeliers that cast decorative patterns on the ceiling. The stage is raked, and the auditorium floor rests on railcar springs. Scenery painted in 15th-century style, photographs, playbills, and original round-backed seats are on display.

MARK TWAIN'S BEGINNINGS

The *Territorial Enterprise*, the city's first newspaper, is where an intrepid young reporter named Samuel Clemens covered the Comstock silver trade. Clemens would go on to fame under the pseudonym Mark Twain, as the author of *The Adventures of Huckleberry Finn*. The former newspaper building's display of print technology includes an 1894 Linotype, type fonts, a binding machine, and a hot-type cabinet.

Visitors can get a vivid sense of mining history at The Way It Was Museum. Chronicling the rugged lives of miners, the museum displays photographs, artifacts, and scale models of stamp mills and Cornish pumps. A replica of the northern end of the Comstock Lode depicts the maze of tunnels that ran directly beneath the city.

The Ponderosa Saloon Mine Tour is reached by a tunnel entered at the back of the Ponderosa Saloon. Guides describe the

hazardous conditions that accompanied the work in the mines: the perpetual threat of cave-ins and fires, and the exhausting heat and bad air. Visitors can examine gold ore, the square-set timbering used to support the infrastructure, and the buckets, drills, winches, rods, and other equipment used to extract the valuable metal.

Miners often squandered their hard-earned wages in saloons and at the slot machines. The gambling and liquor are still flowing at water holes such as the Silver Queen, the Bucket of Blood Saloon, the Red Garter Saloon, and the Old Washoe Club. Venturing into any one of these lively establishments today gives visitors a real taste of the wild and shady side of Virginia City.

FOR MORE INFORMATION:
Virginia City Chamber of Commerce, P.O. Box 464, Virginia City, NV, 89440; 702-847-0311.

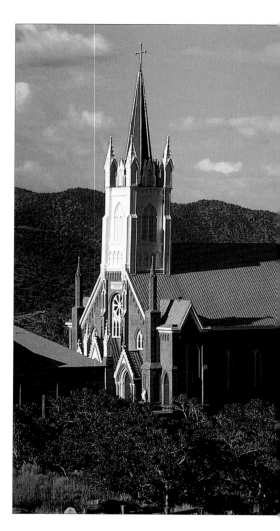

St. Mary's in the Mountains Church, right, once ministered to the spiritual needs of Virginia City's miners.

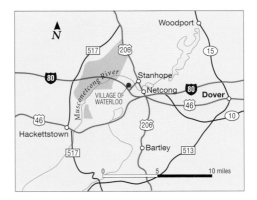

The faded Towpath Tavern sign, left, bids visitors to come in and partake of a light lunch.

With the discovery of iron ore in the area in the mid-18th century, the Philadelphia firm of Allen and Turner opened up a forge along the Musconetcong River in Sussex County, and the settlement of Andover soon grew up around it. The superior iron that was manufactured here was later used to supply Colonial forces with weapons during the American Revolution.

Following the war, Brig. John Smith bought the forge and renamed it Waterloo in honor of Wellington's defeat of Napoleon in 1815. Over time, the name Waterloo became synonymous with the village. Commercial farming operations established themselves, and a flax mill was built.

But it was the opening of a canal between Phillipsburg and Newark in 1831 that brought true economic prosperity to the settlement. In 1836 the Morris Canal was extended to Jersey City, making Waterloo an important stop along New Jersey's first bulk freight transportation line. Along this vital commercial channel moved tons of coal, bricks, iron ore, and lumber to growing cities along the East Coast.

In 1840 the management of the village industries was transferred from John Smith to his capable son, Peter. By the time Peter Smith died in 1877, each of his own sons had built an elegant Victorian or Edwardian mansion in the village. But these were the last buildings constructed in Waterloo. By 1901 the railways had superseded the slow canal route as the main freight network, and Waterloo all but disappeared.

LOVINGLY RESTORED

Restored to its former splendor, Waterloo Village seems more prosperous today than at any other time in its history. This authentic American canal settlement has

Built along the banks of the Morris Canal in 1831, the General Store, right, once supplied boatmen with their basic needs.

been brought to life, with costumed interpreters performing traditional daily tasks in and around its 28 historical buildings.

In the Weaving Barn, artisans demonstrate quilting and wool-spinning techniques. The Apothecary and Herb-Drying Room is a storehouse of natural remedies and the secrets of their use. At the Blacksmith Shop visitors learn how mules were shod and molten iron was shaped.

A stone's throw away stands the Peter D. Smith House, one of the last vestiges of

Smith family power and a hallmark of Waterloo's prosperous past. Built in 1874, this sprawling Victorian mansion was the residence of Peter Smith, who served as a state senator from 1889 to 1891.

A rustic bridge brings visitors to Indian Island where they can step back in time to 1625 when the Lenape Indians inhabited the region. The re-created Lenape Indian Village contains bark wigwams, longhouses, and dugout canoes, and displays the tools and crafts of these Native Americans.

Today tourism and a busy calendar of events have kept this national historic site a popular attraction. With a range of festivals that celebrate everything from the traditional music of Bolivia to Scandinavian cuisine, there is never a shortage of things to do in Waterloo Village. The site hosts historical Revolutionary War reenactments, numerous arts and craft shows, and antique shows. These events ensure that Waterloo Village maintains its reputation as a prosperous settlement more than a century after it reached its height.

FOR MORE INFORMATION:
Waterloo Foundation for the Arts, Inc., 525, Village of Waterloo, Stanhope, NJ 07874; 201-347-0900.

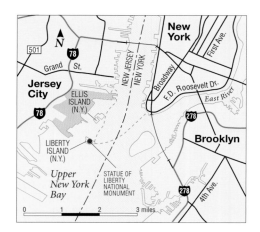

Photographers go to great lengths to capture the beauty of this world-renowned monument, above. The seven-spiked crown symbolizes the seven continents and the seven seas.

On October 28, 1886, New York Harbor came to life with blaring foghorns, waving flags, and the blasts of a 21-gun salute as Americans celebrated the unveiling of their new statue, *Liberty Enlightening the World.* Under a rainy sky the French tricolor dropped from the statue's face and the crowd raised a cheer to the beacon of hope, a triumphant goddess who seemed to stride on water, her flaming torch held high.

Lady Liberty, the statue that has come to embody America's highest ideals, was the brainchild of a group of French citizens. During a dinner party in 1865 hosted by the French jurist and politician Edouard-René Lefebvre de Laboulaye, the guests—a group of French intellectuals who greatly admired the American Republic—conceived the idea of giving it a colossal statue on the occasion of its centennial.

One of the dinner guests was renowned sculptor Frédéric-Auguste Bartholdi, who was given the task of designing the statue. He envisioned a grand beacon in New York Harbor. In 1875 Bartholdi began nine years of work on the statue in his Paris workshop. He made it from sections of a full-scale lath model covered with plaster. Wooden molds were shaped around the massive plaster

forms, while the copper sheeting used to cover the statue was hammered into wood molds in what is called the repoussé method. When the monumental statue was completed it measured 151 feet tall and weighed 450,000 pounds.

Alexandre-Gustave Eiffel, the engineer who later designed the Eiffel Tower, developed an ingenious technology to make the statue strong enough to withstand high winds, yet resilient enough to expand and contract with changes in temperature. A central wrought-iron pylon was constructed to support a secondary framework, and the statue's copper skin was attached to the frame with flexible iron bars. The statue was assembled then taken apart, crated, and shipped to the United States in 1885.

AMERICAN CONTRIBUTION

For their part, the Americans were to provide only a pedestal and a base. They showed little enthusiasm for the cause until Joseph Pulitzer took it up. Using his position as publisher of *The World* in New York, he appealed to American pride and was able to raise the necessary funds for fashionable society architect Richard Morris Hunt to complete the project.

Located on Liberty Island, the statue can be reached by ferry from Manhattan and from Jersey City, New Jersey. Exhibits in the base of the pedestal trace the statue's history. An elevator takes visitors to the top of the pedestal where an outdoor balcony overlooks the waters of New York Harbor. Energetic sightseers can climb 354 steps to Liberty's crown, where windows offer breathtaking views of Staten Island and the New York City skyline.

The ferry continues to Ellis Island, the nation's principal immigration processing depot from 1892 to 1924. The Ellis Island Immigration Museum houses exhibits of manuscripts, objects, and photographs that re-create the experience of new Americans.

In the 1980's Lady Liberty and the museum on Ellis Island, which are administered jointly, were restored at a cost of some $300 million. A team of French and American craftsmen replaced the old torch with a new one equipped with a gilded copper flame. They strengthened the uplifted arm, and replaced popped rivets and corroded iron ribs. Thus refurbished, the Statue of Liberty will continue to raise her light of hope for many years to come.

Exhibits at the Ellis Island National Monument, left, recount its service as a depot for immigrants in the early 20th century and the processing of 12 to 16 million newcomers.

FOR MORE INFORMATION:

Statue of Liberty National Monument, Liberty Island, New York, NY 10004; 718-338-3687.

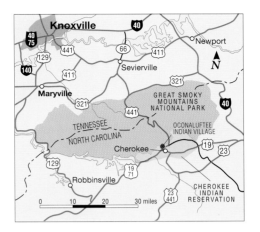

According to Cherokee lore, the Great Smoky Mountains were created by a gigantic vulture flying too close to the ground. Every time the bird's wings brushed the earth they scooped deep valleys and carved jutting mountains in its surface. Today these mountains, with their lush evergreens and gurgling streams, serve as the backdrop for the Cherokee Indian Reservation, a 56,573-acre tract of ancestral land known as the Qualla Boundary. The Oconaluftee Indian Village preserves the heritage of the Eastern Band of the Cherokee and offers programs on the tribe's history and culture during the 18th and 19th centuries.

From May through October each year, the band opens the village to the public, who are encouraged to explore the tranquil grounds. The village was reconstructed by members of the tribe and is renowned for its authenticity and attention to detail.

Native American guides dressed in traditional clothing lead visitors on tours. Cherokee women sit on the porches of log cabins and pound corn into meal with wooden mortars and pestles. Others string colorful beadwork belts and headbands or weave handsome river cane baskets.

TRADITIONAL SKILLS

Elsewhere on the grounds, visitors can observe people carving wooden utensils, chiseling flint arrow points, and fashioning clay pipes, bowls, and jars. The clay used for pottery is dug from the nearby ground, dried by the fire, and pulverized into powder. Water is then mixed with the powder until it forms the right consistency. Cherokee artisans create their pottery without the benefit of a wheel, shaping it by hand instead, sometimes coiling strips of clay upward from the base and blending the coils together. They print designs with a carved wooden paddle and polish the surface with a smooth stone. The type of wood used in firing a pot determines its color. To achieve the proper shine, bran or broken corncobs are tossed into the pots once they become red hot.

Like the potters, the village's canoe builders display skills that are based on techniques developed by their forefathers. They shape their canoes by burning the centers of thick logs and chiseling away the smoldering core with an ax.

The Cherokee were one of several tribes in the South who employed the blowgun to hunt small game. Cherokee men demonstrate how thistle-tufted darts were blown through a long hollow reed.

The physical and spiritual center of the village is a reconstructed council house. These seven-sided structures were the most important buildings in the Cherokee culture and have been used for centuries as meeting places for tribal leaders. They were always built on level ground near a stream so that members could cleanse themselves during or after a ceremony. It was in the council houses that governmental decisions were made and military strategies mapped out. Each side of the council house represents one of the seven clans of the Cherokee. Although ordinary people could not attend council meetings, each clan was represented at the council.

The Eastern Band's 12-member council no longer meets at the council house here, and visitors can tour the large wooden structure within whose walls debates on tribal issues once echoed. Interpreters are on hand to explain the significance of the sacred fire, the traditional carved masks, and other ceremonial objects that are on display inside.

Just down the road, the Mountainside Theater offers a different glimpse into the past. *Unto These Hills* is a moving drama about Cherokee history. The play begins with the Cherokee's first encounter with Europeans in 1540 and takes the audience through the years to the forced march along the Trail of Tears to Oklahoma in 1838, a 116-day journey that cost about 4,000 Cherokee lives. The members of the Eastern Band of the tribe—some 9,000 today—are the descendants of those Cherokee who escaped the exodus by hiding out in the Great Smoky Mountains. The play is presented nightly, except Sundays, during the summer months.

The era when the Cherokee Nation counted about 22,500 people and spanned some 44,000 square miles is long gone, but the group remains among the most independent Native Americans in the country. Thanks to their efforts, the Cherokee's vital history has been preserved and passed on to future generations.

FOR MORE INFORMATION:
Oconaluftee Indian Village, P.O. Box 398, Cherokee, NC 28719; 704-497-2111 or 704-497-2315.

Cherokee women at the Oconaluftee Indian Village make double-woven river cane baskets using materials that include honeysuckle vines, river cane, white oak splints, and bark.

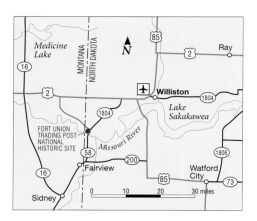

Strategically positioned on a grassy plain above the Missouri River, Fort Union looked out on the hunting grounds of Indian tribes such as the Assiniboin, Cree, Blackfoot, Crow, and the Sioux. Scottish-born fur trader Kenneth McKenzie supervised the fort's construction in 1828, and, under his ambitious leadership, it became one of the wealthiest of the trading posts that line the northern rivers. For almost 40 years furs and buffalo robes destined for the East were shipped via steamboats, which docked right outside the fort on the banks of the Missouri River.

Built by a subsidiary of the American Fur Company, Fort Union was initially established to cater to New England's market in beaver pelts. As silk top hats eventually replaced the craze for beaver hats, the trade in beaver pelts declined at Fort Union.

Hunters bowed to the dictates of a new fashion and began supplying a demand for buffalo robes. The adaptable outpost's brisk trade earned the company an income averaging $300,000 a year.

Fort Union's wealth and its remote locale made it an appealing destination for artists such as John James Audubon, Karl Bodmer, and George Catlin. The men traveled 1,900 miles by steamboat from St. Louis, Missouri, to get there. The vivid paintings and journals of these men describe a dynamic enclave where American, German, Scottish, French, English, Russian, Spanish, and Italian traders bartered peacefully with Native Americans of the region.

THE END OF AN ERA
The bustling fort's demise began in 1857 when smallpox carried by Easterners swept the Native American population, which was still recovering from an epidemic brought by steamboat passengers 20 years before. Fewer and fewer hunters and trappers came to Fort Union, and the fur trade eventually dried up. In 1867 the outpost was sold to the army, which dismantled it and used its materials to build Fort Buford some two miles downstream.

Old stone foundations were all that remained of this once thriving trade center when excavations began there in 1968. Today two reconstructed stone bastions rise at opposite corners of the fort, linking an 18-foot-high palisade that encloses an area

220-by-240 feet. Visitors can tour a reconstructed bell tower and Native American Trade House, rebuilt on their original sites and restored to their 1850's appearance. The Bourgeois House, where the man in charge of the post lived, has been reconstructed and contains the visitor center, a bookstore, and a museum. Guides dressed as traders interpret the fur trade and the Native American artifacts and relics uncovered in the excavations, which include silverware, wine bottles, china, and glass.

As many as 100 employees once lived within the fort quadrangle in its prosperous years. There were the clerks who kept careful inventories of trade goods and furs; hunters who supplied the post with fresh buffalo, elk, and deer meat; tinsmiths who fashioned trade items, such as rings, bracelets, and kettles; carpenters, masons, and blacksmiths who kept the fort in good repair; and herders who tended the horses and cattle. In the spring the fur traders arrived, well supplied with skins after spending the winter among the Native American tribes.

Throughout the warmer season, tribal representatives descended on the fort to exchange furs for trade goods. Grouped according to tribe, they pitched their tepees on the level plain outside the palisade. Language interpreters were an essential part of the transactions and they usually spoke several Native American languages as well as English and French. In exchange for beaver furs and buffalo hides, the Indians acquired iron tools, guns, gunpowder, beads, and blankets. Business was mixed with socializing during these visits, which sometimes culminated in a marriage between an Indian and a fort resident.

During the third weekend of June, onlookers can watch the lively summer festivities in which men dressed as trappers reenact a fur trading rendezvous. The modern-day trappers camp in Indian lodges and tepees and pass the time trading tools, swapping stories, and trying their hands at various frontier contests such as tomahawk and fry-pan throws.

FOR MORE INFORMATION:
Fort Union Trading Post National Historic Site, R.R. 3, Box 71, Williston, ND 58801; 701-572-9083.

The Bourgeois House at Fort Union trading post, left, was the home of Kenneth McKenzie, manager of the American Fur Company.

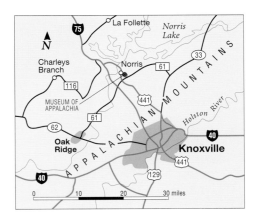

I n the secluded hills of the southern Appalachians, 19th- and early-20th-century mountain people lived hard lives that called for self-reliance and ingenuity. They used every available material or object they had to get by, making, for example, pruning shears from old bayonets, paper from milkweed, and devising self-setting mousetraps and butter churns cranked by a dog-powered treadmill.

These clever contraptions are among the roughly 250,000 items found in the Museum of Appalachia, 16 miles north of Knoxville. Travelers to the museum, set on 70 acres of land, learn what it was like to live in an Appalachian mountain village. Boots, saddles and bits, rifles and bullet molds, ox yokes, cowbells, fishhooks, and a varmint trap—all have a place in the village. But it is the smaller touches that give the museum its authentic feel: an ax stuck in a tree stump, cords of firewood stacked neatly next to a cabin, birdhouses made from gourds. Inside a cabin, dresses hang on wall hooks, kitchen utensils are laid out, and plates of dried beans and peppers sit on the table. Planned down to the smallest detail, the museum receives its highest compliments from visitors who ask, "Does somebody still live here?"

The museum is the brainchild of John Rice Irwin who spent a quarter of a century combing Appalachia for pioneer relics. To store his growing number of collectibles, Irwin purchased land in Anderson County in 1968 and began to acquire buildings from around the area.

Today an underground dairy, a smithy, a smokehouse, and a broom and rope house are among the 30-odd structures belonging to the museum, each with a fully restored interior and a story to tell.

In the one-room Arnwine Cabin, right, realistic displays reveal details of day-to-day life in the Appalachian Mountains.

At the General Bunch House, visitors can imagine what it was like to raise 12 youngsters in a two-room cabin located more than a dozen miles from the nearest store. In the blacksmith's shop the wooden bellows used to fire the blacksmith's forge is on view. The stone corn mill, powered by a large one-cylinder engine, was used to grind maize, also known as Indian corn, for bread and grits. The staple crop fed both livestock and mountain folk.

Sheep graze in a pasture at the Museum of Appalachia, above. Sturdy and attractive split-rail fences surround the fields.

On the museum's working farm, cattle, mules, and goats graze near a massive cantilevered barn with an upper story much larger than the lower. The barn's overhang is peculiar to the region and served to shelter farmers from the rain when they did chores such as splitting shingles.

SENSE OF COMMUNITY

Despite the difficult circumstances of their daily existence, the mountain people took time to fashion things of simple beauty, some of which are exhibited in the museum's folk art collection. Music was also vital to these people. Many handmade musical instruments are included in the collections of the Appalachian Hall of Fame. When the museum holds its annual Tennessee Fall Homecoming during the second weekend of October, this vibrant community comes alive as the village hums with mountain melodies and toe-tapping rhythms. While a dulcimer player strums an old Appalachian tune, artisans parade their wares. On Sunday morning of Homecoming a log chapel, built in the 1840's, resounds with lively harmonies by shape note singers, who read sheet music on which musical notes are represented by different shapes. But at almost any time, old-time music can be heard on the grounds, and visitors are welcome to join in.

FOR MORE INFORMATION:
Museum of Appalachia, P.O. Box 0318, Norris, TN 37828; 423-494-7680.

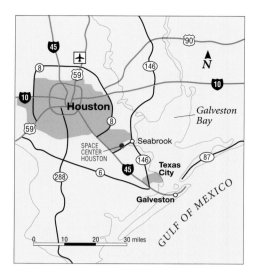

The engines of Saturn V, *above, the 36-story-tall rocket that blasted astronauts to the moon six times, generated the power of 85 Hoover Dams. The craft now rests in Rocket Park at Space Center Houston.*

The Lyndon B. Johnson Space Center in Houston is an active NASA facility that develops spacecraft, trains astronauts, and monitors space missions. At its southwestern corner lies Space Center Houston, a privately funded education and entertainment complex with displays on the past, present, and future of America's manned space program. The 183,000-square-foot facility was completed in 1992 at a cost of $70 million. It contains exhibits of hardware used by the astronauts as well as models of spacecraft and equipment. Accompanying the space exploration artifacts are lively educational programs, as well as films and hands-on interactive displays designed to bring the space program to life.

Visitors begin their voyage of discovery in the central atrium of the Space Center Plaza, where a model of the forward portion of an orbiting space shuttle offers glimpses of how the astronauts live in outer space. Temporary exhibits, set up in the plaza, have included displays such as a rocket constructed of Lego blocks, props from the movie *Apollo 13,* and photographs taken by the Hubble telescope.

Several galleries surround the central plaza, each offering a unique way to understand the space program. Computer simulators at the Feel of Space Gallery show visitors what it is like to land a shuttle or retrieve a satellite, and workshops offer demonstrations on how astronauts eat, sleep, and shower in space. Guests can slide on a space helmet, then try to repair a satellite while sitting in a Manned Maneuvering Unit Trainer, which simulates a frictionless environment using the same principle as an air hockey table.

At the Mission Status Center, trained staff provide minute-to-minute updates on current NASA missions. Visitors can listen in on communications between Mission Control and shuttle crews, or spy on astronauts in training.

Destiny Theater in the Starship Gallery presents a feature film giving highlights of space exploration culled from 1.5 million feet of film footage in NASA's archives. The gallery also chronicles spacecraft development beginning with a model of the Goddard Rocket, which was designed by the father of modern rocketry, Robert Goddard, and launched in 1926. From the Mercury program, there is the *Faith-7* Mercury capsule that carried Gordon Cooper into space in 1963. The Gemini program, designed to test docking procedures in preparation for the Apollo program, is represented by the two-man *Gemini 5* capsule. The Apollo program, in turn, which took three men to the moon, is represented by the *Apollo 17* capsule. The Skylab phase of the program includes the enormous *Skylab 1-G* Trainer, the original craft having burned up on its return to earth. Visitors can also touch real moon rocks in the lunar samples vault, the largest such collection anywhere.

The Astronaut Gallery displays portraits honoring every U.S. astronaut who has traveled in space. An exhibit of flight suits reveals how space fashions have changed since the beginning of the space program. In the adjacent Space Center Theater, visitors view films taken during actual shuttle voyages, and the five-story-high IMAX screens re-create an incredible astronaut's-eye view of space.

MISSION CONTROL CENTER

Visitors can board a tram for a behind-the-scenes look at the manned space flight program of the NASA/Johnson Space Center. One of the tour's highlights is the Mission Control Center, which has been guiding pioneer astronauts since the blast-off of *Gemini 4* on June 3, 1965. During manned missions, Mission Control and the new Control Center Complex are the astronauts' lifeline. Medical attendants monitor the crews' vital signs; technicians check electricity distribution systems, vehicle lighting systems, and cabin pressure controls; and a team of engineers uses high-tech communication equipment to relay essential prelaunch, ascent, and in-flight instructions. Briefings are held periodically on the history and future of NASA and are open to the public.

The Weightless Environment Training Facility, the Space Environment Simulation Laboratory, and the realistic space shuttle models and space stations of the Mockup Integration Laboratory afford visitors a look at astronauts training in simulated environments as they prepare themselves for upcoming space missions.

The tram tour ends at Rocket Park, home of retired spacecraft, where the imagination takes wing at the sight of *Saturn V,* which transported astronauts to the moon from 1969–72, the Mercury Redstone rocket, and *Little Joe II,* a test rocket that never flew.

FOR MORE INFORMATION:
Space Center Houston, 1601 NASA Rd. One, Houston, TX 77058; 713-244-2100 or 800-972-0369.

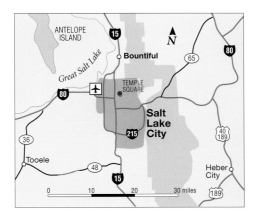

S urrounded by 15-foot-high walls, Salt Lake City's Temple Square is both a center of Mormon faith and a testament to human perseverance. The 10-acre complex of gardens, bronzed statues, and imposing buildings, built by volunteer labor, is the accomplishment of the Mormon settlers who came across the Rockies in the mid-19th century in search of freedom from religious persecution.

The first members of The Church of Jesus Christ of Latter-day Saints to settle in Salt Lake City arrived in July 1847 at the end of an arduous 1,300-mile trek from Nauvoo, Illinois, some three years after the murder of their leader, Joseph Smith. They set to work almost immediately, and by 1867 the Tabernacle, the first of the permanent Temple Square buildings was completed.

The Tabernacle has an immense silver-domed roof, 250 feet long by 150 feet wide. One account credits the auditorium's

Mormon Temple, above, is crowned by six spires that soar 210 feet in height. On the topmost pinnacle stands a statue of the Angel Moroni, who is believed to have delivered the Book of Mormon *to Joseph Smith.*

design to Brigham Young, Joseph Smith's successor, claiming that Young cracked a hard-boiled egg lengthwise and said, "I want the building shaped like that."

The Tabernacle is the result of frugality and lots of hard work. Settlers reused nails taken from worn-out wagon wheels. They felled nearly 1.5 million feet of lumber and secured the roof's wooden lattice truss with wooden dowels and rawhide thongs. No columns support the roof or obstruct the view of the pulpit, and the acoustics are so fine that a pin dropped near the Tabernacle organ can be heard 170 feet away. The organ's 11,000 or so pipes are covered in gold leaf and range in size from 32 feet to less than one inch. Visitors are welcome to attend regularly scheduled organ recitals and performances of the Mormon Tabernacle Choir.

TEMPLE OF GRANITE

Adjacent to the Tabernacle is the Mormon Temple, which took 40 years to build. Mammoth blocks of gray granite were hauled by ox teams and later by railroad from Little Cottonwood Canyon, about 23 miles away. Workers used large derricks to hoist the stones up for the spires. The Temple is used for marriages, baptisms, and other sacred ordinances. Entry is restricted to faithful church members, but accounts of the interior describe its gold-trimmed walls, marble-inlaid floors, richly carved fonts, and frescoed ceilings.

Although the construction of Assembly Hall used up the leftover granite originally designated for the Temple and the Tabernacle, the miniature cathedral was hardly an afterthought. The hall is graced with 40 stained-glass windows, a gabled roof, and white ornamental spires. Inside, pine pews, grained to resemble oak, seat 1,400 people for concerts and lectures.

A block east of the square stands the multigabled Lion House, where some of Brigham Young's many wives and children lived. Young's official residence was the Beehive House, an adobe building named for the carving of the Mormon symbol of industriousness atop its cupola.

FOR MORE INFORMATION:

Temple Square, P.O. Box 112110, Salt Lake City, UT 84147-2110; 801-240-2534.

An aerial view of Temple Square, left, illustrates the striking contrast in architectural styles between the Temple and the Tabernacle.

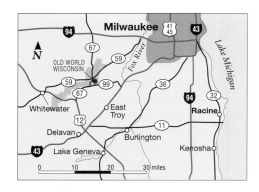

St. Peter's, above, was the first Catholic church in Milwaukee. The modestly furnished church was erected around 1839 and moved to the Crossroads Village in Old World Wisconsin to show the importance of faith in the lives of Wisconsin settlers.

I n the 19th century, thousands of peasants and landless laborers boarded ships docked in the harbors of European cities and sailed to America in search of a better life. After arriving in the Eastern ports, many immigrants made their way across the country to the wooded hills and prairies of Wisconsin. Here German, Polish, Norwegian, Danish, and Finnish settlers built new lives for themselves as farmers, merchants, and craftsmen. An outdoor museum, located in the Kettle Moraine hills southwest of Milwaukee, celebrates the courage and hard work of these early pioneers.

Old World Wisconsin's 60-odd historic farmhouses, barns, and shops have been plucked from all corners of the state and arranged in a series of 10 farmsteads and an 1870's Crossroads Village. The structures are grouped by nationality, with each building reflecting the architecture and heritage of its ethnic community. Trams guide visitors through the 576-acre kaleidoscope of cultures, and interpreters outfitted as farmers explain the folkways of early Wisconsin settlers, demonstrating pioneer methods of baking, plowing, and tending animals.

A single-room cabin in the Norwegian area was the home of Knudt and Gertrude Fossebrekke, who struggled to survive by farming wheat and trapping and selling pelts. Nearby, the 1860's Kvaale Farm illustrates how cabins developed into more comfortable dwellings as their owners adapted to life in America. The farm, which owed its prosperity to dairy and wool production, includes a corncrib, two barns, a granary, summer kitchen, and outhouse.

The Finns settled northern Wisconsin in the late 1880's, drawn by a landscape that resembled their homeland. In the Finnish Area visitors tour a seven-building dairy farm, complete with a sauna. It was constructed by Heikki Ketola between 1894 and 1900, who like many immigrants, worked for years to improve his homestead claim before he sent for his family in Finland to join him.

A common tradition among the immigrants was to build structures that sheltered family and livestock in separate rooms under the same roof. A Polish farmer did just that for his aging in-laws, Barbara and August Kruza. Their 1884 log-and-mortar farmhouse has been transplanted from Hofa Park, Shawano County, to the Polish section of the museum.

FRONTIER MELTING POT

Wisconsin's transplanted cultures merged in small commercial centers, which are represented by Crossroads Village. Farmers might have their horses shod by a German blacksmith, then stock up on essentials at a general store run by a family of Welsh descent. Their shoes might be mended by a Bohemian bachelor and their clothes washed by an Irish-born widow.

Rural traditions grew out of the changing seasons. In spring farmers shear sheep, spin wool, and plow the fields. In the summer visitors play croquet, or watch an old-fashioned Fourth of July parade. Autumn brings the Thresheree, featuring various events such as horses on a treadmill and the steam threshing of the wheat harvest.

FOR MORE INFORMATION:
Old World Wisconsin, S103 W37890
Hwy. 67, Eagle, WI 53119; 414-594-6300.

The vegetable gardens of Old World Wisconsin, above, are designed to resemble those planted by the 19th-century settlers, even down to the clothes used to dress scarecrows.

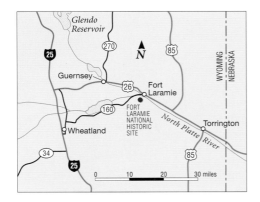

Fort Laramie began as a fur trading post, then served as an immigrant way station and military headquarters. Now a historic landmark, the 830-acre park contains a score of authentic buildings and ruins that evoke its military past.

The region's first permanent trading post was a simple cottonwood stockade. It was built in 1834 by a group of mountain men accompanying the fur trader William Sublette to the annual rendezvous with Native American tribes at Green River. Despite its strategic position on the banks of the Laramie River and not far from the Oregon Trail's one-third point, trading was slow here until the American Fur Company bought the post in 1836. They replaced the already rotting wooden structure with a whitewashed adobe fort and encouraged trade with the neighboring Native American population.

In its early years the Sioux gathered by the thousands at the post, exchanging buffalo robes for blankets, tools, tobacco, and beads. More than 10,000 buffalo robes were sold each year during this period. However, as more and more immigrant wagons rolled into these territories, the amicable trade relations began to fall apart. Then in 1849 the Gold Rush unleashed a frenzy of traffic, and threatening the Sioux way of life. The Sioux responded to the influx of outsiders by harrying wagon trains. The army intervened and purchased Fort Laramie, converting it into a military base.

Over the next four decades, the fort served as a meeting place where peace treaties were signed, a refuge for soldiers, and a stop for travelers on the Oregon Trail. But the fort's broader mission was to lend support to Western settlement and to protect the nation's communication links, such as the the Pony Express, the Oregon Trail, the transcontinental telegraph, and the Cheyenne-Deadwood stage line.

As part of an 1851 treaty, the federal government offered the Plains Indian tribes an annuity in exchange for safe passage for immigrants through their territory. But the situation worsened. The next decades were marked by bloody skirmishes, including the 1854 Grattan Massacre in which 29 soldiers were killed by Sioux warriors. As tensions escalated, Fort Laramie became a staging area for the military campaigns that eventually led to the Plains Indian tribes being forcibly confined on reservations.

By 1890 the army had fulfilled its mission, and the post was abandoned. Local homesteaders bought some of the buildings at auctions and salvaged the wood. Many structures had been stripped down to their foundations when restoration work began in the 1930's. Many original structures have been restored, including the captain's quarters, bakery, guardhouse, post surgeon's quarters, and the fort's magazine.

LONELY MALE BASTION

The stark and treeless landscape provided a view from one of the barrack windows that was as bleak as the living conditions at the garrisoned post. Illness plagued the soldiers due to the unwholesome diet of greasy salt pork, bread, beans, rice, and coffee; discipline was so severe that the smallest transgression could land a man in the guardhouse; and sanitary conditions were deplorable. Soldiers sought solace in liquor and, more rarely, female companionship. The only women at the fort were officers' wives and laundresses.

The cavalry barracks, built of concrete, is the largest building at the fort. Visitors can see the second floor, where rows of cots provided beds for up to 60 men. The nearby officers' quarters has been painstakingly restored, down to its square-cut nails and oak dowels. The post trader's store, which is connected to the officers' club and the enlisted men's bar, was rarely empty. Soldiers supplemented their meager army rations in the store and got drunk in the bar, while immigrants stocked up on tools, weapons, food staples, and whiskey.

Interpreters wearing period clothing tend the bar and trader's store. During the summer park staff sometimes offer guided tours of the fort and educational programs on the history of the opening of the West. Visitors are encouraged to roam among the ruins and to take their time to inspect the meticulous workmanship of the restoration.

FOR MORE INFORMATION:
Superintendent, HC 72, Box 389, Fort Laramie, WY 82212; 307-837-2221.

Built in 1849, the two-story officers' quarters, below, at Fort Laramie is Wyoming's oldest surviving military structure. The clapboard building was dubbed Old Bedlam, perhaps because of the drunken celebrations that were frequently held there by the officers.

INDEX

PICTURE CREDITS

Cover photograph by George H.H. Huey
2   Terry Donnelly
5   Terry Donnelly

HISTORIC BATH
8, 9 Alan Briere
10 (*both*) Alan Briere
12 (*both*) Alan Briere
13 (*both*) Alan Briere
14, 15 (*all*) Alan Briere
16 (*upper left*) Alan Briere
16 (*lower right*) Jan Butchofsky/
   Dave G. Houser
17 Alan Briere

PENNSYLVANIA DUTCH COUNTRY
18, 19 David Muench
20 Carol Kitman
21 (*lower right*) Carol Kitman
22 Ronald N. Wilson
23 (*upper*) Ronald N. Wilson
23 (*lower*) Paul Rocheleau
24 Ronald N. Wilson
25 (*upper left*) Ronald N. Wilson
25 (*lower right*) Lance Nelson/
   The Stock Market
26 David Muench
27 (*upper right*) Dave G. Houser
27 (*lower left*) Betty Crowell

BATTLE AT GETTYSBURG
28, 29 Terry Donnelly
30 (*upper left*) Terry Donnelly
30 (*lower right*) Steve Strickland
32 (*upper right*) Terry Donnelly
32 (*left*) James P. Rowan
33 David Muench
34 (*upper*) Steve Strickland
34 (*lower*) James P. Rowan
35 David Muench
36 James P. Rowan
37 (*upper right*) Dave G. Houser
37 (*lower left*) Michael Melford

SAVANNAH
38, 39 Wolfgang Kaehler
40, 41 (*both*) John Elk III
42 (*upper left*) Wolfgang Kaehler
42 (*lower right*) John Elk III
43 (*upper*) David Muench
43 (*lower*) Bill Weems/Woodfin Camp
   & Associates

44 John Elk III
44, 45 Stephanie Maze/Woodfin Camp
   & Associates
45 John Elk III
46 (*upper right*) Wolfgang Kaehler
46 (*lower left*) James P. Rowan
47 Wolfgang Kaehler
48 Wolfgang Kaehler
49 (*upper right*) John Elk III
49 (*lower left*) David Muench

AMERICAN LEGACY
50, 51 Balthazar Korab
52 (*both*) James P. Rowan
54 Balthazar Korab
55 (*upper left*) Lee Foster
55 (*lower right*) James P. Rowan
56 Lee Foster
56, 57 Balthazar Korab
57 Wolfgang Kaehler
58 James P. Rowan
59 (*upper left*) James P. Rowan
59 (*lower right*) Lee Foster
60, 61 (*all*) Balthazar Korab

LIVING HISTORY FARMS
62, 63 Tim Thompson
64 (*upper left*) John Elk III
64 (*lower right*) Greg Ryan/Sally Beyer
66 (*upper*) Vera Bradshaw/Root Resources
66 (*lower*) Tim Thompson
67 Courtesy of the Living History Farms
68 (*upper*) Tom Bean
68 (*lower*) Courtesy of the Living
   History Farms
69 (*both*) Tim Thompson
70 (*upper*) Courtesy of the Living
   History Farms
70 (*lower*) Tim Thompson
71 (*upper left*) Tom Bean
71 (*lower right*) Greg Ryan/Sally Beyer
72 (*upper left*) Tim Thompson
72 (*lower right*) Tom Bean
73 Tim Thompson

KING RANCH
74, 75 Courtesy King Ranch Archives
76 (*upper right*) John Zimmerman/Courtesy
   King Ranch Archives
76 (*lower left*) Tom Bean
78 (*both*) Tom Bean
79 (*both*) Tom Bean

80 Tom Bean
80, 81 Tom Bean
81 (*lower right*) Courtesy King
   Ranch Archives
82, 83 George H.H. Huey
83 (*upper left*) Bob Daemmrich
83 (*lower right*) Tim Thompson

TAOS
84, 85 Chuck Place
86 Chuck Place
87 Craig Aurness/Woodfin Camp
   and Associates
88 (*upper*) Dave G. Houser
88 (*lower*) Rankin Harvey/Dave G. Houser
89 Jan Butchofsky/Dave G. Houser
90 (*upper right*) Jan Butchofsky/
   Dave G. Houser
90 (*lower left*) Chuck Place
91 (*upper*) Adam Woolfitt/Woodfin Camp
   and Associates
91 (*lower*) Chuck Place
92 (*upper*) Chuck Place
92 (*lower*) Michael Collier
93 (*upper*) Rankin Harvey/Dave G. Houser
93 (*lower*) Craig Aurness/Woodfin Camp
   and Associates
94 George H.H. Huey
94, 95 George H.H. Huey
95 Dave G. Houser

COLUMBIA STATE HISTORIC PARK
96, 97 Fred Hirschmann
98 (*upper right*) David Weintraub
98 (*lower left*) John Senser
100 (*both*) Frank S. Balthis
101 John Elk III
102 (*upper left*) Chuck Place
102 (*lower right*) John Elk III
103 Frank S. Balthis
104 David Weintraub
105 (*upper left*) Chuck Place
105 (*lower right*) John Elk III
106 (*upper*) Marc Muench
106 (*lower*) David Muench
107 David Muench

FORT CLATSOP
108, 109 David Muench
110 Andrew E. Cier/FCNM & FCHA
111 Andrew E. Cier/FCNM & FCHA
112 Andrew E. Cier/FCNM & FCHA

112, 113 (*upper*) Fort Clatsop
   Historical Association
113 Andrew E. Cier/FCNM & FCHA
114 (*both*) Frank S. Balthis
115 Andrew E. Cier/FCNM & FCHA
116 (*upper right*) Frank S. Balthis
116 (*lower left*) Andrew E. Cier/FCNM
   & FCHA
117 David Muench
118 (*upper left*) Chris Bryant
118 (*lower right*) Wolfgang Kaehler
119 Jeff Gnass

GAZETTEER
120 George H.H. Huey
121 (*upper right*) John Elk III
121 (*lower left*) Carol Kitman
122 David Muench
123 (*both*) Wolfgang Kaehler
124 (*both*) George H.H. Huey
125 Robert C. Lautman/
   The Octagon Museum
126 David Muench
127 (*upper right*) Dave G. Houser
127 (*lower left*) David Muench
128 Balthazar Korab
129 (*upper*) Terry Donnelly
129 (*lower*) Paul Rocheleau
130 (*upper*) Jan Butchofsky/
   Dave G. Houser
130 (*lower*) John Elk III
131 Jan Butchofsky/Dave G. Houser
132 Dave G. Houser
133 (*both*) Rob Tringali Jr.
134 (*upper right*) Dick Durrance/Woodfin
   Camp and Associates
134 (*lower left*) Wolfgang Kaehler
135 John Elk III
136 Jan Butchofsky/Dave G. Houser
137 (*upper*) Al Stephenson/Woodfin Camp
   & Associates
137 (*lower*) John Elk III
138 Dave G. Houser
139 (*upper*) Tim Thompson
139 (*lower*) Jan Butchofsky/
   Dave G. Houser
140 (*both*) Terry Donnelly
141 Terry Donnelly

Back cover photograph by Carol Kitman

ACKNOWLEDGMENTS

Cartography: DPR Inc.; map resource base courtesy of the USGS; shaded relief courtesy of the USGS and Mountain High Maps®
Copyright © 1993 Digital Wisdom, Inc.

The editors would also like to thank the following: Chantal Bilodeau, Lorraine Doré, Dominique Gagné, Pascale Hueber,
and Valery Pigeon-Dumas.